Super-History

Super-History

*Comic Book Superheroes
and American Society,
1938 to the Present*

Jeffrey K. Johnson

McFarland & Company, Inc., Publishers
Jefferson, North Carolina, and London

LIBRARY OF CONGRESS CATALOGUING-IN-PUBLICATION DATA

Johnson, Jeffrey K., 1972–
Super-history : comic book superheroes and American society,
1938 to the present / Jeffrey K. Johnson.
p.   cm.
Includes bibliographical references and index.

ISBN 978-0-7864-6564-4
softcover : acid free paper ∞

1. Comic books, strips, etc.— History and critism.
2. Literature and society — United States.
3. Superheroes in literature.   4. Graphic novels.   I. Title.
PN6725.J64 2012   741.5'0973 — dc23   2012008384

British Library cataloguing data are available

Cover illustration © 2012 iStockphoto;
Front cover design by Rob Russell

Manufactured in the United States of America

*McFarland & Company, Inc., Publishers
Box 611, Jefferson, North Carolina 28640
www.mcfarlandpub.com*

For Monika:
"I like pink very much, Lois."

TABLE OF CONTENTS

Recycle-A-Textbook
.com

Thanks for your purchase from Recycle-A-Textbook, I appreciate your business immensely!!!

I strive to provide quality books at a fair price for everyone. The best advertising I can have is word of mouth, and in the online selling world, that is through feedback. If you could, please take a minute and leave feedback on my account.

If for any reason you are planning to leave neutral or negative feedback, basically anything other than positive feedback, please email me directly at textbooktycoon@yahoo.com and give me a chance to correct the issue. I promise you, I want to make it right! I want to make sure everyone is satisfied, and I will make time to ensure everything is correct! I hope you enjoy your book!!!

Thanks again and all the best this semester.

I would love an opportunity to buy your book back when you are finished with it. Please email us when you are finished for a buyback price.

Thanks,
Recycle-A-Textbook
textbooktycoon@yahoo.com

ACKNOWLEDGMENTS

The list of friends, family, colleagues, and other parties that I need to thank for their help with this project is lengthy and unfortunately inevitably incomplete. A large number of people assisted me in numerous and often indescribable ways. While Blanche Dubois may have relied on the kindness of strangers, I have been fortunate enough to be able to rely on the good will of my friends and family. I would like to wholeheartedly thank everyone who has helped me to research and write this book — without each of you this monograph would not exist.

Thank you to my friends and colleagues who have cheerfully given me advice and assistance since this project's inception. I offer special thank yous to Gregory Kupsky, Derek Mallett, Kevin Thompson, and Janisse Davila for their support and encouragement. Nicole Rhoton, you have my heartfelt gratitude for reading several drafts and providing much needed help, feedback, and advice. Cain Vasquez, thank you for all of the research material and comic book discussions.

Thank you to the students in my classes at Michigan State University in WRA (Writing, Rhetoric and American Cultures), IAH (Integrative Studies in the Arts and Humanities), and history for allowing me the opportunity to be your teacher. My students from Lyman Briggs College helped me to think about many of the topics in this book, especially the ideas connected with *Watchmen*, and I owe them a debt of gratitude. A special thank you to Ross Arasim, Gillian Reily, Tim VandenBerg, Katherine Trinkle, Sarah Davis, Anna Hardenbergh, Jillian Cherniawski, Kaitlyn Courville, Rachel Friedman, Kellen Seaton, Maria Swetech, Molly Griffin, Nathan Keniston, Avery Neuman, Laura Freitag, Brett King, Ashley Bradford, May Lin, Jeremy Brooks, and Richard "Skates" Manner.

Malcolm Magee, thank you for helping to me to define this book's main concepts and for all the support and friendship that you have offered over the years. Jesse Draper, thank you for sharing your infectious excitement and deep insight. I never would have dreamed that I would have so much respect and affection for a Cubs fan. Finn McDermott, Superman would easily beat the Flash in a foot race; he'd win because he's Superman.

Thank you Randy Scott and Leslie Behm of the Michigan State University Library Special Collections for scanning many of the superhero images that appear in this book. The MSU Library Comic Art collection is an amazing resource that has 200,000 comic books, and I would strongly encourage anyone interested in comic books to visit. Thank you also to Ted and Toni Mays of Gecko Books & Comics in Kaimuki, Hawai'i. Gecko is everything that a good local comic book store should be, and Ted and Toni have been valuable resources for me while writing this book.

Thank you to the podcasters that keep me updated and excited about comic books. I have never met any of you but I am grateful for the community that you created and the knowledge that you share. Special thanks to Bryan Deemer, Peter Rios, Shane Kelly, Jamie D., Adam Murdough, Brian "Pants" Christman, Matt Keener, and Mike Gallagher of *Comic Geek Speak*; John Siuntres of *Word Balloon*; Vince B., Chris Neseman, David Price, and Jason Wood from *11 O'Clock Comics;* Josh Flanagan, Conor Kilpatrick, and Ron Richards of *iFanboy*; Sean Whelan and Jim Segulin of *Raging Bullets: A DC Comics Fan Podcast*; Chris Marshall from the *Collected Comics Library*, and Tom Katers of *Tom vs. The Flash* and *Tom vs. Aquaman.*

Thank you to Gregory Pan at Marvel Entertainment and Jen Cassidy from Todd McFarlane Productions for providing access to all of the wonderful images that you see in this book.

This book's genesis is tied to the moment when I transitioned from my life as a graduate student to my new career as an academic professional. During my Ph.D. graduation ceremony at Michigan State University, I was lucky enough to be hooded by my mentor Dr. Gary Hoppenstand, who was seated next to me during the remaining portions of the commencement exercise. During the graduation speech, Gary leaned in next me and inquired, "Now that you've finished your dissertation and will have your first book published soon, what is your next project?" Slightly stunned, I admitted that I did not have anything in mind. Gary responded that I should consider writing a book about comic books because I had much to contribute to the subject's study. Although Gary probably soon forgot our brief conversation, I never did. While I had considered doing more comic book research, I never would have untaken a project of this size and scope without Gary's encouragement. It pains that me that I cannot find the words to express my gratitude to you Gary, but I hope a simple, heartfelt "thank you" will suffice. Rarely a day passes that I do not feel fortunate to have meet you and to have benefited from all that you have taught me.

Lastly, thank you, Monika; without you none of this would be possible. I appreciate your love and support more than I can ever express.

INTRODUCTION

I distinctly remember the first comic book I ever read. It was *Action Comics* #489 and although it was cover dated November 1978, I probably first read it in the fall of 1979. A reading teacher had given it to me as part of a literacy program called Reading Is Fundamental or RIF. I was seven years old and the teacher allowed me to select a book out of a stack of free reading material. In the pile, among numerous paperback books, was a comic book with a story featuring Superman. I was amazed and quickly selected the brightly colored comic book and exited the room before the teacher took too much notice of me. I assumed that someone had made a terrible mistake and included a comic book with all of the "real" books. Once the error was realized surely an authority figure would remedy this oversight and take my newly found comic book away. Everyone knew that comic books could not be considered serious reading material and nothing of value could be learned from them. In my heart I understood that my teachers and principal would never endorse my wasting time on lowly funny books.

The story was amazing, though: Superman was battling an alien mastermind named Brainiac who forced the Man of Steel to watch a repeat performance of Krypton's destruction. The issue had everything — action, adventure, science fiction, emotion, and a link to Superman's history — but it also was just a comic book. So I continued to reread my issue of *Action Comics* (literally until it fell apart) and waited in shame for my teachers to one day discover me. Now move forward more than thirty years and amazingly, the same person that was once embarrassed to have read a comic book has written this entire book devoted to comic books' social, cultural, and academic value. My seven-year-old self would be both dumbfounded and aghast (as have been many of the people that have inquired about this project over the last few years).

What my seven-year-old self did not know, and what much of the American public still does not realize, is that comic book superheroes are an important part of America's social fabric. Since its creation in the late 1930s, the superhero has become the United States' dominant cultural icon. Superheroes quickly expanded from their comic book origins to become a part of nearly every portion of American culture and society. Superhero films have become a Hollywood staple, numerous comic book related television shows fill the airwaves, and hundreds of other outlets showcase our fictional spandex-clad guardians. Artists like Andy Warhol and Roy Lichtenstein created comic book influenced art and many museums have presented superhero related exhibitions. More importantly though, superheroes have become part of the structure of American life. Numerous scholars consider comic books and jazz the only indigenous American art forms. Unlike jazz, comic books have rarely received the praise and attention that they highly deserve. For decades many

Americans declared this unique artistic style to be of little or no social value. Most Americans believed comic books were a disposable child's medium that was quickly read and forgotten. This began to change in the 1980s and 1990s when scholars started to study comic books and to publish academic texts about the role comics have played in society. Although there have been a number of comic book monographs published in recent years, there is still a shortage of scholarship that is accessible to researchers and the general public. One area that strongly needs to be addressed is comic book superheroes and their changing roles and influences in American society. Since Superman debuted in 1938 as a Great Depression hero, comic book superheroes have been linked to American hopes, desires, fears, needs, and social norms. Because superhero comic books have always been a form of popular literature, the narratives have closely mirrored and molded American social trends and changes. This means that superhero stories are excellent primary sources for studying changes in American society from 1938 until the present. They are an American mythology that is forever adjusting to meet society's needs. Superheroes are not merely comic book characters; rather they are social mirrors and molders that serve as barometers of the place and time in which they reside. Their stories help us to comprehend our world and allow us to better understand ourselves.

This book explores the ways that comic book superheroes have influenced and have been influenced by American political, social, and cultural events. It takes a decade by decade (and one overarching time period) look at American history as viewed through the lens of superhero comics. This monograph provides an overview of American history from 1938 until 2010 and should be treated as such. No one book could possibly encapsulate every important incident during this over seventy year period, and so I have striven to create a narrative of each decade's central events and most influential comic books.

I fully understand that some historians and comic book readers alike will be frustrated with my decadal surveys because what they deem to be significant events and comic books are not investigated to their satisfaction. Why did *Crisis on Infinite Earths* receive two paragraphs while Ambush Bug was never mentioned? Why do I not provide in-depth analysis of *Secret Wars* or the Beta Ray Bill issues of Walt Simonson's *Thor* run? Why is there an entire chapter about the nuclear era but not a mention of the Panama Canal Treaty? I appreciate these questions and criticisms and sympathize with readers who believe that something of consequence has been overlooked. I would only ask that readers remember that this book is a starting point in understanding American society and culture and I hope that anyone that is interested in learning more will also pursue other outlets.

In this book I use comic book superhero stories to showcase domestic American social changes from decade to decade in the twentieth and early twenty-first centuries. These continuing superhero narratives both reflect and inform major changes in American society from 1938 to 2010. The book contains nine chapters that focus on a different decade or era. Each chapter addresses its period's major social events and uses superhero narratives to display the era's primary cultural and social norms and changes. Every chapter describes how the changes within popular superhero stories reflected the period's important social trends and as the United States continually evolved its superheroes either led or followed. In essence, this book uses comic book superhero narratives to chronicle major American social changes since the Great Depression until the present day. The chapters are arranged as follows:

Chapter 1—"We Need a Hero: New Deal Social Avengers and Vigilantes (1938–1940)"—*explores how this* era gave birth to the comic book superhero. These early superheroes (Superman, Batman, etc.) were products of their time and social avengers that fought for the average man. This chapter describes how the original superheroes were New Deal avengers that concerned themselves with the same social problems as many America citizens. Superheroes quickly changed, but for the first few years these masked avengers were often gritty vigilantes that worked outside the law and did not trust the government or any other agents of the state.

Chapter 2 — "World War II and Super-Patriots (1941–1945)" — describes how comic book superheroes began as social avengers in 1938 but quickly changed even before the U.S. entered World War II. In late 1940, a year before the U.S. joined the war, Marvel Comics published *Captain America* #1, which featured the hero on the cover punching Adolf Hitler. Soon the U.S. was at war and both American society and comic book heroes changed. Superheroes rapidly became patriotic symbols of the nation and pledged to fight and defend the United States. American society also transformed itself into a wartime economy, in which thoughts of combat victory governed most public and private decisions. Both superheroes and American society had to adjust greatly to meet the new wartime needs.

Chapter 3 — "The Nuclear Era (1945–1989)" — investigates how the atomic blasts at Hiroshima and Nagasaki that ended World War II also created a terrifying new age. Suddenly, humankind possessed weaponry that could destroy the Earth and all of its inhabitants. This chapter explores the American public's changing attitudes towards nuclear power and weapons and how comic book superheroes investigate these fears and anxieties. Following World War II, superheroes no longer seemed as safe and powerful as they were before. Much like many American citizens, these costumed avengers had to learn to adjust to the changing face of nuclear power. Although this chapter explores many of the same years as later chapters, it only concerns itself with atomic matters and not other social trends.

Chapter 4 — "The Postwar 1940s and 1950s: Supernormal (1946–1959)" — focuses on the transformation of American society after World War II. Although many contemporary Americans think of the postwar 1940s and 1950s as an innocent period, it also was a repressive and anxiety filled time. Many citizens traded freedom and individuality for stability and consumerism. Superheroes also transformed into super-family men and women that valued home, peace, and stability above all else. These former agents of change promoted the status quo and preached obedience to authority. Both superheroes and American society rarely tolerated dissent or disrespect, which is evident in many cultural venues, including comic book stories.

Chapter 5 — "Counterculture Heroes (1960–1969)" — investigates how the stability and repression of the 1950s soon gave way to the youth movement and counterculture revolution of the 1960s. As Baby Boomers searched for a better way of life, they demanded a new kind of superhero, one that met their cultural and social needs. While 1950s superheroes were often stoic father figures, the 1960s Marvel Comic heroes and many adolescent readers faced similar problems. Marvel heroes like Spider-Man, the Incredible Hulk, and the Fantastic Four confronted real world problems and understood contemporary youths' points of view. DC heroes mostly remained white bread, law abiding citizens, and this contrast helped reflect the growing generation gap.

Chapter 6 — "The American Malaise (1970–1979)" — explores how the political and social traumas of the 1960s gave rise to the 1970s' social downturn. Vietnam, Watergate, oil shortages, the Iranian hostage crisis, and other events tested Americans' faith and understanding. Social conditions often seemed bleak and Americans were forced to rethink their places in society and in the world. Comic book creators also began to question superheroes' social roles, and like many Americans, numerous heroes seemed to have lost their way. Both superheroes and Americans searched for an understanding of a rapidly changing society that no longer seemed to function as it had in days past.

Chapter 7 — "Super-Conservatives and Neo-Cowboys (1980–1989)" — investigates how Ronald Reagan's victory in the 1980 U.S. presidential election signaled the rise of a new national era. Reagan pressed for increased military spending and buildup, a smaller federal government, and a return to a more nationalistic society. The new president pushed for a more conservative society that embraced the idea of a strong national identity. During this era several comic book creators began to reimagine numerous superheroes as harsh conservative vigilantes that no longer exclusively followed the traditional comic book view of right and wrong. Many saw this as a return to the 1930s social avenger, but these heroes also often commented on the new social conservative movement. Stories like *Batman: The Dark Knight Returns* and *Watchmen* embraced violent conservative heroes but critiqued and criticized American society's direction.

Chapter 8 — "Searching for a New Direction (1990–1999)" — explores the decade that was shaped by the 1989 fall of the Berlin Wall and the collapse of European socialist regimes that ended the Cold War. The U.S. and the Soviet Union had been engaged in a political, economic and social struggle since the end of World War II, and this effort had defined much of the U.S.'s agenda since 1945. Americans often understood their society by contrasting it to the U.S.S.R., and many citizens became lost without their old adversary to act as a tether. American government and society searched for a new social and cultural template for the post–Cold War era. Just as American leaders and citizens looked for new purposes, comic book superheroes attempted to define themselves. Numerous superheroes became ultra-violent while others attempted to return to 1950s-like whimsical stories. Both superheroes and society tried to understand what to do after the Cold War was won and the U.S.'s path was no longer clear.

Chapter 9 — "Decade of Fear (2000–2009)" — is dominated by the September 11, 2001, terrorist attacks that quickly redefined America's priorities and characterized the early twenty-first century. Americans looked inward and soon began to view the world through a nationalistic lens of fear and mistrust. American society and culture emulated the country's political and foreign policies and embraced a fear-driven world view. Many Americans worried about terrorism and loss of security and became more isolated and withdrawn. Comic book superheroes also became more fearful and less trusting as villains became more violent and harmful. In DC's *Identity Crisis*, a superhero's wife is raped and murdered while in Marvel's *Secret Invasion*, alien terrorists attempt to overrun society. Comic book superheroes once again mirrored society by embracing the rising fear and terror that surrounded them.

These nine chapters fashion a narrative in which superhero comic books often emulate and sometimes help create the social history of the United States since 1938. During this period, the nation's superheroes have provided Americans with an outlet to express their hopes, fears, joys, and sorrows and have consistently changed whenever the country has needed them to. Our heroes bear witness to who we have been, who we are, and who we may possibly be someday. Sometimes these stories are silly or lighthearted while other times they are dark and grotesque, but they are always a reflection of the America in which they were created. It is easy to disparage comic book superheroes because originally they were designed to be children's personified wishes. They were overly bright and powerfully vulgar representations that only a child could believe in and that an upstanding adult could easily mock. Comic books superheroes have grown up in the last 70 years and most of the stories are no longer for children, but one of the reasons that they are so important is that they are at their heart designed to explain the world in simple terms. I contend that comic books are important because how we explain the world to our children says volumes about ourselves. These characters are often outlandish, violent, campy, aggressive, simplistic, or overly dramatic, but so are we. They also can be virtuous, magnanimous, peaceful, and kind, as can we. Superheroes' flaws are our flaws and their virtues are our virtues. They are mythical protectors that were fashioned in our image and thus possess both our best and worst qualities. By studying the history of comic book superheroes, we can learn much about ourselves and the world around us.

Chapter 1

WE NEED A HERO: NEW DEAL SOCIAL AVENGERS AND VIGILANTES (1938–1940)

When a hero is needed a hero is born. Although this may sound like simplistic or wishful thinking, in reality societies and cultures give birth to the mythological heroes they need. Hercules, King Arthur, Beowulf, and hundreds of other fictional heroes have supplied help and guidance to their homelands. These heroic symbols reflect their societies' values and fulfill their cultures' needs. They unite their followers and create a common understanding of the world. Heroes not only fight for their societies, but more importantly they encourage societies to fight for themselves. They bond a group of people that may have begun separating during a crisis. If ever the United States needed a hero it was during the summer of 1938. The nation was reeling from economic, social, and environmental upheaval with no end in sight. The Great Depression was raging and it was fast approaching a decade since the stock market crash of 1929. Tens of millions of Americans were jobless and the country had witnessed businesses and economic institutions failing in unprecedented numbers. The rest of the nation watched as the Southwest was battered in the environmental disaster known as the Dustbowl. Millions of Texas and Oklahoma farmers lost their land and livelihoods and were reduced to begging for work and migrating to other regions.

Arguably, the nation's most devastating calamity was a loss of trust and belief in the country's central institutions. The system had failed and the government was unable to fix it. This left many Americans feeling isolated and defenseless. As social and economic ills continued to mount, many felt utterly powerless and needed someone powerful to convince them that everything would be all right. The United States needed a hero. Luckily, two teenagers from Cleveland were creating one. The crisis called for more than a man, and soon the nation would indeed have a superman. This new type of hero would be a product of his times and would become a New Deal agent and reformer. Although he would later become so much more, this first superhero would be born a Great Depression social avenger.

Man and Superman

The age of comic book superheroes began in the spring of 1938 when DC Comics published *Action Comics* #1.[1] The comic book's cover showcases a red and blue-costumed strongman lifting a car over his head, and destroying the automobile, as several terrified men stumble about and flee the scene. A story inside introduces the colorful individual as Superman, a super-strong avenger. Quickly it is revealed that Superman fights against injustice and protects the weak. He is a powerful hero that watches out for the misfortunate and punishes wrongdoers. The definition of wrongdoers and the Man of Steel's methods in early Superman stories may seem strange to modern readers though. In *Action Comics* #1, Superman physically threatens a state governor in order to save a woman on death row, severely thrashes a wife beater, and destroys a car full of smalltime hoodlums that made inappropriate advances towards newswoman Lois Lane.[2]

In later stories, in both comic books and comic strips, Superman combats political graft at city hall, stops gangsters from fixing boxing matches, battles smugglers, prevents the assassinations of both a senator and a royal family member, shuts down an orphanage that exploited children, prevents profiteers from starting a war, and creates decent public housing.[3] Superman accomplishes all of these things by being a tough hard-nosed fighter that at times even appears to become excessively brutal. (When combating a wife beater in *Action Comics* #1, Superman pushes a man so hard that the force of impact breaks a wall and scares the offender so badly that he faints.[4]) This early Superman was a superpowered street brawler who fought for the less fortunate and concerned himself more with social ills rather than cosmic threats. He was a product of his time who battled the same societal problems that average Americans faced every day. Superman was a child of his creators and like many children he inherited his parents' hopes and fears, while also possessing their life views. Because of this, Superman, and the costumed superheroes that were to follow, serve as a unique lens in which one can view the changing United States in the years directly preceding World War II.

The cover to *Action Comics* #1 gave Americans their first glimpse of the Man of Steel. (© 1938 DC Comics. Used with permission of DC Comics.)

He Came from Cleveland

While Superman's early adventures provide insight into the late 1930s, the story of Superman's creation is almost as mythic as the hero himself. In this often told legend two young Ohioans, Jerry Siegel and Joe Shuster, create the Man of Steel in the early 1930s in a classic American underdog-makes-good fantasy. Years later, Jerry Siegel claimed that he dreamed up Superman while lying in bed at his mother's house one steamy Cleveland summer night. He immediately began writing down his ideas and creating storylines for the hero. In Siegel's story, when the night was over he ran down the street to his high school friend Joe Shuster's house and the two of them began creating Superman comic strips.[5] The two young men tried to publish the hero's adventures as a newspaper strip but almost every publisher in the industry turned down the duo's strongman. Evidently DC Comics placed a Superman story in *Action Comics* #1 and put the hero on the cover. Soon Superman became a celebrated fictional character as millions read his adventures.[6] Although this story is probably as much fantasy as reality, it does provide a memorable origin story and it gives Superman a mythologized beginning. The Man of Steel was not only a hero that fought for truth and justice, but was also an all–American success story.

By June 1938 the young men raised during the Great Depression had created Superman, succeeded in finding a publisher, and were putting their creation to the task of solving society's ills. Although Superman was a fictional character, the problems he would combat were everyday real world injustices and social evils. The Man of Steel was beginning the fight against the evils that average Americans and real world leaders could not.

The New Deal

Around the time Jerry Siegel and Joe Shuster were creating Superman, many American citizens were placing their trust in another hero, albeit a very different type. During one of the most devastating economic and social upheavals in U.S. history, millions put their faith in the nation's new president, Franklin Delano Roosevelt. In the 1932 election, FDR, the challenger, ran on the platform that he would combat the Great Depression and create a "New Deal" for the average American. At the 1932 Democratic National Convention Roosevelt accepted his party's nomination as their presidential candidate with a speech in which he stated, "Throughout the nation men and women, forgotten in the political philosophy of the Government, look to us here for guidance and for more equitable opportunity to share in the distribution of national wealth.... I pledge myself to a new deal for the American people. This is more than a political campaign. It is a call to arms."[7] This "call to arms" would become a series of governmental programs, reform acts, and legislative initiatives that would change the direction of American government and society. Although Congress crafted and passed the legislation and other entities worked with the Executive Branch to create reform agendas, the general public associated the New Deal and the changes it brought with Franklin Roosevelt. Whether a person liked or loathed Roosevelt, he or she would almost certainly cite him as the architect of the nation's reform movement and the new idea of what the American government's responsibilities were.

A Balancing Act

Although Roosevelt's agenda was in practice a series of bureaucratic wrangling, at its heart the New Deal was a call to balance society and a desire to create a new sense of fairness. FDR wanted to balance urban and rural relations, to abolish child labor, and to create a strong social safety net. The New Deal was as much a vision of a new America as it was a series of policy programs.[8] Because New Deal programs often challenged societal norms and attempted to redistribute wealth and power, not all American citizens thought highly of FDR. A number of conservatives believed that FDR pressed for too much governmental control and many liberals felt that the New Deal was not radical enough. Politicians like Louisiana Senator Huey Long accused Roosevelt of forgetting the working man, while social reformers like Father Charles Coughlin at first backed the New Deal but later declared it to be too business-oriented.[9]

Although FDR had numerous critics, a large portion of Americans did agree with Roosevelt's policies and often venerated the man in an almost hero-like manner. The American electorate voted for Roosevelt as president an unprecedented four times, but many citizens appeared to hold more than political affection for their leader. The president's fireside radio chats brought his voice and his presence into people's homes. Citizens across the country hung pictures of Roosevelt in their houses and sponsored parades in his honor.[10] Americans also sent FDR a deluge of personal written correspondence as if he were a friend or mentor. It is estimated that Roosevelt received five thousand to eight thousand letters a day during his presidency, about ten times the amount that citizens sent his predecessor, Herbert Hoover.[11] The public's fondness for FDR was not just an interesting social phenomenon; it also helped the president to translate much of his New Deal agenda into law. During FDR's first term, he convinced the U.S. Congress to pass most of his reform efforts with easiness rarely seen in American politics.[12] Although some of Congress' willingness can be attributed to the deeply troubling times and the necessity to do something, some part of this action can also be connected to FDR's mammoth popularity. Roosevelt's hero status was a boon in creating a new role for government and a different direction in society. While not all Americans liked or supported the president, enough did so that he was able to fashion real and lasting social change.

A Different Kind of Hero

If President Franklin Roosevelt was a hero to many Americans during the Great Depression, then what were his heroic deeds? What were these social changes that are so often referenced? As mentioned above, FDR's New Deal programs were designed to balance society and create social reforms. Historians generally break the New Deal into two parts, the first in 1933 and the second from 1934 to 1936, but for this study the specifics are not as important as the understanding that FDR was attempting to change American society in an unprecedented manner. The president wanted to give the federal government a larger role in citizens' daily lives and attempted to provide the power to right perceived wrongs.

Examples of these programs include 1933's Civilian Conservation Corps (CCC), a work relief program that hired young men to work on conservation projects. The program provided food, clothing, training, and work experience. The Nation Recovery Administration (NRA), a major component of the National Industrial Recovery Act (NIRA), was a voluntary code that set a minimum wage and a maximum work week, and reduced the number of employers using sweatshops and child labor. The NRA even had its own comic strip–like spokesman, the Blue Eagle, and the slogan "We do our part." Although the Supreme Court eventually deemed the NRA unconstitutional, the bill's passage marked a new public understanding of the federal government's power. The Social Security Board (SSB) (later the Social Security Administration) provided social insurance for retirees, survivors, and the disabled.

Although there were dozens of these programs that critics often referred to as alphabet soup, these three display the major attributes of the New Deal—a desire to change the function and direction of government. Many inside and outside of government believed that economic and social systems had failed the American populace and it was the government's job to remedy this because no one else could. Just over five years after FDR took office and began to enact the New Deal, Jerry Siegel and Joe Shuster would create a fictional vision of social change. This social avenger would have all of the New Deal's goals but would be bound by none of its limitations.

The Social Avenger

Most twenty-first century Americans do not understand how exceptional Superman was when Siegel and Shuster introduced him to the world in 1938. Because the Man of Steel has morphed and changed so many times during the twentieth and twenty-first centuries, the modern reader or viewer generally equates Superman with the "Big Blue Boy Scout" of modern lore. While the twenty-first century Man of Steel is safe, comforting and maybe a little boring, in 1938 Superman was the most alien of characters (pun intended). To be fair, there were very few elements about Superman that were actually distinctive. Crime fighters had existed for years with the likes of Doc Savage in the pulps and the Shadow, the Lone Ranger, and the Green Hornet on the radio. The idea of a costumed hero preceded Superman with such notable examples as the Scarlet Pimpernel, Zorro, and the Phantom.[13] Strong men had been a staple of fiction for decades and characters such as Tarzan, Popeye, and the powerful hero from Philip Wylie's 1930 novel *Gladiator* all noticeably influenced Superman's creation.[14] Even the notion of heroes having adventures on foreign worlds was a science fiction trope used in stories such as *Buck Rogers, Flash Gordon*, and *John Carter of Mars*.

There were very few new ideas in Superman, but what was unique was that the introduction of this character was the first time that all of these traditional science fiction, pulp, and fantasy elements had been combined into one hero. Superman was the first super strong, crime fighting, costumed hero from another world. In other words, he was the first superhero. While young readers had delighted over the exploits of other heroes for years, the Man of Steel was the first avenger to offer all the thrills in one package. Although this now sounds like a logical next step, in truth, publishing Superman was a gamble because no one knew how the public would react to the new character.

A Superman of His Time

Very few people had faith in Superman at the beginning and even fewer dreamed that he would one day become an American mythological icon. As previously mentioned, Jerry Siegel and Joe Shuster shopped their costumed hero to numerous publishers before one agreed to print his adventures. Sheldon Mayer, an editor at DC Comics, the company that finally did publish Superman, claimed that publisher Harry Donenfeld himself was afraid that Superman was too fantastic: "He really got worried. He felt nobody would believe it; that it was ridiculous—crazy."[15] These fears soon subsided as the publisher learned that Superman's stories were selling issues of *Action Comics* better than other comics. Because the Man of Steel's adventures were only one part of the comic book, Harry Donenfeld's sales staff polled news vendors about *Action Comics'* strong sales. They soon found that young buyers were requesting "the comic with Superman in it."[16] Sales of *Action Comics* soon grew to over half a million issues a month and Superman's new self-titled quarterly comic book debuted in 1939 and had a circulation of 1,250,000 by 1940.[17] These high sales figures reveal the connection that readers felt with Superman. Although it is difficult to tell exactly what readers liked about the Man of Tomorrow, it is evident that something about the character resonated with his followers. Not all of Superman's readers were children, but almost all children read comic books. A survey found that in the 1940s over 80 percent of adolescents and more than 90 percent of elementary school aged children read comic books.[18] Additionally, most of the creators and publishers created comic book stories with children in mind. These stories provided action, adventure, and fun, but they also supplied something that set Superman apart from the competition. The Man of Steel appears to be the rare character that came along at the right time and caught the public's imagination. In order for this to be true it can be assumed that Superman fulfilled some need among comic book readers, and he filled some unspoken desire. Superman may have only been a fictional character but in order to pay a dime for his monthly comic book, readers had to have gained something important.

Social Champion

Many non–comic book readers, and even some fans of the genre, believe that comic books are and always have been a type of juvenile literature that offers fantastical stories and has no link to or bearing on society. In this view comic books are lowbrow children's escapist reading material that provides nothing of value. This idea supposes that comic books are a throwaway medium devoid of any social worth. While social worth and value, much like beauty, are in the eye of the beholder, one cannot argue that in the late 1930s Superman comics enjoyed a mammoth circulation. Sales figures do not prove cultural value, but they do establish that something about early Superman comics caught the attention of the general public. As previously noted, Superman offered a variety of understood action-adventure elements in one place, but this says nothing of the stories themselves. While Superman's powers were interesting enough to draw readers in, it was his timely adventures that kept new comic books fans returning for more. These stories showed the Man of Steel fighting social ills and battling low-level type criminals that would be familiar to readers young and old. These comic books did provide escapist literature but not in the pejorative meaning that is so widely used. They were escapist in the sense that they allowed for an outlet from a world gone mad. As newspaper headlines screamed of war, poverty, famine, and disease, Superman's stories provided a fantasy world where good guys won and bad guys were punished. They created a superpowered savior who would protect the innocent and guard the meek. Jerry Siegel and Joe Shuster's fictional America was a place where someone powerful combated society's ills and no one could stop him. Superman's comic books were escapist literature but that is a compliment rather than a derogatory comment. For a few minutes every month, hundreds of thousands of readers escaped to a better place that provided them hope for the future. Pulitzer Prize–winning author Michael Chabon, in an article in *The New Yorker*, described Superman's appeal:

> An entire world of superheroic adventure could be dreamed up by a couple of boys from Columbia, or Cleveland. And the self you knew you contained, the story you knew you had inside you, might find its way like an emblem onto the spot right over your heart. All

we needed to do was accept the standing invitation that superhero comics extended to us by means of [wearing] a towel. It was an invitation to enter into the world of story, to join in the ongoing business of comic books, and, with the knotting of a magical beach towel, to begin to wear what we knew to be hidden inside us.[19]

Comic book historian and child of the 1930s Jules Feiffer explained Superman's benefit this way:

> Those of us raised in ghetto neighborhoods were being asked to believe that crime didn't pay? Tell that to the butcher! Nice guys finished last; landlords, first. Villains by their simple appointment to the role were miles ahead. It was not to be believed that any ordinary human could combat them. More was required. Someone with a call. When Superman at last appeared, he brought with him the deep satisfaction of all underground truths: Our reaction was less "How original!" than "But, of course!"[20]

Superman's value was that he was one of the only people in late 1930s America that could help fix society. No politician, Supreme Court justice, city hall boss, or even the law itself could stop the Man of Steel from doing what was right. Superman was able to accomplish things in his fictional world that Franklin Roosevelt could only dream about in the real one. Comic book writer Grant Morrison notes, "Superman made his position plain: He was a hero of the people. The original Superman was a bold humanist response to Depression-era fears of runaway scientific advance and soulless industrialism."[21] Superman's stories continually tackled real world issues while providing adventure, humor, and happy endings. While critics may still deem Superman stories as trash, the tales provided much needed hope for a weary 1930s America.

The New Hero

The public's first glimpse of Superman left little doubt about the Man of Steel's motives and methods. As previously noted, Superman first appeared on U.S. newsstands in *Action Comics* #1, cover dated June 1938. The comic book's cover displays the red and blue costumed Man of Tomorrow lifting a car above his head and smashing it against a large rock. In the forefront of the image a suit and tie clad man holds his head in his hands as he flees from the bedlam. This was the first Superman image that 1930s America saw. Jerry Siegel and Joe Shuster did have earlier versions of the Man of Steel (even one where Superman was a villain), but this was the first publicly accessible Superman illustration.[22] This image of Superman destroying private property and terrorizing several escaping men was America's introduction to its new hero. If first impressions matter, then Superman seemed to be projecting himself as a violent strongman unworried about law and order. Inside the comic book the story is uneven and jumps from scene to scene quickly because Siegel and Shuster cut and pasted the adventure from several sample Superman newspaper strips.[23] Ultimately, this story cobbling provides the tale with a kinetic energy that mirrors its main character's manic vigor. This first Superman is a force of nature that can neither be stopped nor contained.

Not So Secret Origin

The thirteen page *Action Comics* #1 story devotes the first page to a quick Superman origin, explains what his powers are, and offers a "scientific explanation" for Superman's

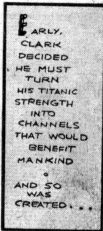

Superman's origin and powers are explained in his first appearance in July 1938's *Action Comics* #1. Jerry Siegel and Joe Shuster introduced Superman as a Great Depression social avenger, although this would soon change. (© 1938 DC Comics. Used with permission of DC Comics.)

amazing abilities. Most importantly though are two first page panels that showcase Siegel's explanation of Superman's purpose. "Early, Clark decided he must turn his titanic strength into channels that would benefit mankind and so was created ... Superman! Champion of the oppressed. The physical marvel who had sworn to devote his existence to helping those in need."[24] This is Superman's earliest mission statement; his reason for being. Notice what is included and what is not. The explanation basically contains two parts; the first is the understanding that Superman is in fact super. He is referred to as having "titanic strength" and is considered "a physical marvel." It is not surprising that Siegel focuses on Superman's superpowers; the Man of Steel was a new character and the public needed to be sold on what he could do. Interestingly though, Siegel does not mention Superman's other powers by name here. Siegel needed to be the literary carnival barker that drew in a crowd and thus hyped Superman's abilities as a whole and not individually.

More importantly for this study is the quotation's second element, which focuses on Superman's purpose. Note that he uses his strength to "benefit mankind" and is referred to as the "champion of the oppressed." Superman also has promised to "devote his existence to helping those in need." Superman undoubtedly is a good guy with noble aims and selfless motives. He wants what is best for humanity and especially the less fortunate. Perhaps what is most important about Superman's mission statement is not what is included but what is not. Nowhere does the text mention the words or phrases "truth," "justice," or "the American way." Superman never claims to have devoted himself to keeping the peace, upholding the law, or maintaining order. By this definition Superman is a vigilante who follows his own understanding of right and wrong. Superman is dedicated to helping those in need but in the manner that he chooses. This early statement of Superman's purpose showcases the Man of Steel as a 1930s superhero, which is quite different from the twenty-first century definition.

Unstoppable

After the brief setup, the first Superman story truly commences on page number two. As the adventure begins, the Man of Steel leaps towards the governor's mansion while carrying a bound and gagged young woman. It is unclear how the young lady fits into the narrative but apparently she held an important position in earlier versions of the story. Superman leaves the incapacitated woman outside as he barges into the governor's residence by knocking down the executive mansion's door. He ignores the governor's butler yelling, "This is illegal entry! I'll have you arrested!" and carries the servant upstairs to the governor's steel-doored bedroom.[25] Superman, of course, rips off the metal door, watches the bullets bounce off his chest as the manservant shoots him, and then convinces the governor to sign a pardon for an innocent woman on death row.

In the coming pages, Superman manhandles a wife beater, destroys the car of a group of gangsters, and stops a lobbyist and corrupt senator from pulling the U.S. into the war in Europe. Superman literally leaps from one situation to the next at a frenzied pace that would seem to mark him as a desirable Ritalin candidate.

This introductory version of Superman is certainly a superhero, but one without superpowered foes. This lack of supervillains may seem antithetical to superhero mythology, but this early text asserts that the 1930s Superman's purpose was to fight against common problems and help average people. Look at this first story's villains: a sheltered and misguided state official, a domestic abuser, several smart-mouthed mobsters, a lobbyist, and a corrupt federal politician. These are hardly the world-conquering madmen that would later be comic book staples, but that is Siegel and Shuster's intention. Although it is almost comical to think of Superman crusading against lobbyists, many Americans of this period considered these kinds of men to be the villains that started the Great Depression. Superman battled the everyday evildoers and problems that destroyed countless lives. Superman warred against the Great Depression's miseries and offered a new deal of his own, although using vastly different methods and often deriving much different outcomes.

Saving the World on a Micro Level

In this first story alone, Superman faces and solves numerous common but important problems. The Man of Tomorrow first intercedes in the political/legal process on the behalf of an innocent woman. The justice system had failed her, the courts wrongly convicted her, the law offered no recourse, and soon the state would unjustly execute her. State representatives would soon shed innocent blood and there appeared to be no remedy. Next, Superman saves a woman from a savage beating. He stops a violent offender from taking advantage of someone physically weaker than him and abusing her. Superman then proceeds to overpower and frighten a group of mobsters. The men kidnap Lois Lane, threaten Clark Kent, and act as if they are above the law. The Man of Steel uses brutal force against men that intimidate and bully society. He teaches those who think they are above the law a lesson. Lastly, Superman threatens and harasses a lobbyist who is attempting to bribe a corrupt senator. If the lobbyist succeeds the politician will make a mockery of the democratic process and worse, harm innocent people. If the lobbyist and senator achieve their goal the United States will be unnecessarily dragged into European problems. Superman works to prevent the impending damage with the story continuing in the next issue.[26]

Although each of these instances at first would appear to be minor wrongs, they are all very socially damaging. Each individual, and the actions he or she produces, harm numerous members of society. Much like an outsider could see the Great Depression as a series of boring financial and political events, the "minor" crimes that Superman combats are only important if one focuses on the victim's suffering.

One example of a real life victim is Ben Issacs, a Chicago resident during the Great Depression, who remembered the hard life and the feeling of hopelessness. He recalled how helpless he felt when he lost his job and the world seemed to turn against him. How powerless he had become when he could no longer support himself and thus could no longer defend himself. He remembered, "I always prayed in my heart that I should never depend on anyone for support. When the time came, it hurted [sic] me. I couldn't take it. Shame? You tellin' me? I would go stand on that relief line, I would look this way and that way and see if there's nobody around that knows me. I would bend my head low so nobody would recognize me."[27]

In reality, Superman is fighting the living conditions the Great Depression created. He is fighting the politicians that cannot or will not fix the situation. He is battling the bullies that prey on the weak because they can. He is fighting those that wish to take advantage of other people's misery. In these early stories, Superman is the fictional embodiment of the New Deal spirit, and the Man of Steel fights to restructure society in a more fair and equitable manner. When the average American needed a champion to protect them, Siegel and

Shuster created Superman as a social avenger. Although Superman was fighting to protect the oppressed, his methods were very different from New Deal programs.

No Holds Barred

Just as important as the evils that Superman battled are the methods that he employed. What many modern readers do not realize is that besides being a social avenger, the 1930s Superman was also a vigilante. Superman worked outside the boundaries of the law and often assaulted or even killed criminals, but this brutality was seemingly acceptable to 1930s readers. The Man of Steel was a product of his rough and tumble Great Depression society and his methods displayed this sensibility. Superman frequently used overly-aggressive and often harsh tactics to create order during a brutal age. Americans of this era tell stories of soup lines that wrapped city blocks, friends and neighbors that struggled to find enough food to eat, a national government that ordered the Army to aggressively disperse protesting veterans, gangsters that arose during Prohibition, and a world where the American dream was replaced with a dark reality. The denizens of such a time demanded a hero that was as scrappy as they were and Superman's violent actions appear to have been acceptable to at least most of his readers. Superman was using the only methods available to him in a society where law and order had failed to protect innocent citizens.

Because Superman only acted in instances in which the law itself had fallen short, one could argue that Superman's methods were not illegal but rather extralegal, the idea of extralegal being that a law cannot be broken if the legislature has never passed a law that addresses the situation. One could contend that neither federal nor state lawmakers had envisioned the need for laws pertaining to how spacemen use their superpowers. (This argument assumes that lawmakers did not create the Alien and Sedition Acts of 1798 to address the space variety of aliens.) If one believes that legislators never crafted laws that concentrate on superhuman acts, then Superman was not breaking the law but rather was laboring outside of its scope. Whether this early Superman was a criminal or an extralegal partisan, his actions were generally violent and often unsavory. The Man of Steel achieved his desired results but often did so only by destructive means. Superman generally left a path of destruction in his wake and the aftermath was often akin to a natural phenomenon like a tornado or hurricane. Superman destroyed, threatened, attacked, and sometimes killed. He was a hard and often cold hero for a time and place that the same adjectives could easily describe. Siegel and Shuster created the type of hero that Great Depression America needed, a New Deal social avenger with aggressive and often brutal tendencies. Your (grand)father's Superman was not someone that you wanted to meet in a dark alley.

A Tough Hero for a Tough Era

Superman's first appearance in *Action Comics* #1 once again serves as an excellent primer to illustrate Superman's aggressive and often destructive behavior. In this first story Superman seemingly kidnaps a young woman, manhandles the governor's manservant, destroys government property, threatens and intimidates an elected official, beats a domestic abuser, destroys a privately owned automobile, harasses, assaults, and batters several citizens, and menaces a lobbyist. In comic books and newspaper strip stories throughout 1938 and 1939

Superman often abuses wrongdoers and sometimes causes circumstances in which people are harmed or even killed. Superman leaps into these situations with an almost manic glee that serves as a strong commentary about the society that produced Superman's creators. Several comic book historians and aficionados, including *The Book of Lies* author Brad Meltzer, believe that Jerry Siegel created Superman because the young man's father was shot to death in 1932.[28] While the elder Siegel's murder undoubtedly played a part in the bulletproof hero's creation, Superman is more than a byproduct of Siegel losing his father. One cannot argue against the idea that Mitchell Siegel's death was part of Jerry Siegel's inspiration for creating Superman, but the younger Siegel put so much more into the character. Superman was far more than a youthful revenge fantasy or Siegel's search for a protector. Rather Superman was a remedy for all of society's ills. The Man of Steel was bigger than just Siegel and his father; Superman became an outlet for addressing the evils of the Great Depression. Superman was an often brutal warrior because he had to be and he understood his job. The Man of Steel served as the protector that society needed and deserved.

The American Superman/Man of Steel

One fascinating Superman newspaper comic strip published in the February 27, 1940, issue of *Look* magazine displays both Superman's purpose and his methods. In this short two page story Superman ends World War II over a year and a half before the United States actually became involved. The tale begins with Superman, "savior of the helpless and oppressed," running towards the Siegfried Line and penetrating the Nazis' defenses as the Germans fire helplessly at the Man of Steel. Superman destroys German fortifications, aircraft, and cannons while trying to convince the French forces to attack. The costumed hero then crashes through Adolf Hitler's roof, knocks out the Fuehrer's bodyguards, and captures the German leader. Superman picks Hitler up by the neck and exclaims, "I'd like to land a strictly non–Aryan sock on your jaw, but there's no time for that! You're coming with me while I visit a certain pal of yours."[29] Superman then drags Hitler to Moscow, where he also seizes Josef Stalin. The Man of Steel takes both Hitler and Stalin to Geneva, Switzerland, where they stand trial before the League of Nations. Superman enters the room and states, "Gentlemen, I've brought before you the two power-mad scoundrels responsible for Europe's present ills." The League of Nations then pronounces the two leaders guilty of crimes against humanity.[30] This story shows Superman violently attacking both German and Russian forces because he blames their leaders for Europe's troubles.

This simplistic idealism mixed with a gritty physicality is the essence of the 1930s Superman. The Man of Steel uses violent methods to fight for the world's innocent victims. Superman is quick to separate himself from both Hitler and Friedrich Nietzsche's superman by declaring himself a non–Aryan (this is also a nod to Siegel and Shuster's Jewish heritage). Superman also attacks and captures Stalin, proving that the American superhero truly is the "Man of Steel." (Stalin's birth name was Yosef Dzhugashvili, but the Georgian often used pseudonyms based in Slavic folklore. The name "Stalin" in Russian means "man of steel." When Superman fought the Soviet leader it was a battle between two very different versions of a man of steel.)

Although Superman normally did not battle such high profile villains, fighting Hitler and Stalin offered him a chance to internationalize his uniquely American mixture of optimism and brutality. Interestingly, after Superman disables large pieces of the German and

Soviet war machines, frightens the armies, and captures and insults the Teutonic and Russian/Georgian leaders, the Man of Steel goes to court. While Superman often works outside the law, he recognizes the importance of the world deciding the two leaders' fates. Superman is the true 1930s American hero; an optimistic yet physically aggressive avenger willing to break or circumvent the law in order to protect the oppressed.

Funnyman

Superman fought crime and wrongdoing with an aggressive and often violent approach, but his manner was anything but serious. While Superman continuously frightened many offenders into submission, he himself had a gleeful appreciation of his duties. The Man of Steel often toyed with wrongdoers and seemed to relish his adversaries' (over)reactions to his superpowers. In *Action Comics* #1, Superman manhandles the crooked lobbyist by grabbing him by the leg and leaping across the city with the man dangling from the costumed avenger's hand. With the man tucked under his arm, Superman playfully runs across telephone lines, which scares the offender into thinking that he will be electrocuted. Superman replies, "No we won't. Birds sit on the telephone wires and they aren't electrocuted — not unless they touch a telephone-pole and are *grounded!* Oops!—I almost touched a pole!"[31] Superman then leaps from building to building in a jovial attempt to scare the man as the Man of Steel proclaims, "Missed — Doggone it!"[32]

In later comics and comic strips Superman amuses himself by letting villains test his powers and thus often harming themselves. In one particularly odd example from a May 1939 newspaper strip Superman allows himself to be subjected to a military firing squad that shoots him again and again. A smiling Superman eggs the men on, extolling them to try again. As the men continue to fire but not harm him, the Man of Steel playfully exclaims, "Ho-hum! This is beginning to bore me." Finally, one of the soldiers, fearing that the rifles contain only blanks, tests the weapon on his own foot. The man shoots himself in the foot and Superman soon leaps away unharmed.[33]

More Good Humor Than an Ice Cream Truck

Gerald Jones, the author of *Men of Tomorrow: Geeks, Gangsters and the Birth of the Comic Book*, claims that Superman's sense of fun was previously unseen in the pulps and the comics. Superman is the first hero who enjoys what he does so much that he outwardly delights in his powers and the good that he can do. Jones believes that the Man of Steel's super sense of humor is a reflection of Siegel and Shuster's youthful exuberance and the perceived joy of being so powerful.[34] (Unfortunately, Superman's fun side later becomes much less pronounced. In a 1990 episode of the television series *Seinfeld*, George and Jerry even argue about whether Superman has a sense of humor.)[35] The character of Superman certainly does provide an outlet for Siegel and Shuster to explore boyhood power fantasies, but more importantly the Man of Steel's joviality also serves as social commentary. Superman not only fights criminals, he toys with them like a cat with a mouse. He enjoys proving that he is not limited by society's normal rules and is not subject to its failures.

This lifestyle would appeal to any period's residents, but would strongly resonate within a 1930s America in which many had lost faith by their social and political foundations.

Superman does not recognize the authority of a system that has failed to protect its citizens. The Man of Steel fights botched authority by working outside the law to provide the services that local, state, and federal governments should but fail to. He can do the things that millions of Americans wished they could without suffering the consequences. Superman can right wrongs and punish the deserving in whatever manner he decides is fair. Superman is an unstoppable force who gets to help the unfortunate, correct society's ills, and do anything else he wants; why would he not be happy?

Job Fulfillment

Superman's sense of humor was not just a reaction to an American system that many viewed as deeply flawed, it was also a weapon against criminals. Although later comic book heroes would fight crime, the 1930s Superman bullied it. He laughed at criminals, he harassed wrongdoers, and he denigrated and degraded his enemies. Superman did not want to merely win but needed to dominate and subjugate anyone that would dare stand against him. The Man of Steel not only punished criminals but he humiliated them in ways they would never forget and probably never recover from. He terrified and embarrassed offenders so badly that they would almost be forced to reform.

Imagine being the lobbyist that Superman manhandles in *Action Comics* #1. You are a white collar criminal that Superman yanks from an office building and begins to threaten. Only a moment ago you were making your backroom deal and now this deranged madman, dressed like a circus performer, is lifting you above the city by one arm. (This would seemingly be quite painful and might result in tendon damage, shoulder dislocation, or worse.) You are now in shock. You do not know what is going on and are stunned that this could be happening to you. How is it possible that someone can act like this and do these things? Is he human? Why is he doing this? This superpowered crazy person now tucks you under his arm and tells you he knows you have been bribing a government official. He cannot work for law enforcement though, his methods are too erratic. What does he want? Your arm is beginning to ache as he leaps dangerously high into the air again and again. You start to believe that he is going to kill you as he begins to taunt you. The red and blue clad freak runs across the telephone wires while teasing you that he might step on the wrong spot and kill you both. He then jumps from the top of one building to another, while joking that he might slip and leave you to plummet to the ground. This creature has total control over you, he not only has physically overpowered (and probably permanently injured) you, he also has both mentally and emotionally broken you. He is not a law enforcement agent that identifies himself, follows accepted rules, and acts in an understood manner. No, this thing is dangerous, erratic, and a menace. How can you ever sleep again knowing that he could be watching you?

Our Superman

When introduced in 1938, Superman, the first modern superhero, was less powerful than he would soon become, but was far more unpredictable and dangerous. The Man of Steel at first did not concern himself with galactic invasions or world dominating madmen (except for a quick two page battle with Hitler and Stalin), but rather fought against social ills that harmed the innocent and the oppressed. He was a reflection of the society that created him, a 1930s America that needed a hero who would fight for the common man and would not be dominated by the flawed and corrupt system of the day. Although the first Superman was much too violent and unpredictable for later eras, he was perfect for the one that created him. Because of this the hero was widely popular and spawned a plethora of imitators. Although Superman was the first Great Depression superhero, many more would come and would attempt to save society from itself.

A Dark and Stormy Knight

Superman was the prototypical Great Depression superhero; a costumed avenger that fought for a better society in an aggressive vigilante manner. He was the first of many comic book superheroes who would soon dominate the American imagination and eventually become a part of the nation's collective mythology. Not long after Superman's first publication, DC Comics also published another superhero that would become an American cultural touchstone. The Bat-Man first appeared in *Detective Comics* #27 cover dated May 1939. Bob Kane, a young cartoonist, created the character after hearing about Superman's popularity. Kane and his collaborator, Bill Finger, based the Bat-Man on diverse sources such as a Leonardo da Vinci sketch, Zorro, and Dracula.[36] Although the Dark Knight was supposed to capitalize on Superman's popularity, in many ways the character was different from Superman, the most notable being that the Bat-Man had no superpowers. The Bat-Man was socialite playboy Bruce Wayne, who trained for many years in order to fight crime during the night.

Bat-Man soon became the unhyphenated "Batman" and within six months readers discovered that the costumed hero fought crime in order to avenge his parents' death. In this *Detective Comics* #33 story the young Bruce Wayne witnesses his parents' murders and vows, "I swear by the spirits of my parents to avenge their deaths by spending the rest of my life warring on all criminals."[37] Unlike Superman, the Batman (whom writers soon referred to without the definite article) is a mere mortal who wants to avenge a personal wrong. While Superman was physically gifted at birth, Batman had to train for many years to become a superhero. (One could argue that Batman is not a superhero because he has no powers. The general counter to this argument is that Batman produces super actions even though he himself does not have natural superpowers.) Even though Batman did not possess Superman's natural abilities, his training and hard work allowed him to be an average man that made himself super.

The Common Batman

The superpowerless Batman was the converse of the overly powerful Superman, but the Dark Knight was also the very model of a modern Great Depression comic book hero. While the Great Depression Superman was a social avenger/New Deal savior, Batman was an example of the common person helping herself or himself. (Billionaire Bruce Wayne was far from common socially and economically, but his lack of superpowers made him average physically. While it may sound odd to describe a rich playboy as "average," when compared to superhumans, Batman is merely a typical person, albeit a wealthy one.) Superman was

Detective Comics #33 (November 1939) introduced Batman's origin and reason for existing. (© 1939 DC Comics. Used with permission of DC Comics.)

the godlike champion whose help the public prayed for, while Batman was an example of what the average citizen could do to help herself or himself.

Because Batman had limited physical abilities, he often had to rely on mental quickness and technological advances to fight crime. Superman was more powerful than the villains he fought, but Batman was smarter and better equipped. Batman's everyman persona and history of creating his own identity and crime fighting ideal fits into the popular "rags to riches" story. While Bruce Wayne started out with money, through hard work and force of will, he was able to build a new super identity for himself. Criminals robbed young Bruce Wayne of his parents and a normal life, so he fights back using training, his intelligence, and American know-how. Using this paradigm, replace Bruce Wayne with the average 1930s American citizen and substitute the criminal that killed Wayne's parents for economic and social forces that robbed many Americans of their former lives. In this reading of Batman stories, the Caped Crusader was the average American battling everyday oppressive forces using hard work and intelligence. Popular culture historian Rick Marschall describes Batman's everyman appeal by noting, "Basically it is the Batman's ultimate vulnerability, not invulnerability, that seizes our attention, affection, and loyalty. We could be him, if...."[38] Batman was assuring readers that they do not need an outside savior, but they themselves could fight against the Great Depression's hardships. Batman was an extension of the American idea that hard work will solve social and political ills. Superman may have fought for the common man but Batman was the common man fighting for himself.

Where Does He Get Those Wonderful Toys?

The first Batman stories showed a belief in the average American's abilities that was not evident in early Superman tales. It provided a superhero lifestyle that a non-powered reader could aspire to and work toward. (This is one aspect of Batman's appeal that seemingly has not changed throughout the years. In 2005, *Forbes Magazine* published an online article calculating how much it would cost to become Batman.[39] In 2008, Dr. E. Paul Zehr wrote a book that scientifically explained how an average person would have to physically and physiologically train to become Batman.[40])

Besides hard work and intelligence, another important element of the 1930s Batman is his use of technology. Even in his earliest adventures, the Caped Crusader relied on gadgets and weapons for his war on crime. Batman's consistent use of technology placed him within the 1930s American mainstream. While the United States was facing a slew of difficult problems at home and abroad, a large number of Americans believed technology could help provide a better future. This technological idealism was evident at the 1939–40 New York World's Fair. This exposition showcased technological advancement and promised a future world made better by technology.[41] The fair preached the same gospel of American innovation that is evident in early Batman stories. The modernist movement had emphasized technology as both a force of good and of ill, and whether they liked or feared new innovations, almost all Americans understand technology's great importance. Batman may not have been superpowered, but he was crafty and possessed all the right technical tools. Much as the Great Depression had trapped the United States, the Caped Crusader often found himself in terrible trouble, but his technological advantage always helped save him just like readers hoped it would help rescue America.

Examples of Batman's advanced technological acumen abound in early tales. In the third Batman story in *Detective Comics* #29, cover dated July 1939, the Dark Knight is shown using suction cups to climb the sides of a building, and he employs a glass pellet from his utility belt to deliver "choking gas" to a criminal. During this adventure Batman is shot and injured, but he is able to survive and win due to his advanced technology.[42] "In *Detective Comics* #31, dated September 1939, Batman employs a helicopter-like flying machine named the Batgyro. The Dark Knight also escapes a death trap using his soon to be famous throwing weapon, the baterang (later spelled batarang) which is described as being 'modeled after the Australian bushman's boomerang.'"[43] Later, in November 1939's *Detective Comics* #33, Batman creates a chemical that is able to neutralize a dirigible-flying madman's death ray and thus saves the city.[44]

Because Batman was a man with average physical abilities, he used technological tools to make his life easier and better. Many average Americans hoped that technological advances would also help to rescue the nation from the perils of the Great Depression.

Vampires, Wolfmen, and Evil Scientists: Good Villains; Bad Dinner Guests

Another unique Great Depression element in early Batman stories is the Caped Crusader's odd assortment of villains. While the 1930s Superman was generally battling common criminals and rule breakers, Batman's early villains were normally megalomaniacal madmen, scientists or supernatural entities. During the time that the incredibly powerful Superman fought average men, the non-superpowered Batman battled foes that were often far more powerful or better equipped than he. As Superman was stopping wife beaters and gangsters, Batman was facing villains that sound like a standard list of pulp and horror story bad guys.

In Batman's first eleven stories in *Detective Comics* #27 to 37, the Caped Crusader battles scientists, jewel thieves, a mad scientist (Dr. Death) and his hired assassin, a costumed villain/werewolf known as the Monk and a gorilla, a vampire, a would-be dictator with a death ray, another evil scientist, an actor/jewel thief, and yet another mad scientist.[45]

Besides causing a generation of comic book readers to fear anyone with a Bunsen burner, these stories also provided the oxymoronic idea of an average superhero (non-powered) that battled the most extreme wrongs. Superman fought against common problems that plagued Great Depression era America, but Batman conquered the fantastical. This difference marked the Dark Knight as an extension of pulp novel and comic strip heroes that had long battled the dark evil forces. Batman provided 1930s America with someone to fight the problems that seemed insurmountable. While Superman fought against the crooked landlords and corrupt politicians that plagued daily lives, someone had to declare war on the era's world shattering evils. Someone had to combat the war, pestilence, and famine that filled both headlines and nightmares. Strangely, the person American comic book readers chose for this exalted position decided to change the world by dressing like a giant bat.

The Migration Patterns of the Gotham City Bat

In addition to being a non-powered, hardworking technology lover with supernatural and megalomaniacal foes, Batman had one other important American 1930s era trait; he was an America-centered isolationist. The United States was a rising world power in the late 1930s, but many Americans wanted the country to focus on domestic issues. The United States' involvement in the disastrous Great War (later known as World War I) had darkened many citizens' and politicians' understanding of America's place in world affairs. A strong American isolationist strain had existed at least since George Washington's 1796 farewell address admonishment to beware of "the mischiefs of foreign intrigue," but World War I's brutality and seemingly useless carnage encouraged a renewed political and social inward focus.[46] The U.S. Senate rejected the country's entry into the League of Nations (although President Woodrow Wilson had spearheaded its creation), and many Americans were happy to be rid of Europe's problems. The rapid growth and social follies of the 1920s pushed world affairs from many people's minds and the Great Depression only strengthened the notion that the country should embark on an "America first" policy. Public sentiment would seem to suggest that an American comic book superhero should stay in United States and fight against America's problems. Even the seemingly all powerful Superman rarely traveled abroad and generally concerned himself with bettering American citizen's lives.

Although Batman battles a number of domestic bad guys, the Caped Crusader's early adventures also feature business trips to fight dangerous foes in both Paris, France (*Detective Comics* # 31 and 34), and Hungary (*Detective Comics* #32). Why would Batman, the every-man superhero, fight against these foreign evils during an isolationist era? Certainly one answer is that Paris and Hungary provide a cosmopolitan backdrop for exciting Batman adventures. More importantly for the study, though, is the notion that Batman was protecting the American people from foreign invaders. The Dark Knight never went to other countries to fight crime and protect foreign citizens; rather Batman chased international criminals from Gotham abroad. Although Batman was a world traveler, his actions were an extension of American isolationism. The Dark Knight was keeping Americans safe from evil international forces and stopping the country from becoming entangled in foreign affairs. The Caped Crusader's international traveling tales have an isolationist underpinning that fits with the "America first" sentiment of the day. Batman was a Great Depression hero who fought for American citizens even when he had to go abroad to do so.

The Superhero Deluge

Superman and Batman were the archetypal Great Depression superheroes both fighting for a society that needed their assistance. While the powerful Superman was American's social avenger, Batman was a self-made crusader that battled grandiose foes both at home and abroad. Because Superman and Batman's stories attracted a large number of readers, scores of imitators soon followed. Comic book historian Mike Benton claims that over 700 new comic book superheroes were created in the period from 1938 to 1954.[47] Many of these heroes were introduced in the late 1930s and early 1940s in order to capitalize on the perceived superhero fad. Almost all comic book creators fashioned their new costumed crime fighters by copying Superman and Batman's perceived successful elements. Although a few comic book writers and artists, like Will Eisner, expanded the medium, most were happy to publish Superman and Batman clones and hope for a large readership. Some of these characters are unintentionally comical to twenty-first century readers, but all of them were attempts to fill a need in Great Depression America. Superman and Batman had paved the way as rough and tumble heroes that fought for society when no one else could or would. Soon other costumed comic book superheroes would take up the quest using many of the same methods and storylines. The citizens of late 1930s America had desperately needed a hero; now they had dozens.

Pick a Color, Add an Animal, Mix in a Superpower and Place on the Newsstand

The general formula for making a post–Superman and Batman Great Depression comic book superhero appears to have been as follows. Select a title, rank or color. Add that to the name of an animal, an adjective, or a description of the hero's powers, and you have the basis for a new hero. Examples of this are Blonde Phantom, Blue Beetle, Blue Bolt, Black Hood, Black Terror, Blackhawk, Black Cat, Cat-Man, Hawkman, Doll Man, Bulletman, Amazing Man, Sandman, Hydroman, Sub-Zero Man, Hangman, Starman, Vapo-Man, Mango the Magnetic Man, Volton the Human Generator, Phantom Lady, Wonder Woman, The Fin, Human Bomb, Doctor Fate, Major Victory, Captain Marvel, and Captain Midnight. (A personal favorite is Whizzer, a speedster who gained his powers by receiving a transfusion of mongoose blood.)

A few of these new heroes gained a large readership, while others never caught on. Additionally, copyright infringement litigation forced some heroes, like Wonder Man, to cease publication.[48] Just as many of the heroes were basically copies of Superman and Batman, so were a majority of their stories. Writers gave most of the new superhero clones formulaic adventures in order to maximize the costumed heroes' potential appeal. With Superman and Batman as their templates, the new heroes, too, tried to become social avengers and protectors of the innocent.

One example of these Great Depression superhero storylines can be found in the adventures of the superhero Bulletman, who premiered in May 1940's *Nickel Comics* #1. Bulletman has a mixture of Superman and Batman's appeal and powers. His origin is standard superhero lore; Bulletman was Pat Barr, who vowed to fight crime after gangsters murdered his father. Barr became a police scientist and attempted to create a serum that would serve as a vaccine against criminal behavior. He tested the crime antidote on himself and soon discovered that the chemicals gave him super-intelligence. This increased potential allowed Barr to develop a Gravity Regulator Helmet that gave him the power of flight, the ability to harmlessly deflect bullets, and the means to crash headfirst through walls or any other solid surface. The powerful helmet was bullet shaped, so Barr tailored a costume and began to fight crime as Bulletman. Barr soon created another helmet for his girlfriend, Susan Kent, and quickly she joined his adventures as Bulletgirl. Before long both of these male and female human projectiles were battling criminals and protecting society in the tradition of Batman and Superman.[49]

Extraordinary Ordinance

All superheroes, including Superman and Batman, borrowed traits, themes, and qualities from science fiction, pulp, and comic strip stories. Bulletman and Bulletgirl not only follow these previous storytelling traditions, but also liberally utilize several of the newly developed comic book conventions. Bulletman dressed in a colorful costume, had a hero name that ended in "man," and fought to protect the innocent like both Superman and Batman. Like the Man of Steel, Bulletman was superpowered and used his powers for the common good. Like Batman, Bulletman fought against crime because his father was killed by criminals, used technology in his quest, and saw himself as a detective. Bulletman also often fought evil scientists and madmen like Batman. An example of this is 1940's *Bulletman* #1 in which Bulletman battles the Black Spider, a mysterious evil madman with world domination plans similar to those of many Batman villains.[50] Bulletman is just one example of the hundreds of costumed superheroes that appeared quickly after Superman's debut. Superman's tremendous popularity pushed many publishers to create heroes that copied the Man of Steel's main traits, and by the end of 1940 the U.S. was awash in supermen and superwomen. These superheroes provided many Americans a much needed reprieve from their problems and fictional champions in which to place their faith.

Conclusion

The 1930s was a difficult time for many Americans. As the United States suffered though the Great Depression, Europe quickly marched towards war. Many American citizens were unemployed and hungry, while even more had seemingly lost faith in the American dream. Like any good comic book story, just as the situation seemed bleakest, the hero arrived. Superman first appeared in 1938 in *Action Comics* #1 and with him he brought a sense of adventure and hope to hundreds of thousands of readers. Superman was a hero for his age, a rough and tumble social avenger and vigilante who was unafraid to break the law in order to uphold the common good. This early Superman concerned himself with protecting ordinary Americans against the everyday villains that plagued society. Although Superman would soon battle alien invasions and superpowered madmen, from 1938 to 1940 the hero's main purpose was protecting everyday citizens. This introductory version of the Man of Steel may seem overly aggressive or even brutal to later generations, but in his era Superman was the hero that the nation needed. Batman, and hundreds of other superheroes that battled threats both large and small, soon followed. These heroes were the start of a new type of American mythology that would continually change to meet American society's needs. Although comic book superheroes were Great Depression characters, war was on the horizon and soon these heroes would be transformed into something far more patriotic and less radical.

Chapter 2

WORLD WAR II AND SUPER-PATRIOTS (1941–1945)

What do you get when you take a puny kid from New York, add a brilliant scientist and a secret superhuman formula, mix in American patriotism, and place it inside a red, white, and blue costume? The recipe for creating the comic book super-soldier known as Captain America. Only a few years after Jerry Siegel and Joe Shuster fashioned Superman to fill a societal void left by the Great Depression, another pair of comic book creators developed a new type of hero to combat growing war fears. Captain America first appeared in December 1940, as war raged in Europe and Asia and U.S. citizens wondered what would be the country's international role. Captain America's first appearance at the end of 1940 showcases a nation transitioning from the horrors of the Great Depression to the challenges of fighting a world war. As most Americans soon accepted new wartime mandates and guidelines, society rapidly focused on providing support for the war effort. While Americans focused on the war, so too did comic book superheroes and many of these heroes, like Captain America, led the way long before the U.S. even entered World War II. The war forced all Americans to make sacrifices, and as many citizens curtailed their basic civil liberties, a number of heroes changed their very natures.

The Beginning?

When did World War II begin? Although this may seem like a simple question, it probably would elicit a variety of answers from different people. An average American may remember the Japanese attack on Pearl Harbor and answer December 7, 1941, forgetting that the U.S. did not officially declare war until the next day and that many European countries had been at war for over two years. A European might cite the German invasion of Poland and mark the date as September 1, 1939. A historian may link the Second World War to the end of World War I and declare the date to be June 28, 1919, the signing of the Treaty of Versailles. In truth, it is often hard to define a beginning and end. Historians like to write about and discuss the idea of historical eras and periods. To many readers, history books seem to present eras in concrete terms. In most historical readings events have a neatly-groomed symmetry in an easy to understand arrangement. Historians generally strive to make events more understandable by linking them together in ways that form these notions of precisely defined eras. In general the perception of periodization is helpful to both the historian and the layman because it creates order and understanding out of events that are often chaotic and confusing. One should always remember that the notion of eras, periods, ages, or epochs are social constructions that generally are developed long after the events in question. The beginnings and ends of historical periods are rarely neat and tidy and often the denizens of a given era did not know they were participating in it until its time had long passed. Although historical reflection or writing can be orderly, daily lives and world events rarely are, which is what makes actual history more complicated than what your high school history teacher taught you.

Many historians state that the Great Depression was a period that lasted from late 1929 until December 7, 1941. They generally mark the era by two events: the stock market crash as its beginning and the Japanese attack on Pearl Harbor as its end. These events are just markers that historians use to segment a period of time in order to better explain it. In reality the Great Depression did not end the moment Japanese forces bombed Pearl Harbor, but the attack did mark a shift in Americans' political, economic, and social understanding of themselves and the world. This shift had begun months before the Japanese assault on the Hawaiian naval base and would continue to grow and change as the war raged. As with many social and culture changes, comic book superheroes were not only mirrors of society, but in many ways ahead of the curve. Comic book superheroes shifted from Great Depression social avengers to super-patriots early on and continued the fight until the end of World War II (and sometimes long after.)

A Nation and an Industry in Transition

Throughout 1938 and 1939 many comic book superheroes modeled the popular attributes and behaviors of Superman and Batman and fought the injustices that plagued Great Depression America. Some heroes tried to create a unique niche though, by relying on the pulps for inspiration, while others like Captain Marvel (Shazam) attempted to promote themselves as less violent and more wholesome. By the end of 1940, Superman appeared to be less aggressive and more law abiding. DC Comics soon gave Batman a young sidekick, Robin the Boy Wonder, in an attempt to lighten up the Dark Knight and make him more appealing to his young audience. Batman became less a brutal vigilante and more a peaceful citizen who wanted to aid the police and other government officials. Superheroes were changing as America was. Some of these changes in superheroes were in answer to public fears that comic books were too violent for young readers. Other changes were because of Americans' interest in the war in Europe. As the real world became more violent, comic book superheroes became less so. Comic book costumed heroes began to tackle large problems using more constructive and less violent actions. These heroes also became more patriotic and proudly displayed their solidarity with the United States. Superheroes who had helped the average American became, by mid 1940, super-Americans who battled global evil forces that threatened the United States and the world.

War of the World

There is an old joke among history teachers about the student who raises his hand during a lecture and asks the professor why World War II started. The professor is momentarily stunned by the complexity of the question and so asks the student if he really wants a run-down of the underpinnings of the Second World War. The student casually looks at him and answers, "Sure, if you got a minute." The reason the joke is (once was) semi-funny is that one of the few things that scholars can agree on is that the events leading to World War II were multifaceted and extremely convoluted. Much like many historical periods or events, the Second World War's beginnings can be traced to European and Asian rivalries that date back centuries.

For the sake of expediency (and sanity) this text will explain the origins of World War II by starting with the new order that was created after World War I. When the First World War (or the Great War as it was then known) ended on November 11, 1918, world leaders had to decide how to proceed in restoring normality to Europe in particular and the world in general. Through a series of postwar treaties the victorious Allies (United Kingdom, France, Russia the United States, and other smaller nations) redrew much of the map of Europe by breaking up empires and repartitioning landholdings. The triumphant nations forced Germany, Austro-Hungary, and the Ottoman Empire to relinquish numerous territories.[1] Additionally, the Treaty of Versailles required Germany to accept the blame for starting World War I and to make payments to other states for war damage. France particularly desired these reparation payments that served to keep the German economy from rapidly rebuilding and, in theory, would stop the Germans from rearming. Furthermore, the treaty limited the German army to 100,000 men, banned any German air force, allowed Germany to maintain only a few small ships, and outlawed German submarines.[2]

In hindsight the Treaty of Versailles was overly punitive and restricted Germany so greatly that the country was doomed to fail. The French were especially vindictive to the Germans because of past wars and territorial disputes. By punishing Germany so severely, the Allies were creating terrible conditions in Germany that would destroy any chance of economic, political, or social stability. The Allies wanted to punish Germany and the other members of the Central Powers, but instead they were only hurting themselves.

Creating a Villain

Several historians, like J.M. Roberts and Anthony Adamthwaite, believe that World War I and World War II were not actually two wars but rather parts of a larger European civil war. Whether this is true or not, in retrospect it seems clear that the Treaty of Versailles did not address the underlying causes of World War I. Instead of fixing prewar problems, the Allies chose to punish the defeated nations (mostly Germany) and move forward. These punitive measures created even greater German instability and made it almost impossible for a democracy to take root. In 1923, the German economy was so depressed that one English pound equaled 500,000 Deutschmarks in value. German workers, who had to be paid bags full of money, quickly spent their pay before the currency lost its value.[3] The German economy briefly rebounded in the mid–1920s, but the worldwide Great Depression quickly sent the country back into economic despair. This economic downturn combined with a widespread German bitterness about the Treaty of Versailles are two of the main factors that led to the rise of the Nazi Party. The Nazis promoted a sense of German nationalism and importance that had been missing since the end of World War I.

At a time when many Germans felt economically and socially battered and blamed outside nations for their troubles, the Nazis promised a return to past glories by building a strong and respected Germany. It was in this context that Adolf Hitler rose to power. The

German leader (an Austrian by birth) was a failed painter who advocated the ideology of fascism, a system of government in which one party controls the state and exalts the nation as supreme by preaching national and racial superiority. As Hitler gained power he pressed for Germany to reclaim some of the territory the country lost after World War I. While Germany began strengthening its military and expanding its borders, many in the world looked on with fear. The Allies in general, and France in particular, had tried to use the Treaty of Versailles to hold Germany in check. The plan had backfired and had instead created an invigorated Germany that seemed driven to right perceived wrongs and strengthen the German state. Although at first many countries seemed to ignore the German threat, soon events would transpire that made it impossible for the world to turn a blind eye.[4]

Rising Up

After serving in the German army during World War I, growing from a regional Munich-based politician to a national figure, and serving time in prison for his political activities, Adolf Hitler became chancellor of Germany in January 1933. Within a month the German parliamentary building, the Reichstag, was set afire and the Nazi party blamed the arson on foreign and German communists. The subsequent anti-communist sentiment increased Hitler's popularity and propelled the Nazi party to take bolder measures. In the course of a few days the German president enacted the Reichstag Fire Decree that severely curtailed civil rights and allowed the Nazis to imprison any opponents. Only a month later in March 1933, the German parliament passed the Enabling Act, which gave Hitler's cabinet the power to make laws without consulting the legislature. The move in practice circumvented the German parliament's authority and made Hitler a dictator. By the end of August 1933, the Nazis became the only legal party in Germany and Hitler assumed the power of the president as well as the chancellor. In seven short months Adolf Hitler had taken over Germany in a manner that would make a comic book villain jealous. Unfortunately, the changes were all too real and soon Hitler would set his sights on Europe.[5]

Pinky, We Try to Take Over the World

Hitler and the Nazi party used the next few years to strengthen the German military. The former Allied powers changed several Treaty of Versailles provisions and Germany merely violated others. In 1935, Hitler announced an alliance with Italian dictator Benito Mussolini. Many aspects of the German version of fascism had been modeled on the Italian example and although the leaders apparently did not personally like each other, the pact made political sense. The alliance became known as the Axis and Japan was soon added to the coalition. Then in March 1938, Austria peacefully unified with the German state, thus expanding Germany's size and power. In September 1938, the major European powers signed the Munich Agreement, which ceded the former Czechoslovakian territory of the Sudetenland to Germany. The move was designed to appease Hitler's expansionist hopes and thus avoid war.

On September 1, 1939, Germany invaded Poland and a few days later both Great Britain and France declared war against Germany. In April 1940, the German military invaded Norway and Denmark and in May 1940 Germany overtook the Netherlands, Luxemburg, and Belgium and invaded France. Ultimately, France would surrender to Germany in June 1940. As these things transpired, many in the United States watched with fear and trepidation. The Great Depression was still raging and Europe was engulfed in a war that could pull in the United States at any time. The world was a scary place and Hitler seemed far more villainous than any comic book bad guy.[6]

Rising Sun

While much of the world was concentrating on Hitler's meteoric rise to power, Japan was building an empire and preparing for war. During World War I, Japan had been a member of the Allied coalition. Although after the war the United States and Europe recognized the Japanese as a colonial power, the West's relationship with Japan was often strained because of discriminatory racial policies. In 1919, Western powers refused to include a "racial equality clause" in the League of Nations' charter and in 1924 the U.S. passed the Exclusion Act that prevented additional immigration from Japan. While Western racial attitudes bothered the Japanese, natural, economic, and political events also severely damaged the nation. Earthquakes, including the Great Kanto Earthquake of 1923, devastated the country and an economic crisis quickly developed. By 1926, millions of Japanese were unemployed and many lost their personal savings. The Japanese government had to deal with political and social disorder and worried that citizens would revolt.

The worldwide Great Depression only made matters worse. Japan needed to obtain resources via international trade and import and was thus very dependent on the world market and other nations. Japan's largest industry was silk export to the U.S. and the Great Depression destroyed almost all demand for the Japanese product. This meant that the Japanese had to find other methods of acquiring the resources they needed. Political and military leaders decided that procuring Asian colonies could supply Japan with these much needed resources. The only way to gain colonies was through conquest though, so the Japanese military needed to fight to acquire new territory. The Japanese army occupied the Chinese province of Manchuria in 1931 and continued to press for more land, but the United States and other world powers would not recognize Japan's newly acquired Manchurian territory as a new independent country. After the League of Nations condemned the military actions, Japan left the organization and ignored world opinion. The Japanese desire to gain resources and the U.S.'s rise to global prominence conflicted and caused the expected tensions. As Japan continued its attempts to militarily gain resources and the U.S. stood as an obstacle, a clash seemed not just possible, but rather probable. In the midst of the Great Depression and the troubles in Europe, the U.S. also had to consider Japanese expansion and wonder what would become of the Pacific region.[7]

A Extraordinarily Dangerous Game of Chicken

There is an iconic scene in the 1955 motion picture *Rebel Without a Cause* in which the James Dean character gets involved in a dangerous game of chicken with another teenager. Both young men attempt to prove their bravery by not jumping to safety until the last moment as their cars approach a perilous cliff. Neither boy wants to back down and damage his reputation, and thus both suffer adverse consequences.[8] In some ways the United

States and Japan entered 1939 engaged in a game of geopolitical chicken. The Great Depression had hurt each country and both needed to find new deposits of raw materials and resources. Just as important, though, both considered it necessary to express their continuing importance and enhance their reputations. Although one rarely thinks of it in such a manner, geopolitics is a lot like high school; one needs to be considered strong in order to avoid the bullies and popular enough to be accepted by the cool kids.

While Japan greatly needed more natural resources and the U.S. desired an economic boost, much of the two countries' struggles had to do with international perception. After Japan overran Manchuria and the U.S. condemned the aggressive action, the two countries continued to drive towards the cliff. In 1939, the U.S revoked its commercial treaty with Japan and soon started to limit deliveries of oil, metals, and other essential goods. In 1940– 1941, the U.S. engaged in an oil embargo against Japan. The American government halted ninety percent of Japan's oil supply from reaching the foreign petroleum dependent country. The U.S. warned Japan to either withdraw from China or lose internationally obtained resources. As Germany appeared to overrun most of western Europe, Japan was presented with a dilemma that seemed to have few solutions. Americans were beginning to question if and when the U.S. would go to war and these worries created a new cultural landscape and filled the nation's thoughts.[9]

Super-Patriots

One of the most important attributes of popular culture is that it quickly changes to meet a society's needs. Popular culture often serves as both a mirror and molder in society and is frequently one of the best gauges of a society's current hopes, fears, wants, and needs. In the early months of 1940, the U.S. was in a transitional period from peace to war and comic book superheroes marked this change. Much as it is difficult to definitively state when the Great Depression ended, it is just as problematic to ascertain when costumed superheroes transformed from Great Depression avengers to super-nationalists. This metamorphosis was a product of cultural evolution and took place over the course of several months, if not years. Some patriotic heroes were introduced in 1940, while other superheroes seemed oblivious to the rising war tensions into early 1942. What can be said is that some comic book superheroes entered World War II far earlier than the United States did. Although the U.S. was aiding the Allied side by 1940 with programs like Lend Lease and Congress was encouraging nationalist propaganda in preparation for war, the nation did not go to war until December 8, 1941, the day after the Japanese attack on Pearl Harbor. Superheroes, by contrast, began to go to war in late 1940. Although patriotic heroes like the Shield existed prior, one can arguably mark the beginning of comic book World War II with the December 1940 release of *Captain America Comics* #1. This new superhero showcased a change not only in comic book superheroes, but also in America itself.

O Captain! My Captain!

The creation and publication of Captain America marks a sea change in comic books and in American society. While Superman had battled imaginary war profiteers in his comic book and Adolf Hitler and Joseph Stalin for a few pages in a *Look* magazine comic strip, he and most other comic book heroes did not fight against real world international wrongs. Batman may have combated fictional international villains, but he did not attempt to defeat the U.S.'s actual political enemies. In other words, although Great Depression superheroes fought for the common man, they did so in a generic fictional manner. The publication of *Captain America Comics* #1 began to change this by creating a new superhero template that most writers and artists would soon utilize. The red, white, and blue garbed Captain America's primary responsibility was to battle the forces that threatened the United States, and his first target was Hitler.

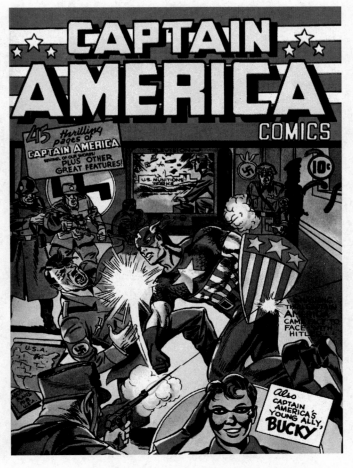

Captain America #1 (March 1941) features the new patriotic superhero punching Adolf Hitler in the jaw months before the U.S. entered World War II. (© 1941 Marvel Comics. All Rights Reserved.)

Captain America Comics #1, containing the first appearance of Captain America, was cover dated March 1941 but went on sale in December 1940, almost exactly a year before the U.S. would enter World War II. The cover of Captain America's first issue depicts Nazis surrounding the star spangled hero as he hits Adolf Hitler squarely in the jaw. Inside the comic book, the reader learns that Captain America is Steve Rogers, a formerly puny and unathletic man who was turned into the perfect physical specimen when he drank the Super-Soldier serum. After giving Steve Rogers the elixir and watching him transform, Abraham Erskine, the scientist who created the Super-Soldier serum, stated, "We shall call you Captain America, son! Because, Like you — America shall gain the strength and the will to safeguard our shores."[10] Note that Captain America's creators designed him to be the symbolic representation of the United States. Writer Joe Simon and artist Jack Kirby created this new superhero to fight the nation's battles. Other heroes had fought fictionalized versions of America's enemies, but Simon and Kirby used Captain America to war against threats on the newspaper's front page rather than the comic strip page. Captain America was uniquely fighting a real world nemesis before the politicians and even the public had decided to do so.

While the U.S. government was already sending aid to the British, not all Americans were convinced that the country should support the Allied cause. Although their views may have changed over time, such notable Americans as Henry Ford and Charles Lindbergh supported elements of the Nazi ideology at one point in their lives.[11] Simon and Kirby later recalled that when they were working on the first issues of *Captain America* they received death threats and had to be protected by the New York Police Department.[12] While it can be assumed that these threats came from a fringe element of the population, it is clear that not all Americans supported the Allied cause. Simon and Kirby had a strong dislike of Adolf Hitler and felt that their new hero could help to rally Americans against the Nazi leader. Marvel's owner, Martin Goodman, also liked the idea of using Hitler as a comic book villain but was unsure if the German leader would still be alive when the comic book was published. Because of this, the first issue of *Captain America* was rushed to press long before the United States entered World War II.[13] Simon and Kirby were thus quickly able to portray Hitler as a villain on *Captain America*'s first cover. The Captain America creators were among the first comic book writers and artists that combined anti-Nazi and pro-American sentiment. More importantly, they had created a character that was not only emulating public opinion, but also shaping it.

In 1939, the U.S. Congress had asked publishers to include patriotic storylines in order to increase nationalistic ideas within the population. Captain America was at the forefront of the new patriotic superhero movement. Although more comic book superheroes would fight against the Nazi threat before the U.S. entered the war, like July 1941's *Daredevil Battles Hitler*, Captain America was arguably one of the first and most important. Soon the U.S. would go to war and most Americans, real or fictional, would rally behind the nation. Captain America was fighting Hitler in December 1940, but after the Japanese attack on Pearl Harbor the entire nation would go to war.

The U.S. Enters the Fray

The United States entered World War II in December 1941 and had to quickly come to terms with fighting battles both in Europe and in the Pacific. Although the U.S. had been aiding Great Britain for almost a year, American government, society, and industry were in many ways unprepared for the war. The U.S. rapidly had to create a blueprint for winning in the Pacific and in Europe. While the U.S. military began waging war abroad, the government was concerned about domestic America's understanding and support. American leaders understood that the military needed the political, economic, and social support of the nation in order to be victorious. This meant the government, and other "independent" sources, needed to create a vast amount of nationalist propaganda to encourage American citizens to act in ways that the government deemed necessary. Although the Japanese attack on Pearl Harbor united almost all of the country against the Axis powers, the American government needed to be certain that American citizens were following national guidelines. American World War II propaganda posters created an outline of the U.S. government's social domestic guidelines that one can compare to the changes among comic book super-heroes. These can be placed into four distinct categories: encouragement to join the military, the importance of supporting servicemen, the need to buy war bonds, and guidelines of how patriotic Americans should act. The U.S. used social propaganda to fight the war on the home front and to change American society. Comic book superheroes started fighting the war in late 1940, but by the end of 1941 American society was fully engaged in the conflict.

I Want You

One of the U.S. government's first priorities in World War II was to encourage young men to join the military. Although a large number of men volunteered for military service shortly after the start of the war, the government needed to keep enlistment numbers high. This meant that the government created a large amount of enlistment propaganda. The most famous of these posters has a painted image of Uncle Sam pointing his finger at the viewer and declaring, "I Want You for U.S. Army." This poster is probably one of the most famous images in American history, and popular culture is replete with references to the illustration. James Montgomery Flagg originally created the poster for World War I recruiting and was it brought back to help with World War II.[14]

Other posters were produced to stress the necessity of joining the armed forces. Several World War II images showed armed forces members at work and stated that the nation needed the support. One poster shows real life sports icon Private Joe Louis wearing a uniform and helmet with a bayonet pointed at the viewer. The caption states, "We're going to do our part ... and we'll win because we're on God's side."[15] Another image presented a picture of two muscular shirtless sailors loading shells into a large gun with the caption reading, "Man the Guns: Join the Navy."[16] Even Walt Disney joined the effort by creating cartoons in which Donald Duck was drafted and went to war. The propaganda encouraged young men to join the armed services and to view military service as a natural and important part of American life. Later posters also encouraged women to join the Women's Army Corps (WAC) or to become nurses. American propaganda easily promoted military service, which was one of the most logical aspects of war. The American public also had to be trained to put the war effort first and their needs second. While American capitalism had before stressed individualism and personal freedom, now the nation would begin to demand sacrifice and selflessness.

War Time Heroes

As American society changed so did its heroes. As noted earlier, Captain America was one of the first war superheroes, appearing a year before the U.S. entered World War II. By mid–1942, nearly all comic book heroes had changed into patriotic citizens that were willing to follow the government's new rules and accept their new societal roles. Comic book historian Jules Feiffer claims that World War II provided an opportunity for superheroes to begin anew, with fresh stories and believable real world villains. Feiffer notes, "There is no telling what would have become of the superheroes had they not been given a *real* enemy."[17] Although it may be true that comic book creators enjoyed the new direction that World War II provided, the war-altered superheroes reflected the same changes that occurred in American society as whole. While superheroes like Captain America looked to inspire patriotic sentiment before the U.S. went to war, most comic book heroes changed with the nation. Just as the government asked Americans to adapt their lives to support the war effort, comic book publishers altered superheroes to better represent the new American society. Before the war comic book heroes like Superman and Batman had been Great Depression social avengers that fought outside the law to right the wrongs that government could not. During World War II these same heroes quickly became law abiding patriotic citizens that encouraged Americans to support the war effort and to follow all new governmental mandates. Much like American citizens, during World War II superheroes voluntarily gave up many of their freedoms to support the greater good. Even the heroes that had previously been radical and uncompromising happily fell into line. Comic book superheroes stories soon became a form of governmental war propaganda and began to provide a clean cut image suitable for young (and old) Americans to model. Much like their readers and American society as a whole, during World War II superheroes changed to meet the needs of the nation and to support the collective good.

The Serviceman Comes First

After the U.S. government stressed the need for military service, it soon began to redefine American societal roles. By mid–December 1941 World War II was the most important element of American society. A 1942 poster that quoted President Roosevelt's December 9, 1941, address to the nation emphasized this new American way of life. The poster states, "WE ARE NOW IN THIS WAR. We are all in it all the way. Every single man, woman and child is a partner in the most tremendous undertaking in our American history. We must share together the bad news and the good news, the defeats and the victories — the changing fortunes of war."[18]

July 1941's *Daredevil Battles Hitler* #1 showcased the costumed superhero Daredevil's fight against the German leader before the U.S.'s direct military involvement in World War II. In typical comic book hyperbolic style the front caption reads, "The most TERRIFYING BATTLE ever waged—HITLER stacked the cards against humanity—BUT—DAREDEVIL deals the ACE OF DEATH to the MADE MERCHANT OF HATE!"

The war effort created a new social structure of how Americans lived, worked, and acted. The unseen but ever present serviceman was at the top of the new American hierarchy. According to the propaganda of the day, the serviceman had given up his normal life in order to fight for American freedom. He had left his home and family and was prepared to die if necessary. Before the war these (mostly) young and inexperienced men probably were lower in the American social system and required to both respect their elders and their superiors at work. During the war the serviceman reached the zenith of domestic

American society. Although the men certainly had to follow military direction and were often not leaders in their daily lives, they became the focal point of propaganda that stated that every part of American society bow to their needs. These men, who only a few months prior had been individually unexceptional, were now collectively the driving force of almost every aspect of American life. War posters demanded that Americans always remember that soldiers, sailors, Marines, and other servicemen were fighting for them. These previously common men had become almost sacrosanct and Americans not in uniform were expected to put the servicemen's needs before their own.

Government agencies used propaganda to consistently reinforce this restructuring of American society. A 1941 poster created by C.C. Beall shows a soldier driving a tank and peering through a machine gun sight. A large white arrow points at the solider and exclaims, "Don't Let Him Down!"[19] The poster does not specifically address how the viewers may harm the serviceman, which makes it more effective. Because the expected actions are never listed, the viewer may police him or herself better than the state could. The viewer is left to search his or her behavior and try to determine how he or she is supporting the servicemen. A 1942 poster displays a soldier lying on his stomach with a rifle in his hand. The man is looking at the viewer and the caption reads, "Kinda give it your personal attention, will you? More Production"[20] This "personal" understated appeal reinforces the idea that American citizens are working to support servicemen. Although the soldier seemingly asks Americans to support his efforts, he is doing so in a facetious manner and is, in reality, telling the American public that they know that they are working for him. While the soldier may not have had much social status before (or even after) the war, he garnered substantial domestic social and cultural support during the war. Although the idea of supporting military men seemed logical, other propaganda efforts needed more finesse and creativity because they were harder to understand and required Americans to change long established patterns.

Super Americans

Some comic book characters like Captain America and Daredevil fought Nazi enemies well before the U.S. entered World War II; these heroes' exploits were fueled by their creators' hopes to prime the American public to fight Germany and to a lesser extent Japan. Many superheroes joined the war effort at the same time as the American public and served as literal and figurative illustrations for readers. Although some superheroes did not serve in the military, almost all of them were concerned with winning the war. (Captain America did, in fact, serve in the military, his secret identity, Steve Rogers, was an Army private.) Superman tried to enlist in the Army but failed his physical when his x-ray vision malfunctioned and he read the eye chart in an adjoining room. The Man of Steel later decided that he would protect the U.S homeland and stated, "The United States Army, Navy, and Marines are capable of smashing their foes without the aid of a Superman."[21] Soon Superman was fighting home front menaces, and the covers of *Action Comics* and *Superman* often depicted a patriotic theme.

A good example of a wartime Superman image is one of the most famous patriotic comic book covers: *Superman* #14 cover dated January–February 1942. The image portrays the predominantly red and blue costumed Superman standing in front of a shield bearing the stars and stripes of the American flag. With his right hand on his hip, the Man of Steel watches as an eagle lands on his left arm. The silhouettes of tanks and aircraft occupy the image's black background. The cover, like most comic book propaganda, provided an array of patriotic images. The American flag turned into a wartime shield/crest, the U.S.'s symbol, the bald eagle, and the war's fighting machines all surround Superman and declare him to be unmistakably American. During the Great Depression, Superman had fought against everyday problems in order to help the common man. After the U.S. entered World War II, he was concerned with helping average Americans, but he now did so by listening to the government and becoming a domestic part of the war effort, just like many Americans. Superman and his fellow heroes were putting the U.S. serviceman first, just as the government told every good American they should.

The Hard Sell

The effort to encourage young men and women to join the military was only one step in the U.S.'s effort to ready itself for war. American society needed to change in order to meet the challenges that the nation faced. One of the most important but mundane issues was how to pay for the war effort. Although war financing is a very significant matter, economics and bookkeeping generally do not produce the same excitement that talk of military battles does. It was easy for the U.S. government to produce propaganda recruiting soldiers, sailors, and Marines. It was much harder to convince the American people to help finance the war. Most of this effort came in the form of war bonds, a government issued debt security used for wartime needs. Essentially, the U.S. government was borrowing money from its citizens to pay for the war. The primary appeal of this investment would be the patriotic urge to keep the U.S. safe from harm. Posters, songs, motion pictures, radio advertisements, and various other types of advertising and propaganda helped to convince many Americans that buying war bonds was their patriotic duty.

Often the posters not only used patriotic appeals but also attempted to make the viewer feel guilty. One gray and red poster from 1942 shows a mother holding an infant and standing next to a young girl. The caption reads, "I gave a man! Will you give at least 10% of your pay in War Bonds?"[22] The creator of the poster wants the viewer to feel guilty about the amount of sacrifices he or she has made compared to the widowed mother. Walt Disney even produced cartoons where such characters as Donald Duck and the seven dwarves buy war bonds. The U.S. government took the seemingly dull but important issue of war financing and successfully turned it into a patriotic act.

During the war, 85 million Americans purchased approximately 157 billion dollars worth of war bonds.[23] The U.S. government had successfully changed the American public's spending and saving habits and had funneled the money into war financing. This was only the beginning of the government's campaign to change Americans. Federal agencies also needed to teach Americans how to best support the troops. Although many Americans had volunteered for war service and others had loaned the government money, the American public need to do much more.

Super Salesmen

While the U.S. government was creating propaganda advertisements to promote societal changes like buying war bonds, many comic book covers were themselves becoming miniature war bonds posters. Superman and Batman had quickly given up their radical pasts and by 1942 were dedicated super citizens and war bonds salesmen. The cover of *Action Comics* #58 (March 1943) depicts Superman turning a giant printing press as he creates fliers that read, "Superman says: You Can Slap a Jap with War Bonds and Stamps!"[24] The next month's cover (*Action Comics* #59) shows Superman dismantling a German tank with the caption, "War Bonds & Stamps Smash Axis Tanks Too!"[25] Numerous covers also showcased Batman and Robin as dedicated war bonds salesmen. Examples are *Batman* #12 (August–September 1942), in which Batman and Robin ride in military style jeep and the caption states, "War Savings Bonds and Stamps Keep 'Em Rolling!"[26]; February–March 1943's *Batman* #15, in which Batman and Robin fire a machine gun and the cover reads, "Keep Those Bullets Flying! Keep on Buying War Bonds & Stamps!"[27]; and June 1943's *Batman* #17, which shows the Dark Knight and the Boy Wonder riding a giant eagle and exclaiming, "Keep the American eagle flying! Buy War Bonds and Stamps!"[28] Although the stories inside did not attempt to sell war bonds, these covers, and many more, promoted the idea of investing in the war. Superheroes like Superman and Batman were selling the state's war agenda while they were hawking war bonds. Much like the rest of society, these characters had changed a lot in just a few short months.

The New War Lifestyle

Millions of Americans bought war bonds during World War II and thus loaned well over 150 billion dollars to the U.S. government. This was an important part of the war effort, but it was only the beginning. Government propaganda convinced Americans that they needed to change their saving habits and invest in government backed war bonds instead of keeping their money at home or investing in other places. The federal government also had to persuade Americans to change their lifestyles in other important ways. These changes were so widespread that in many ways the U.S. government had to retrain the American populace how to act. This retraining effort focused on both large and seemingly mundane issues and appears to have encompassed the whole of American life. This change in Americans' lifestyles reflected the idea that the war effort was more important than individual needs and aspirations. In peacetime most Americans would not have allowed the government to interfere in basic decisions and lifestyle choices. The U.S.'s entry into World War II redefined what acceptable government actions were and changed the way that Americans viewed both themselves and the world as a whole. Government propaganda focused on conservation, gender politics, and how one should interact with others. Conservation and rationing was a big part of the U.S. war effort. At different points during the war the U.S. government limited the availability of certain goods, so that the military could use the limited resources. The government also created propaganda to encourage the public to conserve certain items and to live frugally.

Normally, these conservation and rationing efforts would seemingly violate core capitalist beliefs. During war time most citizens accepted these changes as necessary for the greater good. Conservation efforts included such things as women's stockings, and during the war some women painted a black line on their legs to provide the illusion of wearing hosiery when none was present. The government also rationed such resources as rubber, and one early poster from 1941 shows military vehicles using tires and tells Americans to conserve their tires by utilizing them correctly.[29] A 1942 poster depicts four armed soldiers riding in a jeep with the caption, "They've Got More Important Places to Go Than You! ... Save Rubber. Check Your Tires Now."[30] In stating that the soldiers' driving was more important than the civilians,' this poster clearly demonstrates the new American domestic hierarchy. One other poster from 1943 displays a woman carrying groceries in front of a black and white silhouette of soldiers carrying rifles while marching. The accompanying text reads, "I'll Carry Mine Too!: Trucks and Tires Must Last Till Victory."[31] The poster attempted to use service members' hardships to convince Americans to drive less and walk more.

The Laundry List

Tire usage was just one of the many things that Americans had to conserve. The U.S. government attempted to curtail usage of some goods and encourage people to recycle other things. This list included gasoline, silk, and even scrap metal. A 1942 poster employed the image of a giant hand squeezing old farm equipment in its fist to encourage Americans to recycle scrap metal.[32] Likewise, a 1942 war poster pictured a Navy vessel and read, "Farm Scrap Builds Destroyers: 900 tons of Scrap Metal goes into a Destroyer."[33] Another rationed item was meat, and the government created a 1942 poster to convince Americans to be less carnivorous. The poster states in bold lettering, "Americans! SHARE THE MEAT as a wartime necessity. To meet the needs of our armed forces and fighting allies, a Government order limits the amount of meat delivered to stores and restaurants. To share the supply fairly, all civilians are asked to limit their consumption of beef, veal, lamb, mutton and pork to 2½ lbs. per week." After listing what is considered a fair share, the poster ends with, "HELP WIN THE WAR! Keep within your share."[34] Notice the new hierarchy present in this poster. Americans were no longer categorized as citizens, but rather as servicemen and civilians. The civilians are expected to provide for the servicemen and "meet their needs."

The government tackled the idea of conserving gasoline in a 1943 poster. The advert shows a well-dressed American driving a car with a ghostly outline of a uniform-wearing Adolf Hitler sitting next to him. The caption exclaims, "When you ride ALONE you ride with Hitler! Join a Car-Sharing Club Today!"[35] Another 1943 poster displays how far the government would go to control the economy and the goods that were consumed. The social advertisement shows a female hand pouring oil from an iron skillet and the oil becoming a group of missiles and torpedoes. The poster's caption reads, "Save waste fats for explosives. Take them to your meat dealer."[36] The U.S. government wanted to change American society socially, culturally, and economically. Americans were expected to change their needs, wants, and habits in order to provide for the men serving overseas. The usage and conservation of consumer goods was only the beginning, though. Americans had to change many other things about themselves.

Loose Lips Sink Ships

While the U.S. government was trying to persuade the American populace to change its social hierarchy, invest their money in the war effort, and developed new consumption and conservation habits, it also wanted to retrain Americans on how to interact with each other. The First Amendment notion of freedom of speech is so ingrained in the American psyche that one assumes that even society's youngest and most illiterate members know something of the concept. Though many Americans misunderstand the intricacies of the statement, "Congress shall make no law ... abridging the freedom of speech," an overwhelming majority of Americans view the idea as a basic human right.[37] While government propaganda did not violate the First Amendment, because it was a persuasive tool rather than a legal one, the social advertisements did ask (and in some cases order) Americans to self-censor. In peacetime many American citizens probably would view this concept as an abuse of government power and an un-American concept. During the World War II though, this type of social engineering was tolerated as being necessary for the greater good. The U.S. government convinced the American public that it should not talk about matters involving family members and friends serving overseas. The family is the basic unit of most societies and government interference in familial relations in general met with resistance, annoyance, and often anger. This was generally not the case during World War II as the government attempted to persuade Americans to limit their conversations about absent loved ones. The war allowed the government to convince Americans to curtail their own freedom of speech and to adjust their ideas of individual rights and familial freedom. These parts of American society changed because the government told Americans that they were necessary to win the war.

The most famous propaganda for curtailing the freedom of speech was a 1942–1945 Ad Council campaign entitled "Loose Lips Sink Ships." The phrase is often used in American popular culture and has found its way into films, television, and even song. The slogan was used on posters, in radio advertisements, and in corporate adverts.[38] Other advertisements used the same theme but different slogans. The inherent message in almost all self-censorship propaganda was that if someone talked about the war, then a serviceman may die. A 1944 poster shows the outstretched hand of a drowning serviceman and the caption "Someone Talked!"[39] A 1942 cartoon traces the path of information from step two, when a workman talks about the freight he loaded on a ship, to step six, when the enemy sinks the ship. The piece is entitled "The Sound That Kills," and ends with the line "Don't Murder Men with Idle Words."[40] A 1942 poster features a picture of a sailor staring through a porthole framed by the words "If you talk too much THIS MAN MAY DIE."[41] A 1943 poster displays a dead serviceman with the slogan "A careless word ... A NEEDLESS LOSS."[42] A 1944 propaganda ad shows a picture of bloody-mouthed snakes surrounded by the words "Less Dangerous Than Careless Talk."[43] Perhaps the most frightening of the posters is a 1944 black and white advertisement that looks like a criminal wanted poster. It showcases a picture of a normal looking American woman adorned with middle class pearl earrings and the words "WANTED! FOR MURDER. Her *careless talk* cost lives."[44]

The U.S. government used all available tools, including guilt and fear, to convince the American public to self-censor war information. This campaign was employed with propaganda for a new social structure, war time money management, and usage and conservation of goods to change American society. There were still other ways that the government believed that the U.S. needed to change though.

Changing Heroes

Like most of American society, superheroes also acted much differently than before the war. Comic book covers often depicted superheroes fighting against the Axis powers. While the stories inside the issues rarely matched, the cover presented startling images of American superheroes supporting the war effort. Society no longer allowed superheroes to act and speak freely. Suddenly, Americans expected their formerly self-governing heroes to live within the same social norms as everyone else. World War II comic book covers were often ultra-violent and played to readers' desires that their favorite superheroes quickly dispatch with life's real villains. Examples of this include *Captain Marvel Adventures* #14 (August 1942) in which a giant Captain Marvel prepares to smash a village full of small Japanese people next to the headline "Captain Marvel Swats the Japs."[45] *Master Comics* #29 (August 1942) shows Captain Marvel, Jr., spanking Hitler and Tojo with a belt.[46] *Marvel Mystery Comics* #32 (June 1942) illustrates the Human Torch battling a group of hideous Japanese soldiers.[47] *Superman* #17 (August 1942) pictures the Man of Steel holding a screaming Hitler and Tojo by their collars.[48] All of these comic books, and many more, demonstrate that superheroes changed in much the same way that American society did. Before, superheroes, like many Americans, proudly basked in their personal independence and often labored against societal conventions. American society, and its superhero representatives, transformed amazingly fast as World War II became the country's singular all-consuming focus.

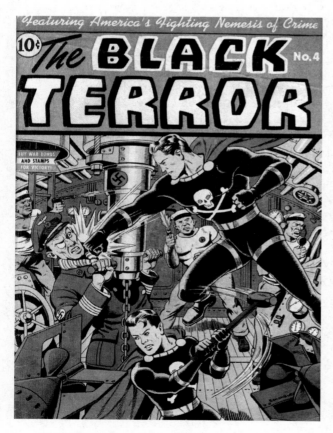

The Black Terror #4's cover (November 1943) displays one of the myriad costumed supermen that brazenly helped fight World War II. Many comic books featured war themed covers even if the stories inside did not mention the war.

Rosie the Riveter

During World War II, the U.S. government attempted to restructure American society to meet wartime needs. These changes affected almost every part of American life, including social status, economics, consumption, conservation, and individual liberties. One of the most dramatic changes during this time was that of gender roles. Because of the enormous number of men sent overseas during World War II, the American economy as a whole and war production specifically needed women to work in traditionally male dominated fields.

Women have always worked outside the home in American society. In rural areas many women worked in agricultural settings and their labor was necessary for the family farm to survive. Lower income white women and black women generally worked outside the home to provide much needed financial support for their families. Additionally, middle class women often worked as secretaries, teachers, and nurses. Two major changes concerning women in the workplace occurred during the war, though. First, the war lifted the social taboo about married middle class women and mothers working outside the home. Although some married middle class women and mothers were professionals before the war, there was a strong social stigma against such activity that government propaganda eased during World War II. Second, the government and business asked American women to perform tasks that prewar had been decidedly considered masculine. The government, manufacturers, and soon society expected women to work on the assembly lines in munitions factories, to learn to weld aircraft and ships, and perform any task that men had engaged in prior to the war.

These new edicts about different classes of women performing all types of labor profoundly changed American society during the war years. Before, society deemed that only a particular segment of women were allowed to work in a few chosen professions. Class structure and gender roles dictated the jobs that certain women could hold. Women that violated these rules were often ostracized by family, friends, and those around them. During the war, the government changed the societal conventions and not only made it acceptable for almost all women to work any job, but also demanded that women work. The government deemed female labor to be an important part of the war effort, and it was a woman's duty to work any job that she could. The U.S. government completely changed women's roles during the war. Female labor that society would have viewed as unacceptable in the prewar years was seen as patriotic and selfless during the war.

Undoubtedly, the most famous World War II female labor propaganda character is Rosie the Riveter. The Ad Council calls the Rosie the Riveter campaign "the most successful advertising recruitment campaign in American history."[49] The campaign featured a fictional character that worked in a factory performing a job that would have been defined as men's work before the war. Rosie was dressed in a blue work jumpsuit with a red and white polka-dotted bandanna tied around her head. The most famous image of the fictional Rosie depicted her flexing her biceps as she exclaims, "We Can Do It!" Norman Rockwell also painted a picture of the factory laborer posed in front of an American flag while eating a sandwich with a rivet gun across her lap.[50] The Ad Council and Norman Rockwell designed these Rosie the Riveter images to convince American society in general and women in particular that it was normal for women to work outside the home. Rosie was dressed in working clothes, looked dirty (at least in the Rockwell painting), and was engaging in a physically demanding job, but her labor was necessary and completely acceptable.

Government propaganda and social pressure greatly changed American society during the war years. Practically overnight, the U.S. had transformed into a wartime society that had given up many of its luxuries and freedoms. Most of these changes would revert to the previous status quo after the war, but from December 1941 until August 1945 the U.S. transformed itself into a new nation. During this time comic book superheroes were also transforming with the nation. Much like average American citizens, superheroes submitted to the government's suggestions and demands and quickly accepted the new guidelines. Like many Americans, heroes that had once basked in their freedom and power now willingly submitted and changed.

Super Rosies

As the U.S. government was encouraging Americans to accept a variety of women in the workplace, comic books were promoting the idea of Axis-fighting superwomen. Much like American factory women, these superheroines took on "male" jobs during the war and performed them as well as any man. The most famous of these superwomen was Wonder Woman, a peace and democracy-loving Amazon who first appeared in 1941. Wonder Woman dressed in the colors of the American flag and fought for the American way of life (and her boyfriend Steve Trevor.) Although Wonder Woman's creator, William Moulton Marston, professed unconventional ideas about peace and sexual relationships, often Wonder Woman fought many of the same types of villains as her male counterparts. (One of the few differences between Wonder Woman and other superheroes was the odd number of times that villains captured and bound her.) Other World War II superheroines include War Nurse, Black Cat, Pat Patriot (America's Joan of Arc), Miss Victory, Miss American, and Liberty Belle. These women battled the Nazis and Japanese like their male counterparts and often were just as harsh and violent towards enemies. One of the most brutal of these wartime heroines was Black Angel, who seemed to take joy in killing Axis forces. In one story, a Japanese adversary named Madame Claw commits suicide and the Black Angel states, "Her kind always picks the wrong side. Well, can't stay here wasting sympathy on her."[51] Society seemingly empowered these superwomen to produce for America's betterment, much like their war-industries-working counterparts. Many of these costumed women worked in the war effort in their alter egos as well. The War Nurse's Pat Parker was also a nurse in her non-costumed time. Miss Victory's Joan Wayne was a stenographer while Pat Patriot's alter ego, Patricia Patrios, worked for awhile in a war factory. As the U.S. government asked Americans to change their ideals and identities, comic book heroes and heroines followed suit. World War II changed the way that Americans saw themselves and the world around them.[52]

Real American Heroes

Even comic book characters like Superman had to modify themselves to conform to a new wartime role. Just like Superman, other prewar heroes changed to meet the wartime public's needs. Wonder Woman became a nurse, Batman and Robin sold war bonds, the Submariner fought against Nazi submarines, and the Justice Society of America disbanded as its members became servicemen. Publishers also created new heroes in order to take advantage of strong wartime comic book sales. Comic books were cheap (usually only a dime), did not spoil, were easily transported, and were very popular among both children and servicemen. The wartime economy allowed for children to have more disposable income and some of that newly found money went towards comic books. Additionally, one-fourth of the magazines shipped to servicemen during World War II were comic books, and the troops received at least 35,000 copies of *Superman* alone monthly.[53] A group of heroes that were designed to take advantage of both the war and youth markets was the *Boy Commandos*, a DC Comics publication created by Captain America's designers, Joe Simon and Jack Kirby. The Boy Commandos was an elite group of young international orphans who fought overseas during the war. The boy soldiers first appeared in *Detective Comics* #64, cover dated June 1942, and soon had their own comic book in Winter 1942. The Commandos consisted of Frenchman André Chavard, Brit Alfie Twidgett, Jan Haasan from the Netherlands, and Brooklyn from the United States. Captain Rip Carter, an adult serviceman, was the group's leader who commanded the boys during their dangerous missions. The Boy Commandos had no superpowers, but were in the tradition of non-superpowered sidekicks like Robin the Boy Wonder. Although it was never stated why the U.S. military would allow four international youths to fight major war campaigns, the boys were extremely popular among readers, selling millions of copies. Joe Simon claimed that for a while *Boy Commandos* was DC Comics' top selling comic book.[54] While no one would have suggested that young American boys join the military, the comic book provided an outlet for children to display their patriotism. The Boy Commandos provided fun, and adventure, but they also made young male readers feel a part of the greater war effort. Simon and Kirby allowed the young readers to join the war and become patriotic members of society, something that the U.S. government wanted every American to do.

Conclusion

The Japanese attack on Pearl Harbor dramatically changed American society. The U.S. government quickly began to not only wage war overseas but also to reconfigure domestic American society in order to meet the wartime needs. Economically, politically, and socially, the nation's primary focus had to be the war effort. Federal government devised propaganda that encouraged men to join the military, preached the importance of supporting servicemen, showcased the need to buy war bonds, and provided guidelines of how patriotic Americans should

The cover of *The Fighting Yank* #17 (August 1946) highlights how comic book creators quickly transformed standard World War II covers for a postwar audience. Villains that had been Nazi or Japanese soldiers during the war became evil scientists or madmen again. Unfortunately, comic book superhero sales dropped dramatically in the postwar era.

act. This reorganization of American society can easily be seen in comic book superheroes. In the 1930s, many superheroes were independent agents that devised their own codes of right and wrong and worked toward their perceptions of the public good. Superheroes had no bosses and often answered to no higher authority. This began to change even before the U.S. entered World War II. Characters like Captain America were designed to be patriotic role models well before the U.S. went to war. Soon almost all superheroes followed suit and became patriotic pitchmen for governmental wartime propaganda. Just like average Americas, comic book superheroes gave up their freedom in order to support the nation's war effort. Superheroes that once had powerful social voices silenced themselves for the greater good.

Most of the changes were short lived and most freedoms were soon restored when World War II ended. Americans had voluntarily subjugated themselves during wartime but expected the good life once the fighting ended. Superheroes were generally not so fortunate. Much of the liberty that these costumed avengers had voluntarily given away would not be returned and it would be many years before the heroes would again be socially powerful and independent. Ironically, the U.S. fought World War II to keep American society free, but the nation's superheroes would lose much of their freedom in the process.

Chapter 3

THE NUCLEAR ERA
(1945–1989)

How does Superman change in and out of his costume so quickly? Since the Man of Steel's creation, many comic book readers have asked themselves, and comic book editors, this seemingly inconsequential question. Comic book fans are often nearly obsessed with the small details about their favorite heroes. Most readers can easily accept the idea that an underdeveloped young man can drink a serum and become a super solider or that a playboy millionaire can dress up like a bat and fight crime. Often minor story points or seemingly mundane questions habitually disturb these same readers though. Before the Internet some superhero fans would write and mail their questions or point out mistakes to comic book editors and explanations would sometimes appear in stories. (In the 1960s, Marvel Comic's writer Stan Lee started giving out a "No-Prize" to fans that found story errors and or created solutions to supposed mistakes.)[1] As mentioned above, one of the mundane questions that readers often submitted was, how did Superman change in and out of his costume so quickly and what did he do with his other set of clothing? The basis for this question was the understanding that change is difficult and changing back is even harder.

The United States faced a similar problem after World War II. The nation had quickly changed into battle mode, and after the war it needed to find a way to change back to its normal identity. During the war, the United States had become Superman, and in late 1945 the nation needed to change back to Clark Kent. The American government had temporarily altered labor relations, commerce, the economy, gender roles, and the very social structure of American society itself. American leadership deemed these modifications to be necessary during the war, but after the conflict's end government officials believed that American society could return to its pre-war status (minus the economic depression). Just like Superman returning from a fight and heading back to work as Clark Kent, many Americans hoped and expected that the domestic U.S. would quickly change back to its civilian identity. Unfortunately, the process of postwar readjustment was far more difficult than changing clothing. World War II transformed Americans' perceptions of the world and themselves and introduced both new nightmares and new marvels. Unquestionably, the most important new element in American life (and the world) was the development and usage of the atomic bomb. When the U.S. dropped atomic bombs on Japan, it changed American society in immeasurable ways. Like every other American, comic book superheroes now had to adjust to a world that contained nuclear weapons. The world had entered the nuclear age and postwar Americans had to change into something new, not something old.

Little Boy and Fat Man

Little Boy and Fat Man started the nuclear age. The pair changed the world and caused humankind to re-evaluate its place in the universe. Although their names are reminiscent of comic book heroes, Little Boy and Fat Man were the atomic weapons that U.S. bombers dropped on Hiroshima and Nagasaki, Japan, on August 6 and August 9, 1945. The secret Manhattan Project had developed the atomic bomb at Los Alamos, New Mexico, and the U.S. essentially tested the weapon on Hiroshima. It is difficult for an American born after 1945 to understand the entire social and cultural impact of the atomic bomb. Post–World War II children have always lived in a nuclear shadow. Although postwar Americans understand the bomb's terrifying destructive potential, the threat has become a common, accepted element of everyday life. To postwar Americans the bomb has always existed and we cannot imagine a world in which it does not. Americans living during 1945 had a much more difficult adjustment. Talk of atomic weapons had existed prior to 1945 in scientific (and science fiction) circles, but most Americans had not come into contact with the idea of the atomic bomb.

When the B-29 bomber *Enola Gay* dropped Little Boy on Hiroshima, it not only destroyed the city, but also destroyed many citizens' ideas about life itself. Suddenly, there was a weapon that could annihilate entire metropolises, and at first this new development shocked and dismayed much of the populace. Humans had developed a technology that could destroy the world and wipe out all of humankind. Most Americans had awakened on August 6, 1945, to a world they thought they understood. This was no longer the case when they went to bed that same day. The world had become unfathomable and this was only the beginning. Little Boy and Fat Man had ushered in a new age, and unlike Superman, there would be no changing back.[2]

Supermen vs. the Bomb

The atomic bomb's advent suddenly caused comic book heroes to seem far less super than before. These costumed mystery men that had once been amazing soon paled in comparison to the atom's real life power. Ironically, a 1944 Superman story was going to feature the villainous Lex Luthor building an atomic bomb almost a year before Hiroshima was destroyed. The Department of Defense asked DC Comics not to publish the story and the tale did not see print until January-February 1946, long after the end of the war.[3] A Captain Marvel story from October 1946 entitled "Captain Marvel and the Atomic War" depicts what would happen in an atomic war. The tale ends with Captain Marvel as the Earth's only survivor and then it is revealed that the entire story was a television dramatization. The story finishes with viewers commenting, "The world just can't afford to have another war, because it would wipe out all civilization and all human life! Remember that kids!" "I guess we'd all better learn to live and get along together — One nation with all other nations and one person with all other persons — So that the terrible atomic war will never occur!"[4] Here even Captain Marvel could not save the U.S. from an atomic bomb's disastrous effects. The hero may have had the strength of Hercules and the power of Zeus but he was no match against the atomic bomb.

Not all atomic bomb stories were so destructive and horrifying. DC Comics published a Superman story in *Action Comics* #101 (October 1946) in which the Man of Steel films an atomic bomb test for the U.S. Army. Apparently, even if Superman could not prove himself stronger and more amazing than the atomic bomb, he could always find work as a civil servant. Later, personnel at the Department of Defense also objected to the proposed use of a cyclotron particle accelerator in another postwar Superman story and asked DC Comics not to publish the tale. It seems that that employees at the government agency thought the comic book usage of a cyclotron would cause the American public to become more relaxed and lose the fear of nuclear power.[5]

These governmental concerns could be seen as well founded when one considers how popular and faddish atomic culture became after the war. Two examples are Atomic Mouse and Atomic Rabbit/Bunny. Atomic Mouse was a superpowered rodent dressed in a black costume with a red cape (and a large white "A" on his chest.) Atomic Mouse appeared to be a Superman clone with the exception that he gained his powers by swallowing Uranium-235 pills. Similarly, Atomic Rabbit acquired his powers by eating a radioactive carrot. He later changed his name to Atomic Bunny, possibly because Atomic Rabbit sounded too menacing.[6]

All of these stories showcase the problem that various creators had in dealing with nuclear weapons and energy in comics. Writers, artists, and editors felt the need to feature atomic weapons and energy in their stories, but were often unsure how to do this or were asked not to. The atomic bomb had made superheroes seem less super while also often baffling and defeating the comic book creators themselves.

The Nuclear Age

Out of all the periods outlined in this book, the Nuclear Age is (poetically) the most unwieldy and nonconforming. It is fairly easy to place most of the chapters in a static timeline and showcase a linear progression. The Nuclear Age defies this linear order, though, and crosses over into many other periods and times. This chapter will progress into years that are included in later chapters, but will only present an overview of the social and cultural impacts of nuclear power in American society. For the purposes of this study the Nuclear Age will be defined using the Cold War timeline of 1945–1989. Although critics could rightly contend that a nuclear era extends into the present day, this book examines the years in which both society and comic books focused on nuclear issues most intently.

As previously noted, the Nuclear Age began abruptly with the U.S. dropping atomic bombs on Japan. Interestingly, many Americans did not immediately see atomic energy as dangerous. Remember that World War II essentially ended when a B-29 pilot dropped the second atomic bomb on Nagasaki. Many Americans were happy to see the war end and felt safe in the knowledge that only the U.S. possessed this destructive weapon. It was estimated that the war's early termination had saved thousands of American lives (at least) and that nuclear energy could usher in a positive new world. In a Gallup Poll taken August 10–15, 1945, 69 percent of Americans believed that the atomic bomb's creation was a good thing, 17 percent felt it to be a negative, while 14 percent offered no opinion.[7] An American citizen of the period, New York's Walter Niebuhr, wrote, "Perhaps the modern scientists have found a means of ending all wars, after centuries of futile efforts by statesmen, pacifists and economic groups.... Modern science has won this war for us. Modern science is winning the peace for us. And modern science will provide a means of living and a security of living for the generations to come which this world has never dreamed of."[8] *Time* magazine's science writer George Wendt wrote that atomic energy would virtually abolish the need for physical labor, and "then at last science will have freed the human race not only from disease, famine, and early death, but also from poverty and work. Then at last science will enable humanity to live, as well as earn a living."[9] In the days following the war most Americans seemed inclined to view the atomic bomb and atomic energy as a potential force for good and a positive technological advance. The bomb had come and most Americans were happy to welcome it.

How to Love the Bomb

In the days immediately after World War II's end, Americans seemed to embrace the atomic bomb and atomic energy, but it was unclear how long this sentiment would last. Soon the bomb's role in World War II's conclusion would fade from many Americans' memories and citizens would have to address the role of nuclear weapons and energy in U.S. culture. American newspapers, magazines, and other media quickly began publishing stories that would (hopefully) explain all things atomic. The news media generally intended these pieces to educate, and many of the stories contained a positive atomic spin. The U.S. had just won World War II and patriotism was still at its zenith. Although some writers and citizens criticized or expressed concern about the atomic bomb, these critics seemed to be in the minority, and most media outlets appeared to be comfortable presenting an optimistic portrayal. This media coverage undoubtedly helped to shape public opinion, but the U.S. government also took a more direct approach at education. The government almost immediately began creating propaganda that showed atomic energy to be both safe and beneficial. The Federal Civil Defense Administration and other government agencies soon produced posters and short films that implored Americans to consider the atom a friend and to trust nuclear power. These advertisements focused on atomic energy's positive uses and rarely mentioned the atomic bomb. Although the bomb had been necessary to end the war, its cousin atomic energy would secure a prosperous future. In the first few years following World War II most Americans still considered the atom to be a safe and reliable part of American society.[10]

Atomic Popular Culture

As the U.S. government created propaganda to convince the American public that nuclear energy was safe, clean and efficient, American popular culture began to embrace all things atomic. Although some Americans were afraid of potential problems, nuclear energy and weapons had not yet developed a sinister reputation. In the years directly following the war, nuclear power and energy became a popular culture sensation that many Americans, young and old, embraced.[11] The word "atomic" became synonymous with the idea of future wonders and technological innovations. Manufacturers began producing atomic toys for American youngsters. These included atomic guns, atomic balls, and even atomic board games. (In one board game from the mid–1950s, entitled "Uranium Rush," the player pretends to search for uranium with a pseudo Geiger counter).[12] The atomic style, which showcased natural patterns, energy lines, and circles depicting atoms in motion, became popular on numerous types of furniture and other household items.[13] America, and much of the world, seemed to have developed nuclear fever as atomic consumer items became a widespread fad. Advertisements flaunted atomic sales, atomic values, and atomic designs. In 1946 General Mills created an "Atomic 'Bomb' Ring" promotion. Over 750,000 children sent in 15 cents and a Kix cereal boxtop to acquire the nuclear jewelry.[14] Scientists became popular culture celebrities on whom Americans heaped praise and respect. The atom was cool and many Americans embraced its power and potential.

A New Kind of Fallout and Overexposure

Probably the most long lasting atomic popular culture icon was not a person or a toy, but rather a new swimsuit design. In 1946 French clothing designer Louis Réard created a daring new type of two piece bathing suit that showed much more skin than the standard one piece design. Réard's swimsuit pushed the boundaries of taste and social acceptability and also made a statement about the limitless possibilities of the postwar era. (Réard once stated that one of the features of his swimming suit was that it was so small that it could "be pulled through a wedding ring.")[15] The bathing suit's designer needed a name that would convey how powerful, advanced, and yet dangerous this new creation was. In order to find a fitting name Réard turned to the atomic lexicon.[16]

On July 1, 1946, the U.S. military conducted one of many atomic bomb tests code named Operation Crossroads on a small Pacific atoll. (Because the U.S. had dropped the first atomic bombs on Japan without much experimentation, military officials deemed tests necessary to determine the bomb's capabilities.) These nuclear tests revealed the atomic bomb's rare power and its inherent destructiveness.[17] The tests showed the A-bomb to be unbelievably powerful, exhilarating, futuristic, and more than a little frightening. These are all the qualities that Réard wanted to emphasize in his new swimsuit, so he named the new type of clothing after the small atoll. Over six decades later many Americans do not know how or why the popular swimsuit got its name, but almost everyone knows what a bikini is.

Atomic Heroes

While the postwar years ushered in a new era of peace and prosperity for many Americans, the comic book industry did not fare as well. Many factors — including increased discretionary spending due to wartime employment, a large number of GI readers, and patriotic storylines — contributed to dramatic growth in comic book sales during World War II. After the war, comic books no longer had the (figuratively) captive military audience or the socially relevant wartime villains. Captain Marvel artist C.C. Beck stated that after the war, "As for the comic book heroes and heroines, they had nothing to do. They had become so humanized that they could no longer fly around, chase outlandish villains, or fight impossible monsters as they once has done; nobody believed in that fairy tale stuff any more."[18] Suddenly, comic book creators were struggling to produce interesting stories that readers wanted to buy. Writers and artists had to find new story gimmicks and interesting, novel villains to keep current readers and attract new ones. Postwar superheroes soon faced social problems, new nemeses, and many other exploratory storylines in hopes of increasing sales.

Arguably, more important than returning GIs and watered-down heroes was that atomic power had made superheroes seem a little less super. When Superman was introduced in 1938 he seemed amazingly powerful when pitted against common criminals. Likewise, even the non-powered Batman seemed incredibly skilled and commanding while battling mad scientists and imaginary villains in 1939. During the war, comic book covers consistently featured superheroes defeating and humiliating Axis members. Before August 1945, comic book heroes seemed more powerful than any villain real or imagined. After the atomic bombings of Hiroshima and Nagasaki, real horrors existed that even superheroes were not powerful enough to defeat. The atomic bomb that had once been only science fiction or comic book fodder was suddenly a real world problem that amazed and frightened the entire planet. Comic book creators had to quickly find a way to incorporate atomic power into superhero storylines or the atomic bomb might destroy comic books like it did Hiroshima.

The Soviets Have the Bomb

In the first years after World War II, many Americans held positive views about nuclear energy and the U.S. possessing atomic weapons. For numerous citizens these optimistic feelings ended abruptly in 1949, when U.S. officials revealed that the Soviet Union had developed nuclear weapons. (The U.S. had detected signs of nuclear fallout from the Soviet test site in Kazakhstan.) Since the new atomic age's beginning, the U.S. had been the A-bomb's sole keeper and the nation had never feared a nuclear attack. Suddenly, the U.S.'s most dangerous international adversary held atomic secrets and was able to launch a nuclear attack on the American homeland. Although the U.S.S.R had been the U.S.'s ally during World War II, the two countries' leaders long had been wary of each other and increasingly had begun to disagree in the postwar era. The Soviet Union's socialist economic system and communistic political system strongly clashed with the American belief in capitalism and republican democracy. Since the war's end, the Soviet and American governments had engaged in minor political skirmishes that marked the beginning of the Cold War, an indirect conflict that relied not on direct military actions, but rather propaganda, the threat of war, and fighting through third parties. The Cold War may have begun when World War II ended, but the war heated up (or cooled down if reverse nomenclature applies) when the Soviets developed atomic weapons. The U.S. government and the American public both worried about the consequences of a nuclear U.S.S.R., and the images of Hiroshima, Nagasaki, and nuclear bomb tests were fresh in American citizens' minds. The Soviets now had the bomb and the world would never be the same.[19]

Happy Days? The 1950s

Many types of American popular culture seem to portray the 1950s as a quiet decade that witnessed the U.S.'s last innocent years. Notable writers, filmmakers, and audience members have nostalgically described the 1950s as a brief American "golden age" between World War II's carnage and the 1960s' social upheaval. Films like *Grease* and *American Graffiti* (set in 1962 but before the 1960s' cultural changes) and television shows like *Happy Days* showcased the 1950s as a virtual American utopia and a *Leave It to Beaver* world. In reality the 1950s were much more of a transitional decade. From 1929 to 1945, economic collapse and war had gripped American society. After World War II, many newly middle class Americans attempted to restructure domestic American life as a safe haven against violence and want. Returning GI's found careers, moved to quiet suburbs, and raised families. To many within a generation forged by war and poverty, boring was a desirous adjective.

A large number of former Second World Warriors strove to create mundane existences, but in reality the 1950s were anything but boring. Hidden behind well-manicured suburban lawns and two car garages was a deep seated fear of an unknown menace. While postwar America seemed peaceful and prosperous, adults remembered how quickly poverty and war had previously disrupted society. Although different Americans saw the postwar menace in various guises, one of the most common was the Soviet nuclear threat.

After the Soviet Union tested an atomic weapon in August 1949, to many Americans the nuclear threat became synonymous with communism. By definition communism is a theoretical political system, but during the 1950s most Americans saw the Soviet variety as a social evil that aimed to destroy American society. Some Americans, like Wisconsin Senator Joseph McCarthy, feared that communists would somehow internally gain control of the U.S., but most citizens worried about a nuclear war. Many Americans built bomb/fallout shelters in their basements, often based on government designs.[20] The Federal Civil Defense Administration (FCDA) produced a large amount of propaganda aimed at educating Americans about the nuclear threat. Numerous short instructional films focused on the Soviet nuclear menace and what the American populace could do to protect itself. These films helped to shape the American public's ideas about nuclear power and the Soviet peril.[21]

Duck and Cover

One of the most well known FCDA propaganda campaigns concerned the concept of duck and cover. The U.S. government created duck and cover as a safety measure for Americans caught in a nuclear attack. The idea was when a citizen saw an atomic flash he or she should duck under some sort of protective structure (like a table or a desk), lie in the fetal position, and cover his or her face with his or her hands. This procedure would have provided little help for a person at ground zero, but duck and cover, in theory, could have prevented shockwave debris from striking and injuring someone.

American public schools appeared to be the focal point of this educational campaign and the U.S. government released a duck and cover instructional film in 1952.[22] This motion picture focused on Bert, a pith helmet wearing turtle, who understands the necessities of ducking and covering. The film begins with Bert ducking into his shell when a tree-hanging monkey attempts to injure the turtle with a stick of dynamite. (It is unclear what political or social hostilities exist between the simian and the reptile.) Because Bert ducked and covered, the monkey's attack does not harm the safety-minded turtle, but instead incinerates both the monkey and his tree base. A catchy jingle accompanies the animated sequence explaining the necessity of learning to duck and cover. Later the film shows live action sequences including footage of schoolchildren ducking under their desks practicing for a nuclear attack.[23] Though this is only one film from the early 1950s, it provides an example of a general American fear of a nuclear attack. The U.S. government and American citizens were so concerned about the Soviet nuclear threat that they educated schoolchildren about nuclear fear. At first glance, 1950s America was prosperous and seemingly bland, but underneath the calm exterior was a society wracked with fear. While the atomic bomb had been a savior during World War II and a postwar scientific marvel that promised a brighter future, by the 1950s it symbolized a possible nuclear nightmare. The same atomic bomb that quickly ended World II created an undertone of fear in the prosperous postwar America.

Anti-Communist and Nuclear Heroes

Comic book publishers mirrored Cold War fears by providing both communist-fighting superheroes and heroes that fought for the American way of life. Although the Cold War was a political, economic, and ideological battle, 1950s comic book heroes turned to the solutions that had worked in World War II, and superheroes personally confronted the enemy and demonstrated American society's superiority. Marvel Comics had cancelled Captain America's monthly comic book in 1950 because of poor sales. Although Marvel had tried such gimmicks as making Captain America's alter ego, Steve Rogers, a school teacher, giving him the female sidekick Golden Girl, and changing the name of his comic book to *Captain America's Weird Tales*, fans no longer seemed interested.[24] Marvel briefly revived Captain America in 1954. Each cover featured the banner "Captain America ... Commie Smasher" and showed Cap battling communists in a manner reminiscent of World War II covers. Issue #77 shows Captain America fighting a ship full of communists, and the cover announces that he is "Striking Back at the Soviets." *Captain America* #78 depicts Cap battling a nuclear powered Soviet character and reads, "See Captain America Defy the Communist Hordes!!"[25] Although this bombastic style sold millions of comic books during World War II it did not work as well in the 1950s, and Captain America was cancelled after three issues. Captain Marvel also fought directly against

Captain America #78 (June 1954) features the Sentinel of Liberty in his new role as "Commie Smasher." Comic book readers did not embrace Cap's anti-communist fight, though, and the series was cancelled after only three issues. Captain America would return again during the 1960s Marvel revival. (© 1954 Marvel Comics. All Rights Reserved.)

communists in several storylines and soon his title was cancelled as well.[26] Readers apparently did not want a patriotic war hero to fight the communists for them. The nature of the Cold War and the threat of nuclear attack made direct action unbelievable even for a superhero.

Unlike Marvel's failed 1950s Captain America, DC Comics generally created heroes that did not directly fight the Cold War but extolled the desirousness of American life. Superman and Batman became proponents of the American dream and soon developed superhero versions of ordinary lives. Both heroes acquired pseudo-families complete with girlfriends, pets, and even daughter-like figures. Monthly stories preached the importance of home, family, working hard, obeying the law, and following society's conventions. While Superman had once been outspoken about the U.S.'s problems, he now openly supported mainstream American ideals. He worked a white collar job as Clark Kent, dated Lois Lane, built a suburban like sanctuary (in the Arctic) and embraced "the American way." The underlying narrative seemed to be that if Superman chose to live as an American, then it must be the best possible society.

During the 1950s, DC Comics also introduced several new versions of old heroes that showcased the superiority of American life. In October 1956, DC Comics established a new version of the 1940s hero the Flash. The updated Flash was Barry Allen, a police scientist who worked closely with law enforcement in both of his identities. The Flash was the typical new 1950s (later termed Silver Age by comic book fans) hero. He fought for law and order and respected the state and American society above all else. Similarly, DC Comics began publishing a new Green Lantern in 1959 that celebrated American freedom and openness. Hal Jordan became a member of an intergalactic police force, the Green Lantern Corps, when a dying alien gave him a ring that could turn thought into reality. Jordan worked as a test pilot in his civilian identity and a cosmic policeman when in costume. In both identities Green Lantern expresses American society's superiority. The dying alien police officer chose an American to become Green Lantern because he was the most qualified candidate. No other nation could have produced someone so exceptional. Likewise, Hal Jordan is a military-type man who understands the importance of the armed services and fights to protect the American way of life. In the 1950s Superman, Batman, the Flash, Green Lantern, and a host of other heroes indirectly fought the Cold War by emphasizing the U.S.'s superiority. Instead of directly fighting an enemy, as in World War II, many popular superheroes became high powered cheerleaders.

Atomic-Americans: The 1960s

American society in the 1950s was a unique mixture of prosperity and fear. The decade's economic and political constancy masked a vast undercurrent of nuclear hysteria. The generation that fought the Second World War craved social stability and worried that a nuclear Soviet Union might destroy normalcy. This generation generally trusted the government to create a livable society and to combat America's enemies. In retrospect the 1950s was not as much a stable decade as a transitional one. While the World War II generation feared the Soviet Union would impose military change on the U.S., this governing generation worried less about the greatest threat to American social stability: their children.

U.S. GIs returned home victorious in 1945 to a soon-to-be prosperous nation. The combination of constrained ardor and the burgeoning economy produced a massive increase in children's births known as the Baby Boom. The U.S. Census Bureau estimates that over

78 million children were born during the Baby Boom years from 1946 to 1964.[27] These children, known as Baby Boomers, lived in a vastly different America than did previous generations. While the Great Depression's poverty and World War II's carnage had shaped their parents' worldview, Baby Boomers only lived in a powerful, prosperous, safe, and slightly dull America. Baby Boomers did not fear economic collapse, but did live their entire lives within the atomic bomb's shadow.[28]

Cuban Missile Crisis

If Baby Boomers resided in a nuclear shadow, then some of their darkest days were during October 1962. Americans' nuclear holocaustic fears were nearly realized during the autumn of 1962 as the world was poised on the brink of nuclear war. In September 1962, the Soviet and Cuban governments began positioning nuclear missiles in Cuba, the Caribbean nation located less than one hundred miles from Florida. On October 14, U.S. reconnaissance planes discovered the nuclear missiles in Cuba. The Cubans and Soviets claimed that the missiles were placed in Cuba to prevent a U.S. invasion. U.S. President John F. Kennedy and other officials viewed the nuclear missiles' close proximity to the U.S. mainland as a threat to American security. The two superpowers appeared to play an intricate nuclear chess game, using Cuba as a pawn. Soviet leader Nikita Khrushchev wanted to test the young and inexperienced U.S. president, while Kennedy desired to end the Cuban nuclear threat and gain a Cold War victory.

On October 22, in a televised speech, Kennedy revealed the missiles' presence and announced that U.S. ships would enforce a naval blockade of Cuba. The U.S. Navy would search all ships traveling to Cuba and would not allow any vessels carrying weapons to enter. Khrushchev declared the blockade to be in violation of international law and U.S. interference in Soviet- Cuban affairs. For the next several days the world waited breathlessly to see what Khrushchev and Kennedy would do. One misstep by either leader could have meant nuclear annihilation not only for the three countries involved, but for the entire world. Two men and their advisors would decide the planet's fate. Many in the Kennedy administration advised the president that the U.S. would have to invade Cuba, an action that would probably have meant nuclear war. The U.S. prepared reactions to a Soviet atomic strike and to many it seemed nuclear war was imminent.

The Soviets and Americans quietly negotiated for several days and by October 28 they forged an agreement. The Soviets would remove the Cuban nuclear missiles in exchange for an American promise not to invade Cuba and a commitment to eliminate U.S. missiles from Turkey. The agreement re-established the Cold War status quo but left the world even more horrified about the prospect of nuclear war.[29]

Many Americans, and citizens of other nations, remember the Cuban Missile Crisis as the time when the world barely avoided nuclear war. As frightening as this concept would have been for American adults, most people that had lived through the Great Depression and the war years had developed the necessary coping strategies. The oldest Baby Boomers were only 16 during the Cuban Missile Crisis and most were younger. For many of these Baby Boomers, the crisis was a seminal event that shaped the generation's collective social and political view. No one can argue that the Baby Boomers were a monolithic generation in which every member perceived the world in a similar way. However, most Boomers shared important social events that defined their generation even if not all members reacted in the same manner. At a young age, these children and teenagers witnessed the unspeakable horror of seemingly impending nuclear war. Two leaders held the world hostage and one misstep, mistake, or wrong decision could have resulted in an atomic holocaust. These events would necessarily shape how the Baby Boom generation perceived society, culture, government, politics, and the world in general. Although the 1960s began with a robust U.S. economy and an America generally at peace internationally, the nuclear threat caused many Baby Boomers to begin to question the idea of American society. The Cuban Missile Crisis had shown many Baby Boomers how close the world could come to nuclear war and how fragile and capricious that society and culture truly were.

Counter Youth Culture

The fear of nuclear war and destruction was only one of many factors that helped transform the Baby Boom generation. The Vietnam War, the assassinations of notable figures like John F. Kennedy, Robert Kennedy, Martin Luther King, Jr., and Malcolm X, along with the civil rights movement, rock and roll, and many other cultural influences worked to shape Baby Boomers' attitudes and create a desire for a new American society. Because of their sheer numbers, the Baby Boomers gained a large amount of economic, and thus social, power as they began to express their wants and desires.

By the early 1960s, Boomers were beginning to create trends and influence society in economic, social, cultural, and even political ways. This social power gave birth to a youth culture that accommodated many of the young generation's wishes and pushed the U.S. from the stuffy 1950s into the increasingly provocative 1960s. Soon rock and roll, the peace movement, the counter culture, and various other ideas and movements would transform U.S. society into something unfathomable only a decade before. During this time period nuclear weapons and destruction were never far from society's surface. Cold War fears and an increased nuclear build up filled the headlines and television soon broadcasted the Vietnam War into millions of American living rooms nightly. As the Baby Boomers emerged and demanded a different society, they also required new heroes. The children born into a nuclear America no longer needed or understood the heroes that had guided their parents through tough times.

Atomic Marvel Heroes

The Baby Bombers began to emerge as an important social element during the 1960s, and American society and culture began to change to accommodate their needs and desires. The heroes of the 1940s, like Superman and Batman, did not appeal to many younger Americans. Although the older heroes' stories still had a large readership, many American youths viewed these comic book tales as old fashioned and dull. To Baby Boomers, heroes like Superman and Batman seemed to belong to an antiquated world in which problems could be solved in one short issue and every story had a happy ending. This new generation born after World War II demanded superheroes that were relevant to young Americans and that spoke directly to a changing society. Marvel Comics began to publish a new type of superhero in the mid 1960s; a hero that faced real life problems and rarely could expect a happy ending. Additionally, most of the early Marvel heroes also shared another common trait — they received their superpowers through a nuclear accident. Older heroes like Superman, Shazam, or the Flash were often aliens or had acquired their powers via magic or a natural or chemical accident. Certainly other past heroes had gained their extraordinary abilities through nuclear sources, but mostly as a gimmick for publishers to cash in on the popular atomic fad.

The new Marvel heroes received their powers through the dangerous and yet potent nuclear energy, but only as a storytelling device. In other words, by 1963 nuclear energy was so much a part of American society that Marvel did not use it as a gimmick, but rather as a "natural" way to give heroes fantastic abilities. Heroes like the Fantastic Four, the Incredible Hulk, Daredevil, and Spider-Man were citizens of the Nuclear Age and thus expectedly gained their powers via nuclear accidents. The Baby Boomers were a generation that had always lived with the knowledge and threat of nuclear power and their heroes reflected such an attitude. Atomic power was socially and culturally relevant and its increased presence in comic books showcased this societal change.[30]

The Nuclear Family

The notion of nuclear or atomic power as the basis for super-abilities was deeply rooted in Marvel Comics stories. The writer Stan Lee and artists like Jack Kirby and Steve Ditko were responsible for creating almost all of the early Marvel characters. These new superheroes gained their amazing abilities through nuclear energy or power, but often it was unclear if these superpowers were a blessing or a curse. The first 1960s Marvel superheroes were a team that Stan Lee developed based on the success of DC Comic's *Justice League of America*.[31] Lee did not create a carbon copy, but rather designed a superpowered "family" known as the Fantastic Four. The quartet consisted of Reed Richards, Sue Storm, Johnny Storm, and Ben Grimm. The group's relationships placed them into semi-familial roles, which was uncommon in previous superhero teams; Sue and Johnny were siblings, Sue and Reed were dating, and Reed and Ben were former college roommates. While on a space flight the four were exposed to strange radiation and thus acquired unique abilities. Reed's body became pliable and elastic, Sue could create force fields and turn invisible, Johnny gained the ability to become engulfed in flames and fly, Ben became an orange rock-like "monster" with super-strength and invulnerability. Although the comic books' creators did not specifically refer to the energy that transformed the Fantastic Four as "nuclear" or "atomic," when placed in a 1960s social context it seems clear that this was the intent.[32] Strange energy had changed a normal "family" into a nuclear family, just as atomic energy had changed society and the American family.

Incredible Radiation

After the success of the Fantastic Four, Marvel Comics created several more nuclear heroes that breathed new life into the superhero genre. Possibly the most recognizable of these is the Incredible Hulk. In this neo-rendition of Dr. Jekyll and Mr. Hyde mixed with Frankenstein, scientist Bruce Banner is exposed to gamma radiation during a nuclear test. The gamma rays build up in Banner's body and when he becomes angry he changes into a super-strong "monster" known as the Hulk.[33] Much like nuclear energy itself, the Hulk can be defined as neither hero nor villain, but rather is a complex and often uncontrollable natural force. Incredible Hulk stories contained many things — action, adventure, and pithy "Hulk Smash" dialogue, but at their core the Hulk stories are about man's inability to control both himself and atomic energy.

Authors Lois Gresh and Robert Weinberg claim that the Hulk was a comic reaction to the Cold War nuclear threat.[34] This reading seems especially evident when one considers the comic book's storylines and characters. The main character is atomic scientist Bruce Banner, who attempts to harness nuclear energy, but instead is changed into a dimwitted "monster." Banner constantly fights against the nuclear monster within, but is unable to control the raw power and energy. Angry and aggressive feelings often cause Banner to transform into the Hulk and thus link these "negative" emotions both to the creature and symbolically to atomic power. Many of the Hulk's adversaries, like the Leader, Abomination and Half-Life, have identities and abilities associated with nuclear accidents. Man's atomic experiments have created not only the Hulk but a myriad of unnatural nuclear villains that threaten human civilization and the Earth as a whole. Much like atomic weapons, these nuclear individuals were too powerful and unpredictable to control, and Americans have to constantly worry for the world's safety.[35]

Additionally, the Hulk's long time nemesis, General Thaddeus "Thunderbolt" Ross, is portrayed as a military officer obsessed with hunting and controlling the Hulk. Military experiments created the Hulk and several of his adversaries, and Ross wants to contain these nuclear threats. Ross is generally portrayed as a villain that is fixated on destroying the Hulk. The general's Ahab-like quest turned him into a moral and intellectual monster. Ross clearly lost his humanity during his fight against his nuclear foe and one cannot help but recall the Friedrich Nietzsche worry, "He who fights with monsters might take care lest he thereby become a monster." If read as a U.S. military symbol, Ross displays the idea that the armed services had lost their direction and morality during the Cold War's nuclear pseudo-confrontations. The Incredible Hulk portrayed a character that symbolized nuclear energy and displayed the U.S.'s inability to command it. Many Americans no longer saw nuclear power as safe and controllable, but rather as a potential monster.

The Man Without Nuclear Fear

If the Fantastic Four was an often unhappy nuclear family and the Incredible Hulk a nuclear monster/menace, then comic books were mirroring society's growing distrust of nuclear power. Atomic energy was threatening the American family and American society and this nuclear menace was seemingly unstoppable. What happened to the late 1940s promise of a clean and efficient nuclear future? Had all of this atomic goodwill wilted and been replaced with a new stark landscape? Although two previous Marvel comic books presented bleak atomic understandings, another 1960s Marvel superhero showcased a positive nuclear view. In April 1964, Marvel introduced the Stan Lee and Bill Everett creation Daredevil. When a radioactive substance fell from a truck and blinded young Matt Murdock, he also gained sonar-like superpowers and took up the mantle of Daredevil to avenge his father's death. Although nuclear materials destroyed Murdock's sight, they gave him a new super-vision that operated differently from normal eyesight.[36] Nuclear energy took away one of Murdock's primary senses, but in return gave him new abilities and a new identity. Without his superpowers Matt would have been unable to avenge his father's death and to make his city safer.

While the Fantastic Four and the Incredible Hulk warned of atomic energy's disastrous problems and liabilities, Daredevil displayed the notion that nuclear power was both potentially dangerous and productive. The atom could harm, but it also could help. Much like American society, Daredevil had to deal with atomic power's positive and negative possibilities. This dilemma, in many ways, served as the Nuclear Age's central problem. Should society fear or embrace nuclear energy and power? How should people feel about something that has so much potential for both good and ill? The idea of nuclear energy and power produced intense feelings of both fear and hope, often in the same person. The 1960s Marvel heroes showcase a spectrum of feelings about the Nuclear Age and most Americans could identify with nearly all of these points of view.

With Nuclear Power Comes Great Responsibility

If the Fantastic Four and the Incredible Hulk served as a warning against nuclear power's destructive presence in American society and Daredevil presented atomic energy's role as both positive and negative, they did so by addressing society as a whole. All six of these characters were adults and their actions symbolized American society's direction. Many Marvel readers were children or young adults, though, and these nuclear comic book symbols did not speak to an atomic presence in their personal lives. Until the early 1960s most teenage comic book characters were either sidekicks or supporting cast members. There were few teenaged comic book superheroes and none in the new Marvel style. This changed in 1962 when Spider-Man debuted in *Amazing Fantasy* #15. In Spider-Man's origin story, a radioactive spider bit the unathletic and nerdy teenager Peter Parker. A science experiment gone wrong caused the spider to become radioactive, and the story's text explains, "Accidentally absorbing a fantastic amount of radioactivity, the dying insect, in sudden shock, bites the nearest living thing, at the split second before life ebbs from its radioactive body."[37] Spiders are not actually insects, but Stan Lee's purple prose does bombastically communicate Spider-Man's nuclear origins. The radioactive spider bite soon endued Peter Parker with new spider-like superpowers, including the ability to climb walls, super strength, extraordinary speed and balance, and a sixth sense that alerted him when danger was present (known as "spider sense.") At first young Parker uses his newfound superpowers for personal gain, but when a thief murders his uncle, Peter vows to fight crime. Nuclear power had given Peter Parker superpowers and tragedy had turned him into a hero.

In order to justify Spider-Man's heroics Stan Lee and Steve Ditko included a literary theme in the crime fighter's first story that would serve as an overarching Spider-Man premise throughout the character's history. The idea of "with great power there must also come great responsibility" was presented in *Amazing Fantasy* #15 and quickly became entrenched in the Spider-Man narrative. Peter's soon to be murdered Uncle Ben extolled this life lesson that became Spider-Man's mantra. As Spider-Man, Peter Parker worked hard to "do the right thing" even though he often suffered severe consequences and his superpowers were seemingly a burden. Spider-Man was different from most early superheroes that lived glamorous and adventurous lifestyles and had few problems that could not be solved during a twenty-two page comic book. Spider-Man's powers helped the hero to create positive change in society, but they were personally encumbersome, often damaging Parker's personal life. For all the good that society derived from Spider-Man's abilities, Peter Parker's relationships with his aunt, his co-workers, society at large, and even potential girlfriends suffered.

The most blatant example of the price that Peter Parker paid for his superpowers appeared in a June 1973 *The Amazing Spider-Man* #121 story entitled "The Night Gwen Stacy Died." As the title suggests, the story featured Peter Parker's girlfriend's death. Spider-Man's nemesis, the Green Goblin, kidnapped Stacy and she eventually died during a subsequent battle between the villain and Spider-Man. The story's author, Gerry Conway, stated that Spider-Man's struggles mirrored an American society in which life seemed futile.[38] Had Peter not been Spider-Man, Gwen probably would not have died, but Peter's inaction had led to his Uncle Ben's death. Peter Parker was trapped in a cycle he could not escape. If he stopped being Spider-Man then innocents would die; if he continued fighting crime then those around him would suffer. This explanation closely matches the U.S.'s dilemma in the nuclear era. Many Americans debated whether the country could abandon atomic energy's positive effects because of the negative consequences.

During the Cold War, cultural and political choices had trapped the U.S. in a nuclear staring match with the U.S.S.R. that could easily be seen in superhero comic book terms. Most American citizens would have considered the U.S. the story's superhero and the Soviet Union the villain. The U.S. gained its nuclear superpowers first, but shortly afterwards the Soviets acquired their own fantastic atomic abilities. In Cold War propaganda terms the U.S. was locked in a struggle with a nuclear supervillain for the planet's fate. In this paradigm, George Kennan's idea of containment provided a road map for how the American hero state should act. The U.S. had to prevent the villainous Soviets from growing their empire and eventually taking over the entire planet. This meant that the U.S. immediately had to stop Soviet expansion before the supervillain could implement its plan to rule the world. In this context the U.S. was not using nuclear power for selfish purposes, but rather was altruistically attempting to save the world. In this historical view, the U.S. understood that "with great power there must also come great responsibility," and was willing to take on this burden for the planet's good. Much like Spider-Man's personal torment, the U.S. suffered many domestic nuclear problems. The nation had little choice though, because to not use nuclear weapons as a deterrent against the U.S.S.R. would mean letting the supervillain win. In this cultural view, like Spider-Man, the U.S. saw itself as a hero that suffers for the greater good. The U.S. had the power to protect the world and thus had to accept the responsibility and the consequences.

Social Stalemate

As the 1960s ended and the 1970s began, the United States entered a period of political, social, and nuclear stagnation. By January 1973, the U.S. and North and South Vietnam signed the Paris Peace Accords, which ended the Vietnam War. After the 1975 Fall of Saigon, all U.S. personnel had left Vietnam. Social unrest calmed and the Baby Boomers' passions seemingly faded, but deep schisms remained within American society. In February 1972, U.S. President Richard Nixon visited China and normalized relations between the two countries. The heightened cooperation between its two greatest enemies propelled the Soviet Union to engage more directly with the United States. The U.S.S.R. and the U.S. entered a period of détente, in which Cold War rhetoric lessened and the countries seemingly learned to work together. The Strategic Arms Limitation Talks (SALT) I had begun in 1969, and by May 1972 the two nations had agreed to set nuclear weapons limits and to peacefully coexist. Although these agreements seemingly provided a structure to end U.S. and Soviet nuclear tensions, they also served to codify and strengthen the Cold War nuclear arrangement.

While détente curbed the two nations' nuclear arms race, the series of treaties and agreements cemented the Cold War reality. The U.S. and U.S.S.R.'s leaders no longer presented the countries as mortal enemies fighting for national survival; now the two "enemy" states conducted the Cold War as a mutually agreed upon nationalistic bureaucratic policy. Détente and the new nuclear arrangement closely mirrored the tone of the American 1970s. The nation was exhausted and many Americans wanted to forget about or ignore the bad news that seemed to surround them. The aftermath of the social upheaval of the 1960s, the Vietnam War, the Watergate Scandal, the Iran Hostage Crisis, and the oil shortages socially took its toll on the American psyche during the second half of the decade. As the economy entered a lengthy recession, President Jimmy Carter believed that the U.S. had a "crisis of the spirit" and few could argue against him.[39] The U.S. had entered the Cold War's stagnant years. The nuclear threat still existed but many Americans had lived in fear for so long that they hardly even noticed.

Malaise Heroes

As in most periods, superheroes epitomized the 1970s' social issues. Comic books entered a darker period in which creators presented more realistic stories as American society and popular culture was filled with many stark and unhappy images. Characters like the Punisher, Luke Cage, and even Batman began to address social issues and even openly disagree with those in authority. Comic books began to question the foundations of American culture and society and many superheroes were no longer simply champions of the "American way." Ironically, two of the decade's only nuclear-themed heroes, Firestorm and Wildfire, are wholesome characters that could have easily been transported from the 1950s. Firestorm was born when teenager Ronald Raymond and physicist Martin Stein were involved in a nuclear accident which allowed them to fuse together and become a nuclear powered hero. DC cancelled Firestorm's comic book after only five issues and the series was not reinstated again until the 1980s.[40] The 1970s version of the hero presented little of social significance during its short run. Much the same can be said of Wildfire, a new member of the Legion of Superheroes, a super-teenage club in which Superboy was a member.[41] Ironically, the most striking nuclear hero of the 1970s had no true atomic powers. Instead, the hero was a self-created living weapon that changed from a pro–Vietnam War advocate to an anti-military spokesman. In April 1963, Marvel Comic released *Tales of Suspense* #39 in which Vietnamese partisans capture and injure weapons manufacturer Tony Stark. In order to remain alive and escape captivity, Stark builds an armored suit that gives him the ability to fly, super strength, and various other weapons. Stark continues to don the armor and becomes the superhero known as Iron Man. At first Stark is an extreme anti-communist who strongly backs the U.S. government's efforts in Vietnam, even at times fighting the war himself. Gradually Iron Man loses faith in the government and by the 1970s he openly opposes the Vietnam War. By the 1970s even the human war machine does not believe in the righteousness of the U.S.'s Cold War struggle.[42]

Iron Man's transformation emulates changes among many U.S. citizens. Stark, the industrialist who made a fortune selling weaponry, began as a conservative symbol, the right wing war hawk who strongly believed in the free market system. The horrors of Vietnam, the Cold War, and by extension the atomic bomb, shake Tony Stark's and many Americans' faith. Stark, an American so patriotic that he became a state weapon, no longer fully trusts or believes in the United States. While this is certainly reflective of a general American malaise, it also displays a growing distrust of weapons of mass destruction. Once many Americans believed that weapons like the atomic bomb could be controlled, then numerous Americans feared that other countries' weapons might destroy the U.S.; by the 1970s many citizens questioned the use of powerful weapons both by both foreign and domestic actors.

No longer did Americans like Tony Stark support the U.S. government unconditionally, including the use of nuclear weaponry. In September 1975's *Invincible Iron Man* #78, Tony Stark flashes back to his involvement in Vietnam war atrocities and vows that he will make amends for following the government blindly in the past. Stark states, "War is the culmination of all those evils. War is the condition that devalues any of mankind's gains, and I swear as the man Tony Stark, as the Avenger fate chose to cast in the role of Iron Man, that I will live to avenge those whose lives have been lost through the ignorance of men like the man I once was, or I will die trying."[43] Like many Americans, Tony Stark had once unquestioningly supported the United States government in all matters foreign and domestic. Now he, and many members of the general public, feels duped and a

Characters like Firestorm displayed comic book creators' difficulties with addressing the Nuclear Age's issues. Both comic book superheroes and the American public debated if nuclear power and energy were saviors or menaces. (© 1978 DC Comics. Used with permission of DC Comics.)

little bitter. Iron Man, and many citizens like him, had once strongly believed in the rightness of the military's decisions and now he was questioning that same military's actions. As the Cold War stagnated and the U.S. and the U.S.S.R. played their roles, many Americans began wondering what the point was.[44]

The Reagan Years

The seemingly stagnant 1970s Cold War policies began to change in the early 1980s with the election of Ronald Reagan as U.S. president. Reagan believed strongly in a capitalistic democratic society and was determined to once again antagonistically engage the Soviet Union. The president quickly reversed the détente policies, massively increased the

U.S. military's size and budget, and greatly amplified Cold War rhetoric. Reagan referred to the U.S.S.R. as an "evil empire," claimed that the Soviet Union would soon collapse, and said "freedom and democracy will leave Marxism and Leninism on the ash heap of history."[45] He once tested a microphone by joking, "My fellow Americans, I am pleased to tell you I just signed legislation which outlaws Russia forever. The bombing begins in five minutes."[46] In 1983, Reagan proposed the Strategic Defense Initiative, a space based missile shield that would be commonly known as "Star Wars." Although Reagan claimed to desire the end of nuclear weapons, the military buildup and the increased rhetoric heightened nuclear fears across the country and the world.

Americans responded with a mixture of anxiety and patriotism. Historian Phillip Jenkins notes that a 1981 poll "found that over 75 percent of Americans expected a nuclear war within a few years."[47] Films like *Red Dawn* and *Rocky IV* showed Americans fighting and beating the evil Soviets, but this bravado barely masked deep seated nuclear fears. In the early and mid–1980s, Americans understood that the Cold War was no longer stagnant and nuclear war could happen at any time.

Who Watches the Watchmen?

Many popular culture outlets reflected the increased nuclear and Cold War tensions of the early and mid–1980s. Undoubtedly, the most influential comic book of this period (and possibly ever) is Alan Moore and Dave Gibbons' *Watchmen*. The twelve part miniseries published by DC Comics from September 1986 to October 1987 showcases costumed superheroes dealing with real life issues including atomic weapons. *Watchmen* was one the first mainstream comic books that explored the idea of what superheroes would act like in the real world. Although most of the costumed crime fighters have positive qualities, each of them is flawed and none are heroes using traditional comic book definitions. These superheroes battle their own insecurities, vices, and inner demons more than external foes. One of Moore's primary themes in the series is the planet's impending atomic doom and how even superheroes appear to be unable to prevent a nuclear holocaust.

Throughout the series Moore showcases the atomic Doomsday Clock and displays the device's slow movement towards nuclear Armageddon. The reader watches as a large American city is forced to face impending nuclear doom while the society's superheroes seemingly do little. *Watchmen* expresses the 1980s cynical post–Watergate attitude about society in general and nuclear weapons specifically. In this comic book world, there are no good guys and the world's true evil is not costumed villains with dreams of world conquest, but rather a socially-constructed nuclear trap. In Moore's dystopia things like nuclear weapons have siphoned away people's humanity and human beings are mere shells of the caring, feeling, loving individuals they once were. Nuclear weapons are not only physically radioactive and toxic, but also spiritually and culturally so. In *Watchmen* superheroes are as powerless as anyone to overcome the haunting and damaging effects of nuclear weapons.

Jon Take Manhattan

In Alan Moore's *Watchmen*, atomic bombs not only kill the body, but also drain away society's humanity. This view is best expressed in the character of Dr. Manhattan, the only superpowered being in *Watchmen*. A nuclear accident transformed scientist Jon Osterman into the atomic powered Dr. Manhattan (named after the Manhattan Project that created the first atomic bomb). Before the accident, Jon was an average man who loved his wife, was good at his job, and connected well with those around him. As Dr. Manhattan, Jon can see the future, instantaneously travel long distances, create energy blasts that can kill a person, and perform other amazing feats. In the *Watchmen* universe Dr. Manhattan led the U.S. to victory in Vietnam and is used as an American weapon to deter the Soviet Union. Jon slowly begins losing his humanity, though, and soon he is unconcerned about what happens to average humans.

By the end of *Watchmen* the being that was once Jon has entirely become Dr. Manhattan. He has lost his humanity and is the embodiment of the 1980s understanding of nuclear power — cold, calculating, and extremely dangerous. This transformation is showcased in many *Watchmen* scenes, but one of the most memorable involves Jon, his wife Sally, and Rorschach, a costumed vigilante. Rorschach asks Jon if a recent death concerned him and Jon replies, "A live body and a dead body contain the same number of particles. Structurally, there's no discernible difference. Life and death are unquantifiable abstracts. Why should I be concerned?"[48]

In Moore's vision nuclear energy drained Jon's humanity, just it had the world's. *Watchmen* mirrored the fears, hopelessness, and regret that many in society felt about nuclear weapons during the last years of the Cold War. Possibly more importantly, it mirrored the apathy of a society that had lived in a nuclear shadow for over forty years.

Not with a Bang but a Whimper

Many historians and foreign affairs experts mark the Cold War's end with the Berlin Wall's collapse in 1989. No matter if one uses this pivotal event or one of many others, by the end of the 1980s the Soviet Union was crumbling and the Cold War over. Scholars argue which of a myriad of impetuses — including the Polish Solidarity movement, Soviet leader Mikhail Gorbachev's reforms, and Reagan's increased military spending — most hastened the Soviet empire's disintegration, but few disagree that the end of the U.S.S.R. marked a new political and historical era. The nearly forty-five year political struggle between the United States and the Soviet Union was over and Americans had to rethink their understanding of the world. For many Americans, the Soviets had always been the enemy and the world was forever divided between capitalists and communists. Now the U.S. had won the Cold War and no one was quite sure how the victors should act. The struggle had left its mark on at least three American generations, but the nation now had to chart and pursue a new course. While American citizens still feared nuclear weapons, the often suffocating Cold War tensions had suddenly dissipated. Americans had lived under a nuclear cloud since 1945 and that had not changed. The geopolitical rules that governed nuclear arms had been altered, though, and that meant both new hopes and fears. The Nuclear Age was over but the possibility of nuclear annihilation still remained.

Comic book superheroes had not saved the world but had instead starred in stories in which the world attempted to save itself. From 1945 to 1989, like most members of American society, comic book heroes adjusted to a changing nuclear world. Some of the stories were good and some fairly bad; some of the tales were helpful but most were at best inconsequential and at worst harmful. In this way, comic book superheroes handled the Nuclear

Age just like their fellow Americans. Some were high-minded and supportive while others were petty and damaging. Some showcased the best of American society while others displayed the nation's flaws. By fighting a menace that they could not defeat, superheroes became less super and more human, which was probably what society needed.

Chapter 4

THE POSTWAR 1940S AND 1950S: SUPERNORMAL (1946–1959)

In a famous scene in the 1986 Rob Reiner film *Stand by Me*, four young men debate their interpretations of comic books and cartoons. The motion picture, set in the 1950s, contrasts the decade's supposed innocence with postwar America's often hidden fears and problems. In the film, the youths debate how Goofy and Pluto could both be dogs in Walt Disney cartoons and then turn their attention to superpowered creations. One of the boys, Vern Tessio, asks, "You think Mighty Mouse could beat up Superman?" Another of the group, Teddy Duchamp, quickly contends that Vern must be crazy to ask such a question. Vern counters by explaining how he recently viewed a cartoon in which Mighty Mouse lifted five elephants with one hand. Teddy then states, "Boy you don't know nothing. Mighty Mouse is a cartoon. Superman is a real guy. No way a cartoon could beat up a real guy." Vern, still not entirely convinced, seemingly agrees but observes, "Yeah, maybe you're right. Would be a good fight, though."[1]

This humorous scene not only showcases youth culture in 1950s America, but also emphasizes that by the 1950s Superman had stopped being fantastical and had become just another "real guy." Paradoxically, as Superman and other comic book characters became more powerful, they also became more mundane. What was once supernatural had become "supernormal." This transformation mirrors changes within American society in the postwar era. After World War II, many Americans strove to create a society that basked in security and normality. American adults who had lived through war and economic collapse desired safety and stability, and many citizens attempted to craft lives that revolved around home, work, and family. As the U.S. seemingly became more "boring," so did comic book super-heroes. Not far below the surface of both 1950s society and comic book heroes lay a less secure and more frightening America. As Americans struggled to create a new stability while masking their fears and frustrations, superheroes reflected the nation's schizophrenic outlook by focusing on both the nation's dreams and nightmares.

War's End

On September 2, 1945, leaders from U.S. and Japan gathered aboard the American battleship USS *Missouri* and signed the Japanese Instrument of Surrender. Less than a month after the U.S. dropped atomic bombs on Hiroshima and Nagasaki, World War II ended with the U.S. able to declare near total victory. In the days following the war, it became clear that the U.S. was in a unique position among the conflict's former combatants. Allied bombing and ground attacks had destroyed much of Germany's infrastructure and the U.S. military occupied a beaten Japan. Even the war "victors" had suffered extreme social, economic, and physical losses. Although over 400,000 Americans died while fighting in World War II, these losses paled when compared to the devastation in much of Europe and the Pacific.[2] Besides the Japanese attack at Pearl Harbor and a few minor coastal bombings, the U.S. homeland escaped from World War II physically unscathed. More importantly, World War II had stimulated the U.S. economy, creating a new era of American prosperity. While World War II devastated much of Europe and the Pacific, American soldiers returned to a nation that saw peace and prosperity for the first time since 1929. In the days following the Second World War the U.S. was facing a new challenge: how to build an American society based on surplus instead of scarcity.

Creating a More Perfect Union

While winning is generally preferable to losing, becoming the victor presents its own set of unique challenges. The U.S.'s post–World War II prosperous position was certainly enviable, but American society quickly had to determine how to best use its new found wealth and status. The U.S.'s situation was analogous to a boxer of humble beginnings who had been down on his luck before winning the championship and decimating his rivals. This imaginary pugilist suddenly achieves his dreams and realizes that all his sacrifices have paid off and he has won. He is swiftly both rich and powerful and must quickly decide how he should live. Does he continue to train at the gym for hours each day in an attempt to stay lean and hungry? Does he live the good life while continuing to box in hopes that his opponents are inferior to him, even in his less than prime condition? Or does he just take his money and retire far away from the world's problems?

Much like the victorious boxer, U.S. citizens had to collectively decide how to react to the nation's new status. Internationally, the U.S. began to play an even more prominent role in world affairs, but domestically Americans started to create a society that reveled in domesticity. By the early 1950s, the nation appeared to have made a choice to embrace a consumer-based culture that venerated the nuclear family. This societal path is understandable when one considers the turbulent years of the Great Depression and World War II. Many Americans desired quiet and constancy after over a decade and a half of trials and tribulations. By creating a culture that relished stability, Americans also propagated the idea of a homogenous society, which only allowed for a narrow understanding of societal norms. Americans created a rigid social order that provided safety and a concrete definition of normalcy, but left little room for dissent or individualistic expression. By the beginning of the 1950s the U.S. was more stable and prosperous than it had ever been before, but these changes came at a high price. Not far below the surface prosperity and "normalcy" lay a nation propelled by fear and insecurity.

The Safe Superhero

While American society prospered in the postwar years, comic book superheroes faltered. The war years witnessed a massive growth in comic book readers due mainly to large

GI readership, patriotic storylines, and more domestic disposable income. Comic book sales plummeted after the war as stories became more predictable and less interesting and many former servicemen changed their reading habits upon returning home. Superheroes had transitioned from social avengers to patriotic super-citizens during World War II, and after the conflict the characters could not return to their previous incarnations. Superheroes had seemingly become socially irrelevant and creators and publishers were unsure how to react. Writers and artists provided numerous new external threats, including those of the social, nuclear, communistic, and space alien varieties, but there seemed to be little for superheroes to do. The U.S. had changed and Americans no longer needed superheroes as they once did. Comic book historian Bradford W. Wright notes, "By appearances at least, the helpless and oppressed who had cried out for Superman in 1938 now lived comfortably and contentedly in the suburbs. Superheroes animated by the crusading spirit of the New Deal and World War II seemed directionless and irrelevant now that those victories has been won."[3]

Many publishers began to focus on other comic book genres, and soon westerns, love stories, and crime tales began to fill newsstand shelves. Left with no real purpose, superheroes began to mirror society's supposed blandness and many faded away as numerous publishers cancelled formerly popular heroes. Most of the heroes that remained became fairy tale caricatures of their former selves. In the postwar U.S, the once mighty social avengers and wartime heroes were reduced to cheery conformists. As American society became more structured and stratified, there was little room for the kinds of change for which Great Depression and World War II superheroes had fought. Postwar American society now reveled in its stability and demanded that nothing, not even superheroes, attempt to change it. American society now expected male comic book heroes to act like every other American man and settle down.

This American Life

The late 1940s and 1950s witnessed unprecedented change in American life. U.S. servicemen returned home from war to a nation far more prosperous and secure than the one they left. Many former servicemen quickly found well-paying jobs while others attended college or technical school using the soon to be famous GI Bill. American men who had previously suffered through unemployment and war suddenly lived in an affluent society that now promised an easier and more comfortable life. Millions of Americans moved to a house in the suburbs, the stereotypical 1950s abode. The clichéd suburban home with its aluminum siding, well-manicured lawn, and neighboring house that looked incredibly similar became one of the era's predominant symbols. It spoke of the American family moving from the noise and danger of the city or the poverty and dirt of the farm to the security and stability provided by a new community. Americans were seemingly trading the problems and vulnerabilities of the past for a new sheltered and protected lifestyle. U.S. citizens began to embrace the notion of consumerism and many started to buy their way towards a better existence. Shops and merchants advertised happiness through consumption and conformity and Americans responded by purchasing more. The postwar 1940s and the 1950s introduced a seemingly affluent, stable, and peaceful America. Many men and women across the nation lived a comfortable lifestyle that would have been unthinkable only a few years prior. This new American way of life came at a cost, though, one that many Americans paid but few spoke of.[4]

In order to prosper in the U.S.'s new era, Americans had to accept (and even embrace) the new social order. Society expected conformity to the supposed homogenized culture and individualism or self-expression that fell outside acceptable limits was punished with ostracism. Cultural norms dictated that the man should be the household's provider, working hard to build a life for himself and his family. The most mythologized American male of the era was the "company man" and to many this white collar worker came to symbolize the postwar period. The company man in his nice but understated business suit and ever present hat (and possibly horn-rimmed glasses) blended in with his corporate brethren who seemingly created an army of grey men in grey suits. In popular understanding these men built American commerce and industry during the day and returned home to enjoy the peace and tranquility of their home and family in the evening.

Popular portrayals of the company man include *Leave It to Beaver*'s Ward Cleaver, *The Adventures of Ozzie and Harriett*'s Ozzie Nelson, and even *Mad Men*'s Don Draper. Each of these characters and countless others showcase the company man's role as a protector and provider and highlight the company man's need to separate his family from the world around them. The stereotypical postwar male sacrificed some of his personal freedom and embraced the new American social order, but in return he wanted to keep his family from and secure. Although some in later generations would view this social agreement negatively, for many Americans of the time it was an easy bargain to make.[5]

June Cleaver's Pearl Necklace: The American Woman

While the stereotypical postwar American male worked outside the home to provide comfort and stability for his family, society expected vastly different things from his female equivalent. If stereotypical American men labored to buy and furnish a house, then American women made the house a home and anchored the family that resided in it. Society dictated that the outside world was the man's domain but the home was the woman's sphere of influence. Single, working class, immigrant, and minority women had worked outside the home for generations in the U.S., but these economic realities were not included in the idealized postwar social code. The romanticized post–World War II American woman was a white, middle-class mother whose primary focus was her husband, children, and home. Personified by popular culture figures like Donna Reed and June Cleaver, the postwar woman concerned herself with all things domestic and left the outside world to her company man husband. Although this idealized woman and mother was not new, and was, in fact, in keeping with the Victorian notion of motherhood, it was a rapid transformation from the new ideas of womanhood that World War II American society expounded and propagandized.

During the war, the U.S. needed all types of women to work outside the home in order to keep war production functioning at an optimal level. After the war, the nation no longer needed a hefty supply of female labor and thus society instructed married women and mothers to return to their homes and families and forget about their war years' roles. Society at large viewed women's factory and war labor as a wartime aberration like rationing and military production that would end quickly after the conflict. As men came back from war, women were once again relegated to the home and expected to be career wives and mothers. Rosie the Riveter was transformed into June Cleaver and the idealized American woman/mother went from working on the home front to working at home. Americans had decided that children would be the new center of life in the U.S. and good Americans were expected to heed society's call.[6]

Baby Boomers

As American men and women transitioned into their new postwar roles, they also experienced and produced an unprecedented demographic shift. Unsurprisingly, birth rates rose as former GIs returned from war to their waiting sweethearts. Increased birth rates following wartime are not abnormal, and historically many societies have seen an uptick in children born when hostilities cease. What was unusual about the postwar American demographic shift was not the number of children born immediately after the war, but rather how long this increase lasted and how many children were born in total. Postwar birth rates remained high for almost two decades. The U.S. Census Bureau calculates that the baby boom lasted from 1946 to 1964, a 19-year period that saw 78 million babies born. In 1946 there were an estimated 141 million people living in the United States and the children born over the next 19 years would equal a 55.3 percent increase.[7] Incredibly, the baby boom's height was in 1957, when 4,300,000 American children were born.[8] This increase in American children can be tied to the strong U.S. economy, the American need for stability and normalcy that family provides, and the amplified societal importance of children.

No matter what the reasons for the baby boom, the new generation was so numerically gigantic that it changed American life in ways too numerous to calculate. The U.S. soon became a youth-centered society and the rising American economy allowed citizens to focus on and spoil their children materially, emotionally, and socially. Children seemed to be everywhere in America and before long they were more socially influential and powerful than ever before. Americans had made a choice to embrace a narrow worldview that promoted stability, home, and family and frowned upon anyone or anything thought to be abnormal. Postwar America no longer needed superheroes to save society but rather called on these heroes to mirror and reinforce newly held values.[9]

Super-Police

During the late 1940s and the early 1950s superhero comics began to mirror the changes in American society. As Americans moved to the suburbs and concentrated on the nuclear family, superheroes acted similarly. With superhero comic book sales shrinking, publishers tried to find new gimmicks, battles, or enemies only to learn that most superheroes could seemingly do little to interest the potential readership. One of the few publishers still enjoying strong sales was DC Comics, home to Superman, Batman, and Wonder Woman. DC Comics quickly became the era's leading publisher and its characters became synonymous with the idea of superheroes until the 1960s. Although Superman and Batman had originally been vigilantes, by the early 1940s DC Comics determined that its heroes needed to be adventurous enough for children but wholesome enough for parents. As newspapers reported protests and comic book burnings aimed at violent superheroes, in 1941, DC Comics preemptively addressed the issue by creating an editorial advisory board staffed with experts that would supposedly keep superhero comics safe and wholesome.[10]

Like most other superheroes, DC characters became patriotic citizens during World War II but were left with little to do at conflict's end. In keeping with their push towards wholesomeness, DC heroes transformed into model citizens that respected authority and aided law enforcement. Superheroes that had once been agents of change were morphed into agents of the state. The most obvious character change was Superman. In 1938, the

Man of Steel uses his powers in an attempt to change the U.S. and remake America into a more liberal society. Less than a decade later Superman fights in order to protect the status quo and often praises law enforcement and elected officials. In *Superman* #62, cover dated January/February 1950, the Man of Steel, while working undercover for the Metropolis police, allows himself to be sent to prison for Clark Kent's murder.[11] By July/August 1956, Superman, Batman, and Robin are all proclaimed "honored guests" at the police ball.[12] Even postwar comic book covers portray Superman as a wholesome agent of the state and protector of the status quo. The cover of September/October 1949's *Superman* #60 depicts the Man of Steel as a baseball umpire, a symbolic portrayal of Superman as peacekeeper and rule enforcer.[13] Compare this to the social crusader Superman featured in 1938's *Action Comics* #1 who manhandles a governor and abuses a wife beater. In a few short years comic book creators (and the American public) had transformed Superman and other DC heroes into the ultimate law abiding citizens. American society seemed to no longer want or need change, so instead new versions of their superheroes fought for those in power and battled to protect society's status quo.

The Super Company Man

DC Comics superheroes also quickly transformed from vigilante mystery men to super-powered company men with homes, families, and domestic problems. Again the most profound changes can be seen in Superman stories. As previously mentioned, Superman becomes a societal umpire who punishes those that break the rules. While the Great Depression Superman was a freelance crime fighter who answered only to himself, the postwar Man of Steel is (an unpaid) public servant who operates within legal, social, and cultural boundaries. Like many of his corporate man brethren, Superman becomes a white collar worker and many of his postwar stories focus on the domestic/non-work parts of his life. This monumental change is easy to gloss over but should be considered for a moment.

After World War II, DC Comics creators and editors made a consensus decision to focus on Superman's personal life and allow readers to become part of Superman's "family." Less than a decade before Superman had been a social avenging force of nature but by 1946 he is a super-citizen with problems that mirror the average American male. The Man of Steel became more physically powerful with every passing year. (In 1938, Superman could not fly and a bursting shell could penetrate his skin. In October 1946, *Action Comics* #101 shows Superman exposing himself to an atomic bomb test.) As Superman became physically stronger he paradoxically became less exceptional and more commonplace. In the 1930s, the Man of Steel was "super" in every sense of the word. By 1946, the character's powers no longer astound readers and writers are forced to explore his "super-life." Superman had once been extraordinary but after the war he becomes simply super-ordinary.

This Is Your Super-Life

In the late 1940s and early 1950s, numerous comic book companies' superheroes failed and some publishers turned to more violent and salacious material of which parents, lawmakers, and educational and medical professionals were beginning to notice and take a dim view. In this environment DC Comics editors needed to make superheroes interesting to young readers without creating violent or lurid storylines that would upset parents. Having already turned Superman into a wholesome agent of the state and a super-ordinary company man, comic book creators decided to explore Superman's family and background. The Man of Steel soon became the antithesis of his previous mystery man self as writers and artists investigated every part of Superman's life.

January 1945's *More Fun Comics* #101 contained the first appearance of Superboy, Superman's teenage self. Over the next few years, creators expanded on Superboy/Superman's origin and revealed that Jonathan and Martha Kent adopted and raised the young baby Kal-El (Superman's Kryptonian name) in an idyllic Kansas town quaint enough to be named Smallville. Superboy was soon given a teenage love interest (Lana Lang), a close friend (Pete Ross), an adolescent connection to his arch nemesis Lex Luthor, and multiple other background ideas. The notion was so popular that writers even began to create stories for Superbaby, Superman as a toddler before the Kents adopted him. Creators also explored Superman's Kryptonian heritage by fashioning stories that focused on Superman's biological parents, Jor-El and Lara Lor-Van, and created a geographic, historic, and political background for Krypton. Although Superman was an orphan and a one-time mystery man, by the late 1940s his family and his past were no longer a mystery and his life was no longer very super.

Although they were aliens from a vastly different culture, Superman's Kryptonian parents loved and cared for him in much the same way that American parents would their offspring. Jor-El and Lara even rocket baby Kal-El to Earth in hopes that he will live even if they will not. Superman became the ultimate American immigrant, the last member of a dying race, sent to the U.S. to fulfill his true potential. It was in Kansas that Superman became super and in the nation's heartland that he learned American values. Superman's adoptive parents, Jonathan and Martha Kent, displayed unconditional love when they adopted the alien baby and treated him as their own son. Superman and his family provide a template for how American families do act and should act. By focusing on Superman's childhood and his background, creators were not only presenting a more well-rounded character but also a non-threatening hero that bolstered the postwar notion of the nuclear family. These changes made Superman less amazing and more predictable, but they also made him more relatable and likable. Although Superman was "a strange visitor from another planet," he also was quickly becoming the quintessential American.[14]

Super-Romance

Postwar American conventional wisdom declared that while every American male needed caring and attentive parents, this was not enough to fulfill his emotional and psychological needs. Young males needed a special someone in their lives to socialize the men to their roles as future husbands and fathers. During the early twentieth century, American society created the idea of dating, and in the 1950s this idea became generally socially accepted. As more teenagers owned automobiles and discretionary incomes rose, adolescent romance became an often inexplicable but acknowledged part of American society and culture. As it became commonplace for males and females to date, it also became unusual for them not to. Although Superman was not an adolescent male, many postwar Americans would find it odd if he did not have a romantic interest. As a hyper-symbolic American male, Superman needed to demonstrate both his heterosexuality and his independence. The strict postwar social code dictated that Superman should have romantic relationships with the opposite sex but also continue to maintain his freedom and bachelorhood. If Superman were to marry he would be forced to settle down and raise a family and comic book creators would lose a wellspring of potential story ideas. Instead the Man of Steel needed to remain a bachelor while preserving the idea of the heterosexual company man.

Lois Lane

Unquestionably, the most important woman in Superman's (and Clark Kent's) life is Lois Lane, a female reporter who appeared in Superman's first story in *Action Comics #1*. Jerry Siegel and Joe Shuster originally portrayed Lois as a tough-talking independent woman but by the late 1940s comic book writers primarily presented her as Superman's potential love interest. While this character lobotomy is unfortunate in many ways, it does provide a unique window to view postwar gender relations. As women's studies scholar Jeanne Pauline Williams notes, by 1948, writers depicted Lois Lane "less often as a reporter and more often as 'Superman's girlfriend.' She became less active and more traditionally feminine. She also began to openly exhibit jealousy toward other women who were involved with Superman."[15] Lois often attempted to prove that Clark Kent was Superman, causing him to spend time tricking her instead of helping those in need. During this period, Lois's main objective appears to be marrying Superman. Many stories showcase Lois's efforts to convince or trick the Man of Steel into matrimony. Superman always avoided these domesticity traps and refused to marry Lois because he did not trust her to keep his Clark Kent identity a secret and thus endanger herself. Lois was silly, conniving, and often child-like in her attempts to ensnare the Man of Steel. Superman writer John Byrne more bluntly states, "Lois was nosey, clinging, inefficient — a royal pain in the butt. And a long fall from 1938."[16]

Although Lois Lane was often called "Superman's girlfriend," it is difficult for modern readers to understand why Superman would have wanted to spend time with her. After World War II, Lois Lane changed from a confident and independent career woman to a jealous girlfriend obsessed with learning her boyfriend's secrets and forcing him to marry her. These changes say a great deal about the pressures within American society for women to conform to romanticized domesticity. Creators could easily portray Superman as a carefree bachelor who enjoyed Lois's company but was not yet ready to settle down. Although the Man of Steel was getting close to the age where he needed to start a family, it still was not unusual for him to want to hold off for a little while longer. Lois, on the other hand, needed to ensure that she would marry the man of her dreams and soon become a mother. She apparently could not conceive of a situation where she remained single and childless and thus she would lie, cheat, or steal in order to become Mrs. Superman.

Notice the inherent power imbalance in Lois and Superman's relationship. Lois is often referred to as "Superman's girlfriend," a term that almost implies ownership and at the very least ties Lois's identity to a strong male. To think of this another way, it is hard to conceive of calling Superman Lois Lane's boyfriend. Lois and Superman's unequal relationship is certainly overly dramaticized and cannot be viewed as normal for the time. Very few women would have tried to trick men into marrying them in this or any other era. If the comic buying public did accept these stories as hyperbolic representations of American life, then they must have some basis in reality. Perhaps Lois represented women who worried they would not be able to fulfill their place in society as wives and mothers. Between 1949 and 1955 over twenty Superman stories appeared in *Action Comics* or *Superman* that focused on marriage. Only in one does Superman appear to be jealous of Lois's affections for another man. (This was in *Superman* #67 when Lois Lane has a "super-crush on super-crooner Perry Como.")[17]

In many issues Lois watches jealously as Superman flirts with or kisses other women, or she attempts to trick him into marriage. One example of this can be found in October 1950's *Action Comics* #149. The cover to this issue depicts a story entitled "The Courtship on Krypton" in which Lois is shown watching Superman's birth parents' wedding video and exclaiming, "You're too late, Superman! I've just seen how your mother won your dad — and that's how I'm going to win you!"[18] Notice that Lois speaks of "winning" Superman as if he is a prize. Lois is not the only one who wants to force Superman into a matrimonial trap. In December 1951's *Action Comics* #163, the mysterious Girl of Tomorrow tells Superman, "Wait, Superman! My ability to read minds tells me that you're Clark Kent — so unless you agree to marry me, the whole world will learn your secret!"[19] Perhaps most bizarre and offensive is the January 1955 cover to *Superman* #94. In a story entitled "Clark Kent's Hillbilly Bride," a young blonde woman tells Clark, "Super-

Superman's Girl Friend Lois Lane #23 (February 1961) features an imaginary tale that allows Superman and Lois to finally marry and have children. (© 1961 DC Comics. Used with permission of DC Comics.)

man is mighty cute — but you're still mah man, Clark, mah beloved." Clark is shown thinking, "I wish I weren't — but it looks as though Superman can't even stop the wedding bells from ringing!"[20]

Lois Lane, and other women in Superman stories, are presented as being consumed by the idea of marriage and will use any method necessary to obtain the husband they want. Superman is portrayed as aloofly watching and sometimes easily stopping these childish efforts to entrap him. He is not worried about getting married; when he is ready it will happen. As a desirable man he holds all of the power and authority. When Superman is ready to have a suburban home and family he will, until then the women around him will not be able to domestically ensnare him.

Superman's Office Pals

Besides expanding his relationships with Lois Lane and other potential female love interests, comic book writers and artists also enlarged and fleshed out Superman's supporting cast. Since his debut Clark Kent had worked for a newspaper (originally the *Daily Star* and later the *Daily Planet*). Many of Kent's co-workers appeared in early stories but received little attention until the postwar years. Stories soon began to focus on Clark Kent's work life and his relationship with those around him. Clark's boss, Perry White, became his bombastic mentor who regularly shouted, "Great Caesar's ghost" and "Don't call me chief!" Jimmy Olsen, a young reporter at the *Daily Planet*, became "Superman's pal," and the two shared numerous adventures together. Although Superman is amazingly powerful, Clark Kent works a white collar job and understands the trials and tribulations of the company man. Clark is familiar with deadlines and angry bosses but also knows the necessity of being a productive part of society. Superman works as a company man for society and law enforcement while Clark wears the traditional suit, tie, and hat and resembles the average company man. By making work friends, Superman and Clark Kent emphasize the importance of work in a man's life and inform young male readers about what to expect in their futures. Superman works because only he can protect society. Clark Kent works because it is the normal acceptable way that an American man should act. Clark's job provides him adventure, excitement and friends that he would not have as Superman. Without his occupation and his Clark Kent identity, Superman would be isolated and lonely. Because Superman works as the company man Clark Kent, he is much more productive and fulfilled, a lesson that creators hoped would not be lost on both young readers and their parents.

Decade of Fear

To an outside observer, early 1950s America seemed to be a stable and peaceful land of plenty. Economic hardship had given way to prosperity and war had begotten peace. Most Americans appeared to embrace the new social order that revolved around home, work, and family. However, beneath society's confident veneer was a vast undercurrent of fear and trepidation. Americans had grown comfortable and the notion of losing their stability was frightening. Politically these fears manifested in anti-communist attacks and the Red Scare of the 1950s. Wisconsin Senator Joseph McCarthy launched assaults against numerous Americans that he believed to have communist ties, and the House Un-American Activities Committee pressed Hollywood businessmen to blacklist various writers, artists, and performers. Prominent Americans warned the U.S. public to carefully observe their neighbors because anyone could be a communist agent attempting to destroy the American way of life. Because Americans constructed postwar society to be rigid and conformist, the notion of the outsider was terrifying. As a society that valued homogeneity, the U.S. was easily susceptible to the fears that created an "us versus them" mentality. Although the communist specter haunted Americans' daydreams and nightmares, it was only one of many of the period's numerous fears. Americans worried about many things, from crime to nuclear holocaust. A large number of Americans were even scared of their own children.[21]

Teenage Wasteland

In the early 1950s, many citizens began to fear that American children were turning into criminals and hoodlums. Many worried that young men and women were becoming juvenile delinquents and that upstanding citizens would soon have to fear for their safety and well-being. In 1953, Federal Bureau of Investigation director J. Edgar Hoover stated, "Persons under the age of 18 committed 53.6 percent of all car thefts; 49.3 percent of all burglaries; 18 percent of all robberies, and 16.2 percent of all rapes. These are the statistics reported to the FBI by 1,174 cities."[22] Because the baby boom was dramatically increasing the number of children and teenagers, some adults began to fear that an unruly criminal teenage mob would soon rule American streets for decades to come.

To prevent this potential teenage apocalypse, authorities began to outline possible causes and solutions for the increased juvenile delinquency. American leaders consulted experts, both real and imagined, and heard conflicting reports regarding the deviant adolescent epidemic. Notable potential causes included more Americans living in urban areas, fathers spending more time outside of the home, and poor supervision at home and school. While these possible reasons seem feasible, they also would be very difficult and time-consuming to offset. "Correcting" these issues would be very challenging and deeply problematic.[23] Another possible cause of the juvenile delinquency outbreak would be much easier to control. According to psychiatrist Dr. Fredric Wertham, one of the reasons that American children were becoming increasingly violent could be tied to their reading habits. Dr. Wertham blamed comic books.

Blacklists, and Legislation, and Book Burnings: Oh My!

The March 29, 1948, issue of *Time* magazine contains an article entitled "Puddles of Blood" that reports on a symposium, at which Dr. Fredric Wertham spoke, regarding the effects of comic books on children. The German born Wertham declared his belief that violent and sexual comic book images contributed to juvenile delinquency. Wertham's assertions were hardly new; in 1938 an organization founded by Catholic bishops blacklisted some comic books as obscene.[24] In May 1940, Sterling North, a *Chicago Daily News* editor, wrote an editorial that castigated comic books for being harmful.[25] In 1948, several towns and cities, including Chicago, Detroit, Los Angeles, and Indianapolis, devised systems to restrict or outlaw a number of comic books that lawmakers or city officials deemed offensive or harmful.[26]

In response to this outside pressure, in 1948 several comic book publishers agreed to create the Association of Comics Magazine Publishers Code, which was designed to set industry standards. No one enforced these voluntary standards, though, and little changed in the industry. Additionally, many comic book publishers like DC Comics already had in-house rules and standards that were very much like the new code. Furthermore, most of these changes were aimed at horror and crime comic books and affected superheroes very little. The code seemingly quieted public criticism of comic book for awhile.[27] In December 1948, a few months after the code's introduction, a group of adolescents did stage a massive comic book burning in Binghamton, New York. While some people like the Binghamton teens would continue to protest, generally the public outcry against comic books would die down for awhile. Within a few years, though, Dr. Fredric Wertham would emerge as a leader of the anti–comic book movement.

Seduction of the Innocent

As the public uproar about comic books dissipated following the Association of Comics Magazine Publishers Code of 1948, some publishers felt emboldened and increased the amount of gore, violence, and titillation in some stories. The offending comic books were mostly horror and crime titles, while superhero fare generally remained wholesome and rather pedantic. Some genres regularly showcased gruesome murder scenes and teased readers with sensual imagery, while titles like Superman and Batman provided child-friendly and parent-approved storylines. To many within the general public, though, all comic books were the same and if some were violent and obscene then all should be investigated. In 1954, Fredric Wertham published a monograph entitled *Seduction of the Innocent* that lambasted comic books for promoting violence, sexual promiscuity, and homosexuality. Although Wertham's methods appear unscientific, in his book he claims to have examined numerous children that comic books harmed. Wertham criticizes Superman for promoting fascism, Wonder Woman for engaging in sadomasochism, and Batman for encouraging homosexuality.[28] Many magazines and newspapers reported about *Seduction of the Innocent* and soon comic books were back in the public conscience.

In April 1954, the United States Senate Subcommittee on Juvenile Delinquency conducted a hearing regarding possible connections between comic books and adolescent misbehavior and violence. Numerous experts and comic book professionals testified, but the most remembered exchanges were between Senator Estes Kefauver of Tennessee and EC Comics publisher William M. Gaines. Bill Gaines's father, M.C. Gaines, had been one of the comic book industry's founders and EC Comics was a cutting-edge horror comic book publisher that thrilled and frightened readers with blood, gore, and violence. In other words, Gaines was the kind of comic book publisher that many lawmakers and parents were worried about. At the hearing, the committee and Gaines verbally sparred before the senators asked the publisher if he would publish anything in his magazine. Gaines replied that he would only publish comic books that were in "good taste." Senator Kefauver proceeded to display several recent issues of *Crime SuspenStories* with shockingly graphic covers. One cover showed a murderer gripping an ax in one hand and holding a woman's severed head by her blonde hair in the other. Upon further questioning Gaines continued to assert that he believed this cover and others like it to be in good taste for a horror comic book.

In the days following the hearing's exchange the media blasted Gaines for his contention that such graphic images could be considered good taste. Although the Senate took no official action, they did not need to. The hearings had been a public relations disaster for the comic book industry and something would have to be done.[29] As a part of a society that valued conformity, family, and children, the comic book industry had little choice. It would have to change whether it wanted to or not.

The Code

The Senate hearings again thrust comic books into the national spotlight. Almost immediately newspapers and magazines began publishing articles bemoaning comic books as dangerous, and local and state officials again started to publicly speak about banning comics. In autumn 1954, a newly founded organization of comic book publishers, the Comics Magazine Association of America, ratified the Comics Code Authority (CCA), a new set of guidelines for the industry. These self-imposed rules were designed to allow the comic book industry to police itself, so outside forces would not step in and require even stricter measures. Although numerous publishers had agreed to the comic book code of 1948, the CCA was far more detailed, restrictive, and enforceable. It attempted to address the public's concern regarding sex and violence by creating ironclad rules against objectionable content. While the CAA was self-limiting and not enforceable by law, the code did have the backing of most comic publishers, newsstand owners, and the general public. Some of the CAA's guidelines were:

General Standards Part A:
1. Crimes shall never be presented in such a way as to create sympathy for the criminal, to promote distrust of the forces of law and justice, or to inspire others with a desire to imitate criminals.
2. No comics shall explicitly present the unique details and methods of a crime.
3. Policemen, judges, government officials, and respected institutions shall never be presented in such a way as to create disrespect for established authority.
4. If crime is depicted it shall be as a sordid and unpleasant activity.
5. Criminals shall not be presented so as to be rendered glamorous or to occupy a position which creates the desire for emulation.
6. In every instance good shall triumph over evil and the criminal punished for his misdeeds.
7. Scenes of excessive violence shall be prohibited. Scenes of brutal torture, excessive and unnecessary knife and gun play, physical agony, gory and gruesome crime shall be eliminated.
8. No unique or unusual methods of concealing weapons shall be shown.
9. Instances of law enforcement officers dying as a result of a criminal's activities should be discouraged.
10. The crime of kidnapping shall never be portrayed in any detail, nor shall any profit accrue to the abductor or kidnapper. The criminal or the kidnapper must be punished in every case.
11. The letters of the word "crime" on a comics magazine shall never be appreciably greater than the other words contained in the title. The word "crime" shall never appear alone on a cover.
12. Restraint in the use of the word "crime" in titles or subtitles shall be exercised.

General Standards Part B:
1. No comic magazine shall use the word "horror" or "terror" in its title.
2. All scenes of horror, excessive bloodshed, gory or gruesome crimes, depravity, lust, sadism, masochism shall not be permitted.
3. All lurid, unsavory, gruesome illustrations shall be eliminated.
4. Inclusion of stories dealing with evil shall be used or shall be published only where the intent is to illustrate a moral issue and in no case shall evil be presented alluringly nor so as to injure the sensibilities of the reader.
5. Scenes dealing with, or instruments associated with walking dead, torture, vampires and vampirism, ghouls, cannibalism, and werewolfism are prohibited.

General Standards Part C:
All elements or techniques not specifically mentioned herein, but which are contrary to the spirit and intent of the Code, and are considered violations of good taste or decency, shall be prohibited.

Dialogue:
1. Profanity, obscenity, smut, vulgarity, or words or symbols which have acquired undesirable meanings are forbidden.
2. Special precautions to avoid references to physical afflictions or deformities shall be taken.
3. Although slang and colloquialisms are acceptable, excessive use should be discouraged and wherever possible good grammar shall be employed.

Religion:
Ridicule or attack on any religious or racial group is never permissible.

Costume:
1. Nudity in any form is prohibited, as is indecent or undue exposure.
2. Suggestive and salacious illustration or suggestive posture is unacceptable.
3. All characters shall be depicted in dress reasonably acceptable to society.
4. Females shall be drawn realistically without exaggeration of any physical qualities.

NOTE: It should be recognized that all prohibitions dealing with costume, dialogue, or artwork apply as specifically to the cover of a comic magazine as they do to the contents.

Marriage and Sex:
1. Divorce shall not be treated humorously nor shall be represented as desirable.
2. Illicit sex relations are neither to be hinted at nor portrayed. Violent love scenes as well as sexual abnormalities are unacceptable.
3. Respect for parents, the moral code, and for honorable behavior shall be fostered. A sympathetic understanding of the problems of love is not a license for moral distortion.
4. The treatment of love-romance stories shall emphasize the value of the home and the sanctity of marriage.
5. Passion or romantic interest shall never be treated in such a way as to stimulate the lower and baser emotions.
6. Seduction and rape shall never be shown or suggested.
7. Sex perversion or any inference to same is strictly forbidden.[30]

The New (Old) Era

The CAA was adopted on October 28, 1954, and soon every screened comic book had to have a CAA logo to indicate that the comic book had met the code's requirements. Without this stamp of approval sellers or buyers could deem the comic book to be aberrant and refuse to associate with it. The CAA served its purpose and straitjacketed the comic book industry. It also caused many comic book publishers to fold and made comic books less popular. Between 1954 and 1956, the number of comic books being published in the United States dropped from around 650 to about 250.[31] Many comic books had been based on violence and titillation, and when they were gone so were their readers. Although superhero comics suffered overall, the CAA merely proved to be a stricter version of the rules that DC Comics had already been following and the publisher seemed to suffer little. In the CCA's immediate aftermath DC continued to publish wholesome superheroes that promoted hard work, fair play, and saw little need to change any part of American society. Superman and Batman were happy company men that half-heartedly pursued the women around them, while stopping outsiders from remaking society. In the DC universe, as in the U.S., villains attempted to change American society while heroes understood that life was already how it should be. The CAA forced many comic book creators to censor their stories and avoid sensitive subjects, but DC Comics had long ago tied its stories to the conservative majority and had little reason to change anything.

A Superman's Home Is His Fortress

Following the passage of the CAA, DC Comics, the major superhero comic book publisher in the industry, continued to create inoffensive stories that reflected an appreciation for the American status quo. *Superman* editor Mort Weisinger fashioned a world in which the Man of Steel, and his Clark Kent persona, were typical company men working to create a home and family much like many men in 1950s American. Under Weisinger's editorial tutelage, writers began to depict Superman's extended cast as his family, of which Superman was the head. Lois Lane received her own comic book in which she was credited as "Superman's Girlfriend." *Daily Planet* "cub reporter" Jimmy Olsen's comic book officially dubbed him "Superman's Pal." By 1959, Superman was even introduced to Kara Zor-El, a cousin that survived Krypton and would soon be known as Supergirl.[32] The Maid of Might (as Supergirl came to be known) became Superman's surrogate daughter, which allowed him to play the roles of both bachelor and father. Writers continued to expand Superman's "family" by adding an entire bottled Kryptonian city (Kandor), a host of superpowered pets (Krypto the Superdog, Streaky the Supercat, Comet the Super-Horse, and Beppo the Super-monkey), and a former mermaid girlfriend (Lori Lemaris). Once a lone avenger and the last son of a doomed planet, by the late 1950s the Man of Steel had become the patriarch of an ever expanding clan; Superman had turned into "Superdad."

As Superman's cast was growing his stories had generally become mechanical and pedestrian. Often Superman would lose his powers or have a "life changing" event that would cause him some difficulty before the situation was rectified by the end of the comic book issue. Several noted comic book creators, including Grant Morrison, claim that the editor developed many of his Superman plots during psychiatric therapy sessions and that Weisinger saw Superman's stories as a reflection of the modern American man's problems.[33] Superman, the first comic book superhero, had once been daring, dangerous, and amazing. In the past, he had promised to help make society a better place. In the late 1950s, Superman, and almost every other comic book hero, was no longer an agent of social change but rather an agent of social order; the CAA made certain of that.

Wanted: Costumed Everymen — No Outsiders Need Apply

In October 1956, DC Comic's *Showcase* #4 introduced the Flash to comic book readers. Actually, *Showcase* #4 introduced the Flash again. The original Flash, Jay Garrick, first appeared in *Flash Comics* #1 (January 1940). *Showcase* #4's Flash was an updated version of the original character, complete with a new alter ego and origin. The new Flash was police scientist Barry Allen, who gained the ability to run at super speeds after being doused by chemicals that were struck by lightning. DC Comics editor Julius Schwartz, along with writer Gardner Fox and artist Carmine Infantino, modernized the Flash to appeal to young readers. The Scarlet Speedster was quickly a runaway hit and DC Comics soon updated other 1940s superheroes, sometimes only keeping the original hero's name. Newsstands soon teemed with refurbished DC superheroes, including Green Lantern, the Atom, and Hawkman. This marked the beginning of the "Silver Age" of superhero comics and introduced fresh versions of older heroes to new readers. (Fans would soon label the original heroes as being part of comics' "Golden Age.")

Not surprisingly, these new old heroes featured new identities, powers, and storylines, but almost no gender or ethnic diversity. *Showcase*, which served as a "tryout" comic book for new characters and ideas, featured only one female lead character during the 1950s, Lois Lane: Superman's Girlfriend. The few female superheroes that DC did introduce, like Supergirl, were part of a male superhero's "family" and were expected to do anything the patriarchal hero instructed. (Superman kept Supergirl hidden for years and made her adopt a secret identity that required her to live in an orphanage.) This understanding of the male as head of the family fit with gender stereotypes of the era. Comic books were essentially a boys' club that, with a few exceptions, were created by men for young men. This exclusion or underestimation of women in superhero comic books mirrored the stereotypical societal view of women as girlfriend, wife, or mother.

While few female superheroes appeared in comic books, there was at least a handful that did. In the 1950s, as the Civil Rights struggle was beginning, every major comic book superhero was white. The new Silver Age superheroes were almost always middle class white males who worked white collar jobs when they were not fighting crime. Barry Allen, the new Flash, was a police scientist. The new Green Lantern, Hal Jordan, was an airplane test pilot, while Ray Palmer, the Atom, was a scientist. The Supreme Court decided the landmark case *Brown v. Board of Education of Topeka, Kansas,* in 1954 making school segregation illegal. Over the next six years, the Civil Rights movement pressed for an equal and equitable America. Activists organized boycotts and sit-ins across the South. In 1957, Central High School in Little Rock, Arkansas, was integrated, with the help of federal troops and the National Guard. During this time, organizations like the Southern Christian Leadership Conference and the National Association for the Advancement of Colored People pressed for change, and the Civil Rights struggle became one of the 1950s' most important issues. Superhero comic books contain almost nothing about one of the era's most essential struggles. There are no major comic book black superheroes until Marvel's Black Panther appears in 1966 and virtually no 1950s Civil Rights superhero storylines. Interestingly, EC Comics, which the CAA deemed too violent and offensive, had multiple non-superhero stories featuring black heroes and often spoke out against racism.

While the Civil Rights movement was questioning basic American assumptions and working to remake American society, comic book superheroes were fighting generic villains and attempting to prevent social change. Superhero storylines never addressed the Civil Rights struggle, but rather chose to ignore the problem and hope it would go away. In the 1930s many superheroes had fought against social injustice, but by the middle of the 1950s superheroes had become a part of the system they had once tried to change. Superheroes were now full scale supporters of the state and any threats against it. While a 1930s version of Superman may have fought for civil rights, the 1950s hero did not. The 1950s hero had become the company man of steel and a protector of the status quo. He, and the society he represented, no longer wanted change but instead wanted stability. As the 1950s ended, American society was still relatively peaceful and stable but that would not last for long. Change was coming, no matter if society wanted it or not.

Conclusion

During the late 1940s and 1950s, most superheroes followed American society's lead and transformed into safer and more mundane versions of themselves. A generation of Americans who had known over a decade and a half of economic depression and war now found themselves creating a new postwar reality. The United States was suddenly both at peace and economically prosperous, and many citizens wanted to insure that nothing upset this seemingly splendid new reality. Remembering the country's recent difficulties, many citizens pressed for stability, normalcy, and social conformity. Many Americans chose to trade freedom of expression for a newly acquired high standard of living. At the heart of the new American prosperity and conformity lay fears and insecurities that the good times would not last and soon another disaster would irreparably harm the nation. Americans labored to create a peaceful and stable society in hopes that they could ward off the outside world's dangers.

Comic book superheroes also soon succumbed to this new postwar reality and changed into super-ordinary heroes who no longer fought to change society but rather were content to enforce the status quo. Superheroes transformed from tough streetwise rule breakers into social watchdogs who above all fought against change. The Comics Code Authority of 1954 even further restricted comic book creators and led to even stricter standards and more mundane content. At first glance the postwar 1940s and 1950s appear to be a golden age of American life in which the nation faced few of the problems that it had before and since. Although the society as a whole was amazingly affluent, this new found wealth came at a steep cost as many Americans struggled to overcome their fears and insecurities by imposing strong restrictions on themselves and those around them. Society then co-opted superheroes into becoming watchmen instead of protectors and attempted to create a new utopia based on fear and insecurity.

Chapter 5

COUNTERCULTURE HEROES
(1960–1969)

One of the most often used clichés in comic books is the idea that a small action can change the world forever. Much of the superhero mythos is based on the notion that both big and small events define our lives. If baby Kal-El had been sent to a planet other than Earth he never would have become Superman. If a thief had shot someone else instead of Thomas and Martha Wayne then Batman would have never existed. If lightning had not struck a very specific group of chemicals Barry Allen would have never become the Flash. These pre–1960s comic book actions, much like many citizens' ideas of American history, carried with them a sense of predetermination. A lot of people believed that a higher power had preordained the U.S. to exist and the nation's heroes were a reflection of this cultural, social, and historical certainty. Superman, Batman, the Flash, and most other DC Comics characters were Manifest Destiny heroes; they existed because there were supposed to. The actions that created the heroes may seem random but they were actually part of a larger plan. Pre–1960s superheroes were a component of an American society that valued order and firmly believed in the rightness of its own existence. This would quickly change in the 1960s, as a new generation began to question American society's very foundations. A social and cultural war was about to begin and, just like most of the nation, superheroes would be pitted against each other and almost every American, both non-powered and super, would never again be the same.

The Eve of Destruction

The survivors of the Great Depression and World War II built an incredibly prosperous postwar America that cloaked itself in a thick layer of paranoia and fear. These Americans, who had once lost so much and had survived their society's near destruction, understood how fragile their lives were. They had seen pestilence, war, famine, and death and knew that it could all happen again. Most of these people lived with the knowledge that everything could be taken away in an instant and thus they never truly felt safe. Many men and women spent the postwar 1940s and 1950s trying to build a buffer against possible threats. Well-manicured suburban lawns, dependable well-paying jobs, and safe, child-friendly neighborhoods seemingly provided a safety layer against potential threats and problems. Although most of society's apprehensions remained unrealized, one group would conspire to create a social upheaval that eventually would destroy the peaceful and stable American landscape that postwar Americans had created. While many worried about communist uprisings and foreign invasions, most could not have fathomed that the biggest threat to their way of life was their own children.

Teach Your Children Well

While postwar adults attempted to create a safe and peaceful society, they paradoxically took on the task of raising children who would never truly understand their hopes and fears. Forces like poverty and war had shaped these older Americans' lives in ways that they hoped their children would never know. These parents changed society in order to protect their children from the horrors they had witnessed. A lifetime of worry and pain propelled them to create a society in which their children would never need to fear or want. Ironically, these social changes also served to create a gap between parent and offspring that often could not be fully bridged. The values and understandings the older generation learned while suffering through difficult times were entirely different from the ones that their children developed during the postwar economic boom.

While almost all parents and children experience problems because of a generation gap, the distance between these older adults and their Baby Boomer children was arguably the greatest in American history. The postwar America was socially a very different nation than its earlier Great Depression and World War II version and in many ways parents and children grew up in different countries. Although they lived together and generally loved each other, World War II parents and their Baby Boomer children were often foreign to each other. Frequently, neither understood the other's values, fears, and hopes. Maybe most importantly, each generation expected something very different from their nation and generally disagreed on the social issues of the day. Although both generations felt secure in their beliefs, neither possessed the proper tools to understand the other. Two generations of Americans had been born a few decades apart, lived parts of their lives under the same roof, most loved and respected the other, but because of the U.S.'s massive social changes they seemingly came from different worlds whose inhabitants had not learned to communicate with each other.[1]

The Times They Are A-Changin'

Historians disagree when the cultural 1960s began and ended. Although the actual 1960s, of course, lasted from 1960 until 1969, these are merely calendar markings that provide little in the way of cultural and social importance. Instead of using only the traditional decade, historians generally attempt to define the 1960s by central themes and their cultural beginning and ending points and events. While the 1960s has many major themes and ideas, most of them are represented in the idea of the generational struggle between old and new. The 1960s are the story of the Baby Boomers' rise to social power and the struggles that ensued. One can use many events to make the beginning of this change, including John F. Kennedy being sworn into office as president of the U.S. in January 1961, the Cuban Missile Crisis in October 1962, JFK's assassination in November 1963, the Beatles' first appearance on the *Ed Sullivan Show* in February 1964, and the Gulf of Tonkin Resolution that expanded the Vietnam War in August 1964. Possible endings for the imagined cultural decade include the Woodstock music festival in 1969, The Beatles' breakup in April 1970, the removal of U.S. troops from Vietnam in 1973, and the fall of Saigon in April 1975. Because there is no clearly drawn line of demarcation, this study will define the 1960s in the traditional manner of 1960 to 1969. It should be noted, that like any time in American life, society was rapidly changing and evolving and one must always differentiate between the early, middle, and late 1960s.

Here Comes the Sun

When John F. Kennedy took office in January 1961 he announced the beginning of a new era in the U.S. and the world. Although JFK was born was born in 1917 and had served in U.S. Navy during World War II, many Baby Boomers revered him for his youth and energy. Kennedy, who narrowly defeated Richard Nixon in the 1960 election, represented a change from Dwight Eisenhower's conservative and grey leadership during the previous eight years. JFK brought to office a shift in tone and style along with a more liberal idea of government's role in society and the U.S.'s duty to the world. In his inaugural address, the new president stated:

> Let the word go forth from this time and place, to friend and foe alike, that the torch has been passed to a new generation of Americans — born in this century, tempered by war, disciplined by a hard and bitter peace, proud of our ancient heritage, and unwilling to witness or permit the slow undoing of those human rights to which this nation has always been committed, and to which we are committed today at home and around the world.[2]

At his inauguration, Kennedy issued a clarion call to create a new version of American society under his leadership. He called for a new America society built through slow political and social transition that would strengthen the nation and allow Americans to adjust. Neither Kennedy nor many of his followers were pressing for a radical shift at this time. Although "the torch [had] been passed to a new generation," little would change during the Kennedy years. The start of the 1960s looked much like the 1950s, but soon political and social events along with the Baby Boomers' desire for independence would create changes of which Kennedy never dreamed.[3]

Superfather and Superperson

Much like the World War II generation and their Baby Boomer children, comic book superheroes would soon find themselves engaged in a social and cultural battle to determine the new balance of power. Unlike American society at large, comic book heroes would not begin the decade with a new leader who promised to radically change the way their world(s) operated. In 1960, DC Comics had by far the largest share of the superhero comic book market. Superman was the most popular superhero comic, selling an estimated 810,000 a month, and DC controlled at least the year's top twenty selling superhero titles.[4] The superhero 1960s generally began as the 1950s had ended, by featuring safe and unimpressive stories that encouraged conservative values and obedience to the state. Superman, Batman, and several other DC superheroes led the way by starring in mostly hokey tales that promoted super-niceness and strong family ties.

The most socially conforming of these stories were so-called "imaginary tales." Although all superhero stories are imaginary tales, these narratives take place outside of the normal monthly comic book continuity and free the writer and artist from standard boundaries. By making a story "imaginary," a creative team could change history, kill characters, and even destroy worlds without having to worry about this issue's consequences, because an imaginary tale would have no effect on the characters' present or future. In essence, comic book writers and artists could tell whichever stories they wanted without changing anything. What if Lex Luthor killed Superman?[5] What if Superman married Lois Lane?[6] What if Batman needed to find a new secret identity?[7] What if Superman and Batman were brothers?[8] These stories were essentially cheats that gave creators opportunities to write tales in which theoretically anything could happen. Generally, little to nothing truly radical ever took place in imaginary tales. Most of these stories revolved around either a superhero getting married, having children, or finding a sibling. Even in the stories in which a hero dies, another character takes his place and little changes because of his sacrifice.

One the most interesting of these imaginary tales presents a scenario in which Superman splits into two versions of himself known as Superman-Blue and Superman-Red. Working together, the two supermen create a new Kryptonian home world, implement satellites that bombard the Earth with a "hypno-ray" that "erase[s] all thoughts of evil from the minds of the world's criminals," and eradicates all disease. Eventually Superman-Red marries Superman's current girlfriend, Lois Lane, while Superman-Blue marries his high school sweetheart, Lana Lang. Both Supermen have a son and daughter and the story ends with this editorial question, "What's your opinion, readers? Suppose this imaginary story really happened, which couple do you think would be happiest?"[9] This story, and all of the other imaginary tales, showcases what the most popular superhero comic books of the early 1960s were like.

While an imaginary story seemingly gave its creators unlimited freedom to produce brave new tales, in reality DC Comics editors and managers wanted stories featuring conservative heroes that promoted patriotism and family values. Although these stories promised limitless possibilities, they almost always served as vehicles to reinforce middle-class morality. The 1960s began as the 1950s had ended in comic books with DC producing nice guy company man heroes that smiled while upholding American values and seemingly having few problems that could not be solved in the span of one comic book story. Although DC would continue with this formula throughout much of the 1960s, a rival would soon appear on the scene that would change the superhero publishing world forever. Just as Baby Boomers were beginning to struggle for social and cultural control of American society, soon a new type of hero would emerge. Marvel Comics was coming and the world would never be the same again.

Happy Together

DC Comics opened the 1960s as the only major comic book company producing superhero stories. Archie, Harvey, and Dell were very successful at creating funny animal, adventure, and teenage stories, but generally stayed away from superheroes. Marvel Comics — which had previously published such heroes as Captain America, the Human Torch, and the Sub-Mariner — ended 1960 with three titles in the top 48, *Tales to Astonish*, *Tales of Suspense*, and *Kid Colt Outlaw*, none of which were superhero fare.[10] In 1960, DC Comics created a team consisting of seven of its most popular superheroes. This team, known as the Justice League of America, was so successful that DC gave the group its own comic book in 1961. During its first year, *Justice League of America* was one of the top ten selling superhero comics in the nation and a resounding success.[11]

Martin Goodman, the publisher who owned Marvel Comics, noticed *Justice League of America*'s success and instructed his comic book editor, Stan Lee, to create a new superhero group that could cash in on this perceived trend. Stan Lee had worked for Marvel Comics (which had twice changed its name from Timely and Atlas) for over twenty years and had seen superhero comic book sales boom and then bust. Marvel's efforts to publish superhero titles in the 1950s had quickly failed and there was little to indicate that this new super-group comic book would last more than a few issues. Marvel generally made its money by capitalizing on the newest fad until its popularity dwindled and then quickly moving on to the next big thing. Martin Goodman had not charged Stan Lee with creating a new and lasting work of art and literature; rather Goodman only wanted a *Justice League of America* ripoff that could sell a few issues. Luckily for comic book fans, Stan Lee and Jack Kirby had much more in mind.[12]

Start Me Up

Virtually every good comic book superhero has a secret origin. This tale informs the reader how the hero received his or her powers and why he or she decided to don a costume and fight to uphold established social norms (i.e., "good.") Most secret origins are anything but secret and are generally a necessary element in understanding a superhero's behavior. Understanding a comic book character's literary creation is often much harder, though, and sometimes the parties involved cannot agree on how they fashioned a given superhero. Because comic books are a merger of words and pictures, it is frequently difficult to determine how and by whom a comic book character was created. Comic book writers and artists must collaborate to create a character and story and generally no one except those involved in the process knows with whom the ideas originated.

To better clarify this idea, think of Superman's creation. Jerry Siegel reportedly came up with the original idea and wrote the first story, but Joe Shuster designed the character's appearance and created the comic book's style. Would Superman be Superman is he looked and dressed differently? Does not Shuster deserve some of the credit for creating the character? What if the two creators thoroughly disagreed about Superman's origin? How would comic book fans and historians know the "truth" about Superman's creation? This process is even further complicated when creators use "Marvel method" scripts to produce a superhero's design and story. Traditional comic book scripts look much like movie scripts and the writer provides the artist with scene descriptions, dialogue, and other major story elements. In the Marvel method the writer gives the artist a brief summary of the story and then supplies the dialogue once the artist has rendered the pages. Because the writer has not fully fleshed out the story and sometimes the characters, the artist must write most of the story. The Marvel method blurs the line between writer and artist and makes it even more difficult to determine which person created what. Although comic book historians would often like to emphatically proclaim how their favorite superheroes were created, in general no one but the creators themselves really know.[13]

The Fab Four

After Marvel's publisher Martin Goodman told Stan Lee to create a Justice League-style super-team, the writer began to think of ideas. Lee, who believed that traditional comic books were beneath him, wanted to create a new type of super-hero that would be more realistic than previous incarnations. He later recalled, "For once I wanted to write stories that wouldn't insult the intelligence of an older reader, stories with interesting characterization, more realistic dialogue, and plots that hadn't been recycled a thousand times before. Above all, stories that wouldn't hew to all the comicbook [sic] clichés of years past."[14] In other words, Lee wanted to break with the period's conservative norms and create a new type of hero. According to Lee, he created the characters and worked out the first issue's plot details before handing the typed plot outline to artist Jack Kirby, who drew the issue. Kirby disagrees, claiming that the two men had a story conference in which both created the new super-team.[15] Although comic book enthusiasts often argue over Lee and Kirby's roles, what ultimately matters is that the creative duo had successfully fashioned a new kind of superhero unique to the 1960s. Lee and Kirby had created the Fantastic Four, the first Marvel Comics superheroes and the introduction to Baby Boomer superheroes that would soon change the landscape forever.

Fantastic Four #1 (November 1961) is the comic book that ushered in the new Marvel era. The Stan Lee penned and Jack Kirby drawn story created a superhero family that appealed to young Baby Boomers. (© 1961 Marvel Comics. All Rights Reserved.)

Although Martin Goodman envisioned the Fantastic Four as a Justice League clone, what Stan Lee and Jack Kirby produced was a super-team unlike any seen before. Popular culture commentator Pierre Comtois writes, "Here's the book that neatly divides the history of comics into two eras: everything that came before and the progeny of the Fantastic Four that came after. It was the book that rewrote the rules on comics and, in order to survive, all others eventually had to follow its lead."[16] The new team consisted of four friends and relatives that gained superpowers after encountering cosmic radiation while conducting a scientific space mission. Reed Richards, a scientific genius, witnessed his body becoming elastic-like and stretchable and he donned the identity of Mr. Fantastic. Reed's fiancée, Sue Storm, became Invisible Girl and displayed invisibility and force field rendering powers. Sue's brother Johnny Storm gained the ability to fly when his body turned into a flaming mass and he soon became known as the Human Torch. Reed's college roommate Ben Grimm changed into a super-strong and invulnerable orange rock creature known as the Thing.

What made the heroes unique was that they were more human than any other super-human that had preceded them. The Fantastic Four fought super-menaces and stopped criminals but they also bickered among themselves and faced personal problems that many readers could understand. They also were not the seemingly perfect human beings that many DC Comics superheroes had become. Reed was an arrogant intellectual bore who sometimes treated Sue coldly. Johnny was a young hothead who often acted before thinking. Possibly the most interesting of the group was Ben, who faced isolation and loneliness after becoming the Thing. Ben became as much monster as hero and had to learn to live in a world that feared him and was repulsed by his appearance. The Fantastic Four's debut introduced a new type of superhero that faced his or her inner demons as much as he or she fought external foes. American society was changing and comic book superheroes were beginning to change with it. The Fantastic Four was only the first version of the changing superhero, but it was the comic book that started the Marvel revolution.[17]

The Monster Mash

The Fantastic Four was highly successful, and Martin Goodman soon asked Stan Lee to create another new comic book hero. Lee, along with Jack Kirby, in keeping with the writers' new philosophy of creating novel kinds of superheroes, developed a character that was more monster than hero. The character was based on Dr. Jekyll and Mr. Hyde and Frankenstein. *The Incredible Hulk* debuted in May 1962 and quickly become a smash hit for the publisher. Due to gamma radiation exposure Dr. Bruce Banner transforms into the super-strong and invulnerable Hulk whenever the scientist becomes angry. The Hulk originally was gray skinned but the publisher quickly changed him into a green goliath after experiencing printing problems. The green giant was a pitiable monster whom many average people feared and despised, much like the Fantastic Four's the Thing. The Hulk

The Incredible Hulk #3 (September 1962) features the nuclear-altered hero/monster as he battles both villains and society itself. The Hulk served as a hero for many adolescent readers who felt isolated and alone. (© 1962 Marvel Comics. All Rights Reserved.)

only wanted to be left alone, and many of the character's early stories contained instances of some person or entity pursuing the green-skinned loner.

The character appealed to many adolescent and teenage readers who felt alienated from mainstream society. These young readers not only experienced typical adolescent identity struggles but also were becoming increasingly involved in the growing societal and cultural divide between the Baby Boomers and their parents. As Baby Boomers became progressively more disenfranchised with mainstream American society, they began to seek new culturally expressive outlets. The Incredible Hulk was a new monster/hero for a new age. He was a character that spoke to a changing society and to many Baby Boomers that felt that American ideals and values were too rigid and outdated. Although Lee and Kirby had not developed the Incredible Hulk as a mouthpiece against conventional American culture, he soon became a symbol of a new American generation. He and the Fantastic Four would help to usher in a new age of comic books and create discourse that would mirror many young voices in American society. The Marvel Age had begun, and it all started with a superhero family and a sympathetic green-skinned monster.[18]

The Itsy Bitsy Spider

After discovering the success of the Fantastic Four and the Incredible Hulk, Stan Lee, Jack Kirby and other Marvel creators developed several additional comic book superheroes over the next few years, like Ant-Man, Thor, Iron Man, and the X-Men. Each of these heroes provided new modern elements that challenged the traditional superhero status quo. Each battled inner demons, real world problems, and social stigmas as well as fighting crime. These Marvel heroes had both unique voices and severe flaws that allowed them to greatly differ from DC Comics' seemingly perfect and yet bland heroes. Many young comic book readers identified with the Marvel heroes' personal problems and seemingly respected the new heroes for having foibles and shortcomings. DC heroes were the clean-cut and well-mannered individuals that most parents wished their children to emulate. Marvel heroes were edgy and complex characters that many younger readers believed to be realistic (or as realistic as people who fight supervillains and dress in spandex can be).

In August 1962, arguably the most popular and important Marvel superhero would make his debut. *Amazing Fantasy* #15 featured the first appearance of Spider-Man, the hero that would soon become Marvel's most popular character. Spider-Man's mythos revolves around the teenaged Peter Parker, who acquired superpowers from a radioactive spider's bite. In the early stories, the orphaned Peter was a shy young man who faced the same money, romance, and peer pressure problems as many teenagers did. After Peter develops his superpowers the problems do not stop, and often they are only intensified. At first Peter does not even want to fight crime but decides to become a costumed hero after a thief kills his beloved uncle Ben. When Marvel's publisher, Martin Goodman, first heard of Spider-Man, he thought the character was a terrible idea and would surely fail because it violated too many established superhero norms.[19] Goodman was wrong though, and the publisher himself soon gave Spider-Man his own comic book. Spider-Man was the first young Baby Boomer superhero that was not another hero's sidekick. The web slinger acted like other adolescents and many readers reacted by buying his comic book.[20] Spider-Man and all of the other Marvel heroes' sales and popularity were an early indication that the Baby Boomers were beginning to exert cultural and social power.

The Day the Music Died

The early 1960s were but a prelude to the social and cultural change that would occur later in the decade. Although John F. Kennedy brought a new youthful exuberance to the nation, very few social changes followed. The U.S. remained the same conservative society that it had been in the 1950s. Although underground movements and cultures were beginning to form and grow, none had yet reached the national consciousness. The nation was still locked in a Cold War struggle with the Soviet Union, as evidenced by 1962's Cuban Missile Crisis and the U.S.'s growing involvement in Vietnam. The Civil Rights Movement pressed forward making substantial gains but lacked support among politicians and the middle class. The World War II generation continued to steer American society in a conservative and safe direction.

The first major event that delineated the 1960s from the 1950s happened on November 22, 1963. On this date in Dallas, Texas, Lee Harvey Oswald shot and killed President Kennedy. Shortly after assassinating the president, Oswald himself was murdered by local businessman Jack Ruby. The president's murder shocked and stunned the nation and caused many Americans to question their core beliefs. Kennedy's assassination especially devastated many Baby Boomers, who were young enough to fully believe in the charismatic young politician. To many younger Americans the president's death was the first major step towards a disenchantment with the mainstream American way of life. If someone could kill President Kennedy, then who or what could be trusted? Many Baby Boomers were becoming adults in a country they no longer knew if they understood, believed in, or liked.[21]

A Change Is Gonna Come

Kennedy's death may have been an early flashpoint but it was not the cause of the social and cultural rebellion that is associated with the 1960s. Rather the counterculture 1960s was the product of a confluence of events that swirled together in a way that was unpredictable. Looking backwards it becomes clear that as the oldest members of the largest American generation in history were reaching adulthood, they would begin to demand social changes.

After being raised in a conservative and repressive environment that encouraged stability and obedience, Baby Boomers were approaching the age at which they could demand freedom. Every American generation changes society and demands new types of freedom and self-determination. The Baby Boomers were unique because their numerical size and relative affluence allowed them to fight for social and cultural control while their generation was still composed of young adults and adolescents. This postwar generation refused to follow the traditional waiting period and instead many Baby Boomers pressed for social changes immediately. Once social injustice, war, race, sex, political assassinations, drugs, and rock and roll were added to the mix then a messy social and cultural struggle between parents and children became almost inevitable. John F. Kennedy's assassination did not cause the cultural revolution, but it is one of the first in a series of events that changed the American social landscape forever.[22]

Blowing in the Wind

As the nation reeled from John F. Kennedy's assassination, Vice President Lyndon Baines Johnson became president. The politically powerful Johnson urged the Congress to honor Kennedy by passing civil rights legislation. The Civil Rights Act of 1964, which expanded voting rights and barred racial segregation in locations like schools and workplaces, became law within a year of the young president's death. The Civil Rights Act was the year's bright spot. On the downside, problems and issues that would plague the nation throughout the decade were beginning to grow.

Although Congress was finally addressing civil rights, there was growing disenchantment and resentment among blacks. Society's attitudes towards civil rights were changing much too slowly for some and many blacks were upset about the perceived overall unfairness of life in the United States. The Nation of Islam, a black nationalist organization, was gaining supporters by preaching the doctrine of separatism. This created a rift between more conservative blacks that pushed for mainstream inclusion combined with cultural, social, and economic equality. The debate between inclusion and separation was not new to the 1960s and can be seen in earlier times such as in the 19th century writings of W.E.B. Du Bois and Booker T. Washington. The 1960s saw a growing outrage among many blacks that seemed to increase with every passing year. In 1965, an unknown assassin would kill the popular Nation of Islam spokesman Malcolm X. Another American leader had been murdered and discontent was growing. Race relations were changing in the U.S., but the pace was much too slow for many.[23]

War (What Is It Good For?)

The Civil Rights struggle was an issue that Americans would slowly address over the coming decades and that would define much of the 1960s' cultural ideology. It would provide a forum and an outlet for many Americans to express their disappointment with society. The other 1960s issue that would polarize Americans and have major social and cultural effects on the nation for well over a decade was the Vietnam War. Although the U.S. had a substantial political presence in Vietnam since the 1940s and a small military role early in the 1960s, large scale U.S. military involvement in Vietnam did not begin until 1964. At the end of 1963, the U.S. had approximately 15,000 military advisors in South Vietnam.

In 1966 that number would rise to over 400,000 U.S. service personnel and by December 1968 there would be roughly 540,000 U.S. servicemen fighting in the Vietnam conflict.[24] Lyndon Johnson strongly believed that South Vietnam should not be allowed to fall to the communists and openly expressed this opinion to many.

Historians debate whether Johnson engineered events that would force the U.S. to become more involved in the Vietnam conflict, but no one can deny that one of the first major turning points of the war happened on August 2, 1964. On that day, North Vietnamese Naval torpedo boats reportedly attacked the USS *Maddox* while it was on an intelligence mission in the Gulf of Tonkin's international waters. President Johnson quickly convinced Congress to pass the Gulf of Tonkin Resolution that gave the president the ability to lead military operations without the legislature declaring war. Johnson promptly used his new found power to escalate the Vietnam conflict. Within a few years over 500,000 Americans would be fighting in South Vietnam and a substantial portion of this number were draftees. The Vietnam conflict may have started for political reasons, but soon it would become one of the major social and cultural events of the 1960s.[25]

She Loves You, Yeah, Yeah, Yeah

As the Civil Rights movement, the Cold War, and the Vietnam conflict began to increase political and social tensions within the U.S., many Baby Boomers turned to new means of expression. Some younger Americans began to rebel against convention and demanded new social and cultural outlets. The most obvious of these was rock and roll. Although rock and roll had existed for more than a decade (and its ancestors blues, jazz, country, folk, and bluegrass were even older), the popular music style was constantly changing. Artists like Elvis Presley, Buddy Holly, and Little Richard had enthralled fans and scandalized critics during the 1950s, but by 1964 many fans' tastes were changing. Rock and roll transformed forever in 1964 when The Beatles appeared on *The Ed Sullivan Show* in February. This marked the band's introduction to many in the U.S. and started the so-called British invasion by popular musicians. Although The Beatles probably seem tame to twenty-first century eyes and ears, they were a startling sight and sound to many when they first appeared. The four Liverpudlian youths refused to conform to conservative American standards in the way they sang, dressed, and even cut their hair. While The Beatles may have begun as a faddish boy band, the Fab Four soon became a voice for Baby Boomers that felt trapped and disenfranchised with American society.

Soon other musical artists like Bob Dylan, Joan Baez, the Rolling Stones, Jimi Hendrix, and Janis Joplin would also lend their voice to the new generation. As the world seemed to begin to spin out of control, popular music both fanned the flames of social upheaval and offered comfort from the storm. Although most of the cultural and social issues and icons that later generations would associate with the 1960s were still in their infancy in 1964, that would soon change. A new era was beginning and rock and roll would provide the soundtrack for the decade that would change the nation forever.[26]

My Generation

As the Civil Rights movement shined a spotlight on the shocking disparities in American society, the Vietnam conflict sent hundreds of thousands of young Americans to fight in Southeast Asia, and President Kennedy's assassination shattered the air of tranquility, members of the Baby Boom generation began to seriously question American values and ideals. This notion of a counterculture that started after Kennedy's death was earnestly embraced by many in 1965 when college students began to protest the Vietnam conflict. Numerous young Americans resented the idea of fighting in a war that seemed to have no clear goals or desired outcomes. Protestors especially took exception to the fact that deferments and exemptions created a system in which poor and working-class citizens and minorities served in the armed forces in disproportionate numbers. As the Vietnam conflict soured the idea of government and military service in many Baby Boomers' minds, these same citizens turned to new counterculture outlets like drugs, free love, and the aforementioned rock and roll. Marijuana, LSD, and other drugs purportedly offered young Americans the opportunity to expand their consciousnesses and obtain personal growth. Former Harvard professor Timothy Leary began experimenting with LSD and told Americans to "tune in, turn on, and drop out." He informed his fellow citizens that the modern lifestyle was a sham and remembered his former self as being "an anonymous institutional employee who drove to work each morning in a long line of commuter cars and drove home each night and drank martinis ... like several million middle-class, liberal, intellectual robots."[27] Free love promised to strip sex of its puritanical associations, while seemingly offering young men and women sexual equality and the freedom from judgment and guilt. The counterculture envisioned a new system of values that focused more on the individual's needs and desires and less on society's stability. This focus is understandable when one considers the conservative and structured society in which many Baby Boomers grew up. Baby Boomers were not only rebelling against their parents, their childhoods, and their lives, but also against American society in general. Many young Americans were developing a counterculture and not everyone in society would embrace it.[28]

Stop Children, What's That Sound?

As American society was increasingly changing so were comic book superheroes; well, some of them were. Marvel Comics stories were becoming increasingly daring and unconventional, while DC Comics tales continued to employ the conservative elements that had worked so well in the past. Marvel writers and editors used an audacious and self-deprecating style that appealed to many hip young readers. Marvel comic books were not slick and over-produced fare; the final product was often an unpolished magazine that looked unprofessional to the older generation. By contrast, DC employed rigid 1950s style professionalism and made certain that each comic book adhered to a strict code of quality control. In fact, DC publishers and editors did not regard Marvel comic books as competition for a long time because the more established DC employees believed that Marvel's products looked shabby and unprofessional.[29] Although Marvel superheroes were creatively at the forefront, DC's conservative stories continued to greatly outsell the competition.[30]

DC's sales dominance mirrors a trend in American society at large that many historians either do not mention or gloss over quickly. While a large number of younger Americans became involved in protests, social movements, or the counterculture during the 1960s, this group was always by far a minority. Those of us who were born after the 1960s often focus on the relative few individuals that changed American society, while we forget that most people were either ambivalent toward or opposed to these social changes. It is easy to look back at the major 1960s social and cultural events and imagine that everyone was locked into a powerful struggle that transformed society forever, but in reality many people were too busy or uninspired to participate. We now see the 1960s as the birth of the Marvel superhero style, an idea that would soon revolutionize the comic book industry, but forget that throughout the 1960s most American preferred traditional and conservative superhero stories. In comic books and in American society, new cultural ideas were gaining traction, but most people still favored the status quo. The 1960s was a revolutionary time, and although all Americans were affected by the social and cultural changes, most people either did not participate or preferred life as it was.

Changes

While most Americans either did not support the idea of large scale social and cultural changes or did not want to become involved, the notion of a new kind of American society gained appeal among young people in the mid–1960s. After these early adapters lent their support to numerous movements, changes began to slowly trickle down into mainstream culture. The anti-war movement started to find increasingly diverse supporters that were often very different from the young, white, middle and upper class university students that founded the movement. The Civil Rights movement slowly expanded politically and socially, and gradually began to change some Americans' ideas about race and society. The counterculture at first seemed odd to many, but little by little several of its aspects became part of the social norm. Although it did not happen quickly and mainstream society required the most radical ideas to be remade or watered down, some counterculture elements became acceptable to most and desirable to many. None of these changes happened swiftly and often they involved a process of engagement, reconciliation, and adaptation. It would be a mistake to assume that the changes were either immediate or straightforward. They were difficult and slow, and by the mid–1960s would test the nation's mettle, because the toughest days were still ahead.[31]

Long and Winding Road

Much like mainstream American society, Marvel superhero stories initially did not embrace many of the 1960s' new social and cultural ideas. Although Marvel created a new kind of superhero and used an irreverent style that appealed to many Baby Boomers, the company incorporated few social or counterculture elements. Marvel did introduce the first black superhero in July 1966's *Fantastic Four* #52. Possibly more importantly, Marvel began featuring random blacks as background characters in 1965.[32] Although the inclusion of black characters in Marvel stories was an important step that reflected the changing American culture, by and large Marvel continued to create mainstream stories. For all of its nonconformist bluster and self-created maverick image, in the mid–1960s Marvel generally produced conservative stories that reinforced the power and rightness of the state. While Marvel heroes were more unusual and socially relevant than DC's clean-cut white bread crusaders, Marvel comic books were still state-friendly fare that encouraged readers to be good Americans and to support the status quo. Present day comic book fans often think of Marvel as a counterculture company that produced liberal texts that pressed to change American society. This may be true in later years, but in the early and mid–1960s Marvel stories celebrated American exceptionalism and preached against social change.

Marvel stories produced from 1961 until 1968 reflected certain changing social and cultural elements but remained highly conservative in nature. Marvel's most popular hero, Spider-Man, continued to fight crime and express little social commentary. Captain America remained a symbol of American patriotism and honor.

Iron Man was perhaps the most conservative of all the Marvel superheroes during the early and mid–1960s. Technologically powered industrialist Tony Stark became Iron Man and battled Cold War adversaries while working hard to defeat communist foes across the world. Iron Man often fought grotesque Soviet and Eastern European villains who initially challenged the American way of life but ultimately surrendered to the glorious supremacy of American values and ideals. Although by the mid–1960s Tony Stark began to question the American government and the Vietnam conflict, he remained committed to a traditional conservative understanding of the U.S.'s problems, both at home and abroad. Iron Man, and all of the other Marvel heroes, borrowed liberal cultural aesthetics to appeal to young readers but remained solidly conservative in theme and story. Much like American society, the Marvel heroes were beginning to accept a few cultural and social changes while considering even greater ones, but were not ready for radical ideas. Although many think of Marvel as a comic book leader in American society, it was very much a follower. In the mid–1960s, Marvel was still a conservative company that produced pro-state stories for adolescents and children. Like much of American society, it supported the U.S. government and believed deeply in the status quo.

Dazed and Confused

Throughout the mid–1960s the U.S. increased troop numbers and escalated the war effort in Vietnam while the streets of some U.S. cities also seemed like war zones. In August 1965, the Watts neighborhood of Los Angeles erupted into chaos and terror as tensions boiled over, resulting in a six day riot. The racial injustice, police brutality, and economic hardship that had long plagued the predominantly black community finally became too great to handle and many citizens took to the streets. Detroit, Michigan, and Newark, New Jersey, suffered similar riots in 1967 when police mistreatment lit the fuse on a powder keg filled with decades of discrimination and exploitation.[33] The world seemed to be spinning out of control. The U.S. was escalating the Vietnam conflict while the nightly television news displayed the flag-draped coffins of young American men and women. Protesters took to the streets and openly disagreed with the war in Vietnam. Rioters destroyed American cities. Blacks staged rallies, sit ins, and marches. Young men grew their hair long. The younger generation talked about free love, dressed oddly, and questioned American society and its values. To many, the world seemed to have gone mad, a far cry from the postwar American society that many citizens had worked so hard to build and maintain. The peace and security that many so desired during the 1950s was replaced with conflict and uncertainty. Soldiers died, cities burned, children turned away from their parents, and young citizens no longer seemed to celebrate the nation and its values. In many Americans' eyes the world seemed to be falling apart by the end of 1967; unfortunately for them, these situations and events would only intensify in the coming year.

Revolution

War, riots, and social unrest upset the nation's delicate balance and made the years from 1960 to 1967 frightening for some and exhilarating for others. But those events pale in comparison with 1968's long list of life-altering happenings. As students protested across the world and a political spring seemingly briefly thawed the Cold War in Prague, American society also reeled. On January 31, 1968, the North Vietnamese launched a massive attack known as the Tet Offensive. Over 70,000 North Vietnamese and Viet Cong combatants began assaulting South Vietnam during the Vietnamese holiday of Tet. Although South Vietnamese and U.S. troops pushed back and defeated the communist forces, many Americans were shocked that North Vietnamese and Viet Cong fighters could launch such a large war effort. The Tet Offensive marks a turning point in which many average and apolitical Americans began to question the U.S involvement in Vietnam. Although numerous young people had long protested the Vietnam conflict, the Tet Offensive caused many conservative Americans to rethink the U.S.'s policy.[34] As the U.S. war effort was losing support at home,

President Lyndon Johnson was reeling from a credibility gap in which many Americans did not believe his claims about Vietnam.[35] Anti-war protests increased and trusted voices of reason like anchorman Walter Cronkite informed the American people that the war in Vietnam was going badly. While many Americans began to question the country's role in Vietnam, in April 1968 a tragic murder would both shock and divide the nation and again press American society to address the issues of racism and inequality.

On April 4, 1968, an escaped convict named James Earl Ray shot and killed Dr. Martin Luther King, Jr., at a motel in Memphis, Tennessee. Dr. King's murder horrified and angered many Americans and served as a catalyst for riots that gripped several U.S. cities, including Chicago, Washington D.C., Louisville, and Baltimore.[36] King's assassination came only a few years after John F. Kennedy's murder and stunned many Americans who could not believe that another important leader could be killed so soon after the beloved president. As millions still reeled from the news of King's shooting, on April 11, the U.S. Department of Defense announced it would raise the number of American troops in Vietnam to 540,000.[37] Protests grew larger and more common and some American males burned their draft cards as an act of civil disobedience. In the early morning of June 5, 1968, the country again lost an important leader when a 24-year-old Jordanian student named Sirhan Sirhan shot presidential candidate and former Attorney General Robert F. Kennedy. The young and charismatic Kennedy was many Baby Boomers' favorite candidate and a front runner to win the presidential election and follow in his brother John's footsteps. Kennedy's assassination took place less than five years after his brother's death and barely two months after Martin Luther King's murder.

As a nation that prided itself on providing law, order, and stability, Americans were aghast at the chaos. Two prominent leaders had been murdered within nearly two months' time, riots destroyed parts of cities, protests filled the streets, and thousands of young Americans were dying in a war that seemed difficult to justify or understand. In August 1968, the Democratic National Convention was held in Chicago, where delegates would nominate Hubert Humphrey as their presidential candidate. Anti-war protestors and other demonstrators flocked to the city and remained relatively peaceful for the convention's first few nights. Then on Wednesday, August 28, the protestors clashed with Chicago police. The city's finest beat dozens of protestors until they were unconscious and sent more than 100 people to local emergency rooms.[38] Chicago mayor Richard Daley famously stated, "The policeman isn't there to create disorder, the policeman is there to preserve disorder."[39] Americans watched on television as even the process surrounding their president's election degenerated into a street brawl. The events of 1968 shocked and horrified most Americans. The nation seemed to be spiraling out of control and there was apparently little anyone could do to stop it. American society was changing and very few Americans seemed to like it.

Everyday People

As society appeared to become ever more frightening and chaotic, DC and Marvel attempted to create comic books that appealed to modern readers, while still adhering to the comic book code and not becoming so radical as to disenfranchise readers. DC mainly continued to produce conservative fare with enough of a hint of modern culture to make the stories appear contemporary. Generally this updating of clothing, hairstyles, slang usage, and minor revisions only served as a cultural whitewash of stories that remained inherently conservative. Marvel, on the other hand, produced increasingly left-leaning stories that mirrored contemporary social and cultural ideals. Early and mid–1960s Marvel tales had been hip and youthfully-stylized while remaining conservative at their core. Numerous 1968–1969 produced stories featured progressively more liberal elements that appeared to be in step with ongoing social and cultural movements. These tales made it clear that most Marvel characters had liberal leanings but believed in centrist non-violent resolutions that avoided radical and aggressive social outcomes. Comic book historian Bradford W. Wright notes, "Super-heroes like Spider-Man endorsed liberal solutions to social problems while rejecting the extreme and violent responses of both the left and the right." Wright then notes, "Nevertheless, in an American society facing deepening political divisions, Marvel heroes worked to preserve what remained of the vital center."[40]

Heroes like Spider-Man, Captain America, Dr. Strange, Nick Fury, and Thor displayed their increasingly liberal biases but still advocated middle of the road solutions. While these comic book stories were far from radical, they also were different from the trendy yet con-

The Mighty Thor #144 (September 1967) presents the brash Norse god as he develops his humanity. Thor was one of many popular Marvel superheroes that battled internal struggles as well as external foes. (© 1967 Marvel Comics. All Rights Reserved.)

servative fare from only a few years before. Generally, Marvel superheroes were becoming more liberal and DC characters remained conservative, but creators at both companies were producing stories that advocated patience and restraint, a centrist approach that many Americans supported.

The End's in Sight

The 1960s ended very differently than the decade had begun. The early 1960s were an extension of the safe, stable, and conformist 1950s. By contrast, 1969 displayed the later part of the decade's counterculture pedigree. The 1960s' last year featured massive anti–Vietnam War demonstrations, the Stonewall Riots protesting the mistreatment of gay citizens, and increased violence between police officers and student protestors across the country. Almost on cue, the 1960s' social and cultural movements were beginning to decline, though. Many were starting to rethink the decade's reforms and liberal programs and were questioning if Americans had strayed too far from their traditional social roles. Richard Nixon was elected president in November 1968 and took office in January 1969. The conservative Republican leader promised to follow the "silent majority's" will and to end the Vietnam War.

While many Marvel and some DC comic book superheroes continued to display increasingly liberal and progressive elements, American society was beginning to shift again. The country (and the world) paused to watch on July 20, 1969, as Apollo 11 landed on the moon and Neil Armstrong became the first human to step on the lunar surface. This was merely a momentary reprieve, though, as the chaotic 1960s came to an end and the unknown 1970s were ushered in. The 1960s had begun with the end of a conservative era and after much liberal change, the decade ended with many unsure about the future or the past. While superheroes would continue to follow the same general paths that they had for the last few years, it was unclear how American society would proceed.

Conclusion

The 1960s were one of the most turbulent and unpredictable periods in the United States' history. The decade featured the end of the conservative and repressive 1950s and the beginning of a youth movement that changed American society forever. During this period, a new generation stepped forward and began to press for changes that would have been impossible only a few short years before. As the Vietnam conflict escalated the new generation began to question society's foundations and then remade the United States both culturally and socially. This new American vision extended into comic book superhero stories and soon fresh heroes that co-opted the spirit of the 1960s youth movement were introduced. By creating superheroes like the Fantastic Four, the Incredible Hulk, and Spider-Man, Marvel comics revolutionized the comic book industry and developed characters that spoke to the needs and desires of the Baby Boom generation. While Marvel was publishing heroes that appealed to trendy 1960s youths, DC continued to market characters that espoused traditional values and conservative beliefs. The differences between these two comic book companies' superheroes showcase American society's tensions during the 1960s and, more importantly, help to display the growing generation gap that in part led to both chaos and change during this pivotal decade. As with most social changes, comic book superheroes transformed to meet society's wants and needs. In this instance, superheroes also experienced the generation gap and began to fight the culture wars while continuing to also battle supervillains. Although many Americans disagree about the desirability of the decade's changes, few can argue with the notion that the 1960s was an important decade that greatly changed the United States.

Chapter 6

THE AMERICAN MALAISE (1970–1979)

In 1978, a motion picture version of Superman premiered in theaters across the United States. The film, starring Christopher Reeve, became wildly popular and millions of viewers left theaters agreeing with the motion picture's tagline, "You'll believe a man can fly." The film helped to change many movie goers' opinions of the Man of Steel, while social forces were compelling Americans to rethink their changing lives. The 1970s was a decade of transition in which most Americans had to amend many of their social and cultural beliefs, not just the ones concerning celluloid Kryptonians. At the start of the decade, people were questioning the place of traditional institutions in American society following a shift in the 1960s toward more liberal philosophies. Others wondered whether the country had changed too much during the 1960s and even more citizens asked if the nation could bond newly established freedoms with older ways of life. If the 1960s was a decade of newness and change, then the 1970s was about melding the old with the new and sometimes creating fresh understandings of a world that often seemed bleaker and more imposing than before. The 1970s generally witnessed and produced a darker and more despondent national tone and a citizenry that often questioned what had gone wrong with the United States. In classic comic book fashion, by the end of the decade many superheroes began to become as angry and dejected as the nation.

The Nightmare Begins

While many speak fondly of the 1960s and the 1980s, few people seem to hold the 1970s in such high esteem. Many equate the decade with the Watergate scandal, the end of the Vietnam conflict, the energy crisis, or a myriad of other disturbing or unappealing events. Scholar Philip Jenkins described the period between the 1960s and 1980s as the "Decade of Nightmares" and as an important transitional period. Jenkins claims that the cultural 1970s lasted from 1975 to 1986 and notes, "A marked change of the national mood occurred in the mid–1970s, bringing with it a much deeper pessimism about the state of America and its future, and a growing rejection of recent liberal orthodoxies."[1] Although many scholars disagree with Jenkins about the cultural 1970s' dates, most concur that the decade produced and witnessed a bleaker and more unhappy nation.[2] The collectivist ideals were transforming into a "me first" mentality and the nation was beginning to see the darker side of the 1960s changes.

One of the decade's seminal events highlighted this intersection between old and new and set the tone for the decade. On May 4, 1970, members of the Ohio National Guard fired on several unarmed students at Kent State University in Ohio. Guardsmen killed four stu-

dents and wounded nine others after firing 67 rounds of ammunition into a group of protestors and passersby. A large group of students had been protesting the U.S. military's invasion of Cambodia and the clash between student protestors and servicemen highlighted deep
divisions within American society. Pictures and videos of young American guardsmen shooting young American students horrified many.[3] While Americans debated whether the students or the servicemen were at fault, many agreed that something was amiss in the country
and things needed to change. The Kent State shootings exemplified the clash between conservative and liberal elements at the beginning of the 1970s. Although this is an overly simplistic presentation of the events surrounding the Ohio shootings, the Kent State Massacre
does provide a foundation for understanding some of the issues that perplexed Americans
at the beginning of the 1970s. Did the liberal reforms of the 1960s go too far? Were traditional
social and cultural elements being forgotten and should Americans embrace more conservative social mores? Americans found themselves in the midst a cultural and social identity
crisis that would test the nation's resolve and again change perceptions of the country itself.

The New Old DC

As American society attempted to reconcile the nation's numerous political, social,
and cultural changes with traditional American values, comic book superheroes were also
working to understand the country's new direction. By the end of the 1960s, Marvel's superheroes had embraced youth culture and some of the social changes associated with the
decade. DC's costumed avengers had slowly, and seemingly reluctantly, begun to follow
suit. As the 1970s began, Marvel comic book stories were continuing to embrace 1960s
youth culture-centered ideas while DC creators and editors were attempting to slightly
change to meet the new generation's tastes. Although Marvel would soon need to transition
to a 1970s mindset, DC was still attempting to produce 1960s-style stories even after the
decade and its ethos had ended. Undoubtedly, the symbol for this delayed transition among
DC superheroes was Superman, the first superhero. The fictional Kryptonian began as a
1930s social avenger but became almost infinitely powerful and deeply conservative as the
decades progressed. The conservative, clean-cut, and outdated Man of Steel symbolized
DC during the 1960s and the start of 1970s, as both the hero and the comic book company
battled to remain relevant in an ever changing society. As 1970 started, Superman was still
a conservative 1950s style hero whose stories contained numerous, often silly, gimmicks
that creators and editors apparently thought would appeal to modern readers. Although
DC writers and artists had created several new heroes like Deadman and the Creeper during
the 1960s, as 1970 commenced the majority of the publisher's heroes appeared outdated.
Ironically, DC attempted to renovate some of their superheroes and these characters' roles
in American society, just as many Americans were heatedly debating social norms. By 1970
several DC superheroes were displaying 1960s-style ideas and traits while many of these
concepts were falling into disfavor.

May the Schwartz Be with You

As American society was coming to grips with the 1960s and its aftereffects, DC Comics
was also attempting to merge the traditional and the new. Much like the nation, the comic

book publisher needed to blend important core concepts with new ideas in order to stay strong and vibrant. Both the U.S. and DC strove to find the right balance between revolutionary and traditional while worrying about becoming either too radical or outdated. DC's management implemented several important editorial and creative changes in 1970. One the most significant was the departure of longtime *Superman* editor Mort Weisinger, who had shaped the Man of Steel since the early 1950s.[4] Former *Batman* editor Julius Schwartz took over the *Superman* title, a transition that many superhero fans claim marks the end of the Silver Age of comic books and the beginning of the Bronze Age. Schwartz quickly hired Denny O'Neil as the new *Superman* writer and Neal Adams as the cover artist. The pair had previously worked for Schwartz on *Batman*, where they were noted for bringing a more modern sensibility to the character. While Batman had earlier been portrayed in a silly or campy manner, O'Neil and Adams transformed the Caped Crusader into a dark and brooding vigilante who scarcely resembled his formerly cheery self. Schwartz asked O'Neil to reinvent Superman, much as he had Batman, and make the Man of Steel more relevant to contemporary readers. The creators set out to reinterpret the first superhero by modernizing him, while keeping his core ideas and values, a process that could also aptly describe the social and cultural transformations that were taking place within American society as a whole.

The Man of Bronze

Superman #233's cover showcases a dynamic Neal Adams drawn cover of Superman busting free from kryptonite chains and proclaiming, "Kryptonite Nevermore!" The January 1971 issue marked a new direction for Superman and promised the beginning of a new comic book age. For decades, Superman had become increasingly more powerful, while also more conservative and stuffy. Denny O'Neil wrote and Curt Swan penciled a story in which Superman lost much of his power to a mysterious sand creature, while a failed experiment destroyed all of the kryptonite on Earth. In this single issue, O'Neil and Swan not only depowered Superman but also destroyed an overused nemesis. The less powerful Superman promised to be more relatable, while the absence of kryptonite would theoretically force writers to come up with more creative story ideas.

Although the idea of revamping the Man of Steel seems prudent in retrospect, the changes did not take hold and before long Superman again displayed almost godlike powers. Years later O'Neil claimed that Superman reverted to his former power levels because editor Julius Schwartz believed that sales had dropped during the new storyline.[5] While minor characters and situations changed, Superman remained a conservative beacon of law and order in a society that was questioning such institutions. Although some DC writers and artists had attempted to change Superman, editors and public opinion quickly pushed the hero back into his more traditional state. Superman had briefly changed and then changed back, would the same be true of American society?

The King Is Coming, Long Live the King

Many comic book historians believed that three major events led to the end of the Silver Age of comic books and the beginning of the Bronze Age. The first two, Mort

Weisinger leaving as *Superman* editor and Julius Schwartz taking the helm, created a major shift in the comic book industry. The third change that symbolized the start of a new era marked the breakup of an influential Silver Age team and the movement of a comic book great to a new superhero universe. In the late 1960s, legendary artist Carmine Infantino became DC art director, and soon afterwards DC editor-in-chief. The renowned artist became DC's publisher in 1971. Infantino knew that he needed to attract readers that were flocking to Marvel's hip antiestablishment heroes, and the easiest way was to copy Marvel's ideas and poach the publisher's creators. In 1970, Infantino convinced Jack Kirby to quit his job at Marvel Comics and take a writer-artist position at DC.[6] Kirby was one of the architects of the Marvel style of comics and helped to create most of Marvel's highly popular characters. Kirby had almost single-handedly designed the Marvel visual method and was instrumental in the development of most of Marvel's storytelling elements. It would not be hyperbole to state that without Jack Kirby, Marvel comic books, and in turn comic books in general, would be very different today, if they even still existed.

By the end of the 1960s, Kirby was chafing both personally and creatively at Marvel. The King (as Kirby was nicknamed) had grown tired of working with Stan Lee, who often singularly took credit for many of the achievements that he and Kirby shared. Because the "Marvel style" of comic book creation required the penciler to develop much of a story's plot, Kirby believed that he should be credited as more than "just" an artist. The promise of a salary increase, more creative control, and star billing lured Kirby from his former Marvel home to the greener pastures of DC publishing.[7] DC Comics already consisted of numerous demigods but now the universe had a king. Ironically, one of comic books' greatest creators would begin his DC career working on a series headlined by a superhero's friend.

This advertisement featured in July 1970 issues of DC Comics foretold the coming of Jack "the King" Kirby to DC. Kirby's move from Marvel to DC was one of the events that signaled the end of the Silver Age of comics. (© 1970 DC Comics. Used with permission of DC Comics.)

Jack Kirby's Pal

Comic book fans often laugh when they recall Jack Kirby's first DC comic book title, *Superman's Pal Jimmy Olsen*. This second or third tier comic book seems to be a poor choice for such a well known creator. The often told tale surrounding this decision states that Kirby took over this less than desirable title because it had no assigned creative team that would have to be fired and he did not want to cost any creators their jobs.[8] No matter which book Jack Kirby was assigned, DC quickly rushed to promote his arrival. In-house DC advertisements began announcing Kirby's arrival before the company even revealed his name. A full page ad in *Superman's Pal Jimmy Olsen* #130 from July 1970 announced "the word from high is — The Great One Is Coming."[9] The advert later provided hints to Kirby's upcoming projects focusing on the New Gods. Although the teaser ad never reveals what creator is coming to DC, it does encourage fans to be excited and to guess who the "great one" is. When Kirby began producing DC stories a few months later, the October 1970 cover of *Superman's Pal Jimmy Olsen* #133 proudly proclaimed that "Kirby Is Here!"[10] Kirby had worked for DC in the past but his return promised a new DC direction and the end of an era at Marvel.

While at DC, Kirby would author an original series of comic books known as the Fourth World, along with several other new characters like OMAC, Kamandi, and the Demon. Although the King's handiwork would later become important parts of the DC universe, the creator, the company, and the new era seemed to be mismatched. Kirby created wildly imaginative stories with a 1960s' cultural slant for a conservative company in a society that was beginning to question both liberal values and heroes themselves. A prime example of this is the Jack Kirby authored comic book *Forever People*, which debuted in March 1971. A part of Kirby's Fourth World epic, the Forever People were a group of young New Gods that acted like 1960s flower children. In *Forever People* #1 the group consisting of Vykin the Black, Big Bear, Mark Moonrider, and Serifan travel from Supertown to rescue their friend Beautiful Dreamer. During this first adventure the Forever People encounter Superman, 1930s style gangsters funded by evil aliens, and purple monsters while riding a superpowered all terrain vehicle known as the Super-Cycle.[11] The Forever People are effectively a 1970s adaptation of the "kid gang" concept that Kirby and Joe Simon had used during the 1940s and 1950s in titles like the Newsboy Legion and the Young Allies. Many of Kirby's creations were essentially rehashed concepts from earlier eras. The once popular 1940s Newsboy Legion reappeared in Jimmy Olsen stories, 1950s post-apocalyptic science fiction is revisited in Kamandi, and OMAC is basically a future version of Captain America.[12]

After a five year tenure at DC, Kirby left at the end of 1975 and returned to Marvel. Kirby's term at DC showcases the company's attempts (and often failures) at changing. The publisher was often trying to meet the needs of a rapidly transforming American society by reusing conservative ideas from the past. Even when new ideas were introduced the company's institutionalized conservatism (and the fear of lower sales) generally quashed any opportunity for long lasting change. This battle between conservative institutions, liberal ideas, and fear of change not only affected comic book publishing but also American society as a whole. As DC Comics executives and creators were desperately trying to re-imagine their universe, Americans were also trying to re-imagine their country.

It Isn't Easy Being Green

As DC Comics creators were attempting to modernize and re-imagine the publisher's superheroes culturally, some stories also began to delve into the political realm. Although characters like Superman had demonstrated liberal leanings during the 1930s, all of DC's

Denny O'Neil and Neal Adams used the Green Lantern/Green Arrow series of the early 1970s to question superheroes' roles in society. (© 1970 DC Comics. Used with permission of DC Comics.)

superheroes became staunch state-guarding conservatives during and after World War II. While many of Marvel's heroes began to embrace a more liberal political agenda during the late 1960s, almost every one of DC's characters remained deeply conservative. The most notable change in this publishing philosophy occurred in April 1970's *Green Lantern and Green Arrow* #76. In this issue the creative duo of Denny O'Neil and Neal Adams took over the series and created stories centered on social and political issues. Green Lantern remained a conservative space policeman, while Green Arrow was transformed into a liberal activist who was more worried about correcting social wrongs than catching criminals. As writer Denny O'Neil puts it, Green Arrow "could be a lusty, hot-tempered anarchist to contrast with the cerebral, sedate model citizen that was Green Lantern."[13]

In the first story of the team's 13 issue run, Green Lantern stops a young man from attacking a local businessman, but Green Arrow eventually informs him that the older man is a slumlord who is trying to force his building's occupants to leave so that he can build a more profitable parking lot on the land. Green Lantern feels remorseful and eventually helps to have the man arrested for his illegal activities. During the issue, Green Arrow and others demand that both Green Lantern and the reader question the social order and the conventional understanding of such things as right, wrong, and justice. In one famous scene, an elderly black man confronts Green Lantern and states, "I been readin' about you.... How you work for the blue skins.... And how on a planet someplace you helped out the orange skins ... and you done considerable for the purple skins! Only there's skins you never bothered with —! The black skins! I want to know how come? Answer me that, Mr. Green Lantern!"[14] During the following 12 issues Green Lantern and Green Arrow would explore social ills and question the very nature of American society. Although the series was a critical success and received praise in *The New York Times*, *Newsweek*, and the *Wall Street Journal*, the storyline barely lasted a year before the comic book title reverted to more traditionally conservative tales. Low sales doomed the title and comic book fans did not appear to be ready for these new political/social stories.[15] The Green Lantern/Green Arrow pairing wrapped up in three short backup stories in *Flash* #217–219. These stories sees Green Arrow joining a monastery before eventually returning to super-heroics. Denny O'Neil notes that in creating this last storyline he and Neal Adams were addressing the changing times: "For once, we were turning inward instead of outward and perhaps unintentionally commenting on the failure of the dream of the Sixties."[16] Most comic book readers had not accepted the political/social storyline, just as many Americans had not accepted the 1960s' social changes.

Make Mine Marvel

Marvel Comics entered the 1970s with a distinct advantage over its crosstown rival DC. The House of Ideas (as Marvel is nicknamed) continued to publish stories that addressed political, social, and cultural problems and catered to the assumed liberal leanings of young readers. These innovative and sophisticated stories expanded the medium's boundaries and some of the best tales displayed comic books' artistic potential. Media outlets like the *New York Times Magazine*, *The Wall Street Journal*, and *Newsweek* noted this transition and opined that comic books were no longer only for children.[17] During this period, many Marvel superheroes shifted from merely having left wing leanings to becoming established countercultural identities and openly opposing either governmental actions or traditional ideas.

Marvel heroes had always walked the line between nationalism and anti-authority displays, but as the 1970s commenced these same characters began more openly questioning traditional American values. Marvel superheroes mirrored the many American citizens that questioned the nation's identity and this confusion about American's values and character would only grow as the decade progressed. Marvel Comics seemed to begin the decade in step with a new generation of Americans but this shared understanding would be tested as the 1970s moved forward.

Code Words

Marvel superheroes began to embrace youth culture and started to question traditional American society during the 1960s. Most of Marvel's heroes acted in a conservative manner but liberal elements began to make their way into many stories. Although Marvel characters had begun to push social and cultural boundaries, the Comics Code Authority still greatly restricted their stories. The CCA, which had been agreed upon during the conservative 1950s, severely limited comic book creators and publishers, thus often not allowing the industry to either innovate or copy social trends well. The Comics Code was a conservative stabilizing force, which held many of the 1960s era liberal agendas at bay. While a number of creators and publishers had complained, there had been no serious challenges to the code since the comic book industry enacted it in 1954. By 1971, the Comics Code had become so archaic that it was often comical. In 1969, DC Comics had to ask for approval in order to credit writer Marv Wolfman in *House of Secrets* #83 because the code banned the use of wolfmen or werewolves.[18] The outdated code displayed how much American society had changed in less than two decades, but also represented the conservative values that many Americans wanted to retain at all costs. Although the CCA had many supporters and detractors, it would soon face its first major challenge. Surprisingly, this challenge against the conservative Comics Authority Code would be instigated by the United States government.

Just Say No to the Comics Code

In 1970, the U.S. Department of Health, Education, and Welfare wrote a letter to Marvel's editor-in-chief, Stan Lee, requesting that Marvel Comics produce an anti-drug comic book. The agency believed that Marvel could use its clout among adolescents and college students to help spread the message against drugs. Lee and artist Gil Kane created a story entitled "Green Goblin Reborn!" that showcases the negative consequences of drug use.[19] Marvel personnel submitted the story to the code's governing body, who ruled that because the CCA banned the depiction of drug use in comics even an anti-drug storyline could not be code approved. Marvel published the story without the Comics Code Authority's stamp of approval in three issues in *The Amazing Spider-Man* #96–98 from May to July 1971. The CCA governing board soon made changes that slightly liberalized the code but insured that at its heart the Comics Code remained essentially conservative.

Although the code was altered for the first time since its creation in 1954, it continued to be a restrictive agent for traditional values. Comic book historian Amy Kiste Nyberg argues that by not liberalizing the code, comic publishers squandered a chance to expand the medium. She writes, "Publishers were generally content with the status quo and unwilling to risk their economic health on experimentation that would challenge the public's perception of comic books."[20] The newly revised code allowed for moral ambiguity, a greater flexibility in presenting stories about corrupt politicians and policemen, alcohol and drug use, and the ability to display graphic depictions of violence, but the revamped code did not open up the field as many hoped it would. DC soon followed Marvel's lead and published a drug story in which Green Arrow's sidekick Speedy becomes a drug addict (which was now acceptable under the revamped code.) At the start of the 1970s the comics industry had an opportunity to rethink their creative code but chose to merely make cosmetic changes to the existing conservative structure. As many Americans were questioning the nation's political, social, and culture foundation, comic book publishers decided to only slightly change the status quo. The U.S. was changing but, like most Americans, comic book publishers and creators did not understand what these changes would be or for how long they would last.

The Good, the Bad, and the Ugly

As creators like Jack Kirby, Denny O'Neil, and Neal Adams attempted to push comic book storytelling boundaries, many DC Comics superhero tales remained clichéd, uninspired, or just plain unappealing. Most of DC's efforts to revitalize its line failed and stories quickly reverted to the conservative status quo. DC's new ideas were generally either rehashed versions of older stories or unfathomably bizarre characters and tales that left readers bewildered and unimpressed. These included *Superman's Pal Jimmy Olsen* #139 (July 1971) in which real life comedian Don Rickles appears as a costumed hero and battles cos-mic gangsters. *Superman* #249 (March 1971) introduces Terra-Man, a cowboy armed with alien weaponry who rides a winged horse, and luckily fights a Superman who is powerless due to sixth solar cycle Kryptonian sorrow. Wonder Woman stars in issue #203 (December 1972) of her self-titled series in which the cover proclaims it to be a "women's lib issue." This story ends with a powerless karate fighting version of the Amazonian princess helping to close down a department store, which leaves numerous women unemployed and angry. As DC was mostly producing reheated leftovers, Marvel was continuing to create liberal-leaning stories that incorporated topical issues that did not directly challenge core conservative social values. Spider-Man, Daredevil and Captain America all appeared in stories that addressed social issues like Vietnam protesting, racial inequality, and draft dodging. While the heroes sometimes fought crooked businessmen and right-wing politicians, the creators attempted to develop storylines that did not offend too many conservative readers while appealing to the core youth audience. Marvel superheroes still seemed to be in touch with young readers while most DC comics appeared to be outdated. The U.S. was quickly changing, though, and both publishers would have to evolve or suffer the consequences.

Nixon's America

The 1970s had begun with many Americans attempting to redefine their society by questioning a number of social understandings and institutions and endeavoring to determine how the country should function both in the present and the future. As the decade progressed, new problems and situations challenged the notion of what it meant to be an American. The country's conservative core demonstrated its power when a large percentage of the populace elected Richard Nixon to a second term in 1972. Nixon had previously termed his supporters the "silent majority" and believed that his overwhelming victory over Democratic challenger George McGovern proved that most of the nation shared his conservative ideology. Nixon's victory would be short lived, though, because he had already set into motion events that would ensure that he would not finish his presidential term. Although Nixon's election seemed to confirm a change in American politics and life that might have brought about stability and a new social direction, this was not to be. Both Richard Nixon and the United States were soon to be engulfed in scandal and recrimination. People who were unsure about American society's direction would be further pushed towards bitterness and acrimony.[21]

Things Fall Apart

On June 17, 1972, five men were arrested for breaking into the Democratic National Committee headquarters at the Watergate office complex in Washington, D.C. The press soon learned that the men had ties to Richard Nixon and that the burglars has been paid with money from Nixon's re-election campaign in an attempt to gain information that could help solidify his re-election. The men were hired and paid through a convoluted system of back channels but eventually the burglary order and the payments were traced to people inside the Nixon White House. Many politicians, newspersons, and the general public at large began to question if Nixon knew about the break-in. The Watergate Scandal (as it came to be known) quickly became a national obsession as new and more damaging news continually surfaced. By April 1973, the scandal was becoming so politically threatening that Nixon had to ask for the resignation of two of his top aides, H.R. Haldeman and John Ehrlichman, along with White House Counsel John Dean. Later, audio tapes of White House conversations recorded only a few days after the burglary revealed that Nixon knew about the break-in and supported a cover-up. Richard Nixon resigned as president of the United States on August 9, 1974. By this time the scandal had been growing for well over two years. Months earlier the House of Representatives had begun impeachment investigations and all evidence indicated that if proceedings were held President Nixon would be impeached. When Nixon stepped down in August 1974, Vice President Gerald Ford became the new president.[22]

The Watergate Scandal had dominated the headlines, but a number of other events also changed American society during this period. A peace agreement was reached with Vietnam in January 1973 and the U.S. troops were quickly pulled out, practically ending the war, although the last American military and governmental personnel would not leave Vietnam until April 1975. Vice President Spiro T. Agnew had stepped down in October 1973 because of questionable financial dealings, becoming the first vice president in U.S. history to resign. During 1973 and 1974, OPEC members created an oil embargo that cut oil supplies across the world and caused shortages and price increases. This in turn was most likely one of the catalysts for the stock market crash and recession that gripped the country during 1973 and 1974. Making matters even worse, the recession produced high inflation with increased unemployment a rare and miserable economic condition known as stagflation. By the end of 1974, a nation that started the 1970s with an identity crisis now had witnessed the disgrace and downfall of a U.S. president, oil shortages and massive gas price increases, and an immense economic recession. U.S. citizens now suffered though political, social, cultural, and economic hard times. The decade may have had a difficult beginning but by the end of 1974 things seemed to have fallen apart.[23]

Rethinking the All-American Hero

As society was filled with turmoil in 1973–1974, the comic book industry felt the effects of this turbulent period in numerous ways. DC writers and artists continued to produce a mixture of rehashed old ideas and bizarre new creations, but watched as their sales stayed stagnant. Marvel creators, on the other hand, were authoring numerous new storylines that seemed to resonate with their young audience and a large portion of society in general. Marvel began publishing stories that questioned modern American beliefs and life, and by early 1973 Captain America was wondering what his place was in society. As people were questioning the government, institutions, and most parts of American life, Captain America served as their proxy. Cap no longer could accept the traditional order of American life in which he had long believed. The red, white, and blue-clad hero did not know who he could trust and began to not even trust himself. In *Captain America* #153–156, Steve Rogers, the true World War II Captain America who was frozen in ice and then recovered in the 1960s, fights the 1950s Commie Smasher Captain America. The 1950s Captain America changed his name to Steve Rogers, altered his face to look like Rogers, and donned the costume during the real Steve Rogers' absence. Although the story is complicated, it basically allowed Steve Englehart to write a tale in which the real Steve Rogers faces a deformed 1950s version of himself and all that Captain America stands for. The false Captain America is a representation of the 1950s and thus embodies the decade's fears and weaknesses. The 1950s Cap is still overcome with Red Scare paranoia and his anti-communist agenda is laced with racism and xenophobia. He also displays the overly aggressive and overconfident nature of the postwar America. The two Captain Americas fight and as expected, the real Steve Rogers wins. Rogers internalizes the battle, though, and wonders what wrongs he is responsible for and what flaw he also has. Cap thinks, "I've never fought the evil side of my own nature. And that's what he is, after all — a man who began with the same dreams I did — and ended as an insane, bigoted superpatriot. He is what he is because he admired me — wanted to copy me. In a very real way, I'm responsible for all the evil he's done."[24]

In this fight, the real Captain America not only battles an impostor, but also fights against himself and what he could have become or might one day be. He serves as the changing introspective hero of a nation that is questioning itself and attempting to determine how to proceed. Past heroes, like the 1950s Captain America, were deeply self-assured and almost never self-questioning or changing. They, often like the nation itself, believed that they knew best and relied on their basic rock solid beliefs as guidance. By the end of 1972, this national self-assuredness was quickly becoming a thing of the past. As the country fought seemingly unnecessary wars, society had changed dramatically in only a few short years. As core values and ideals could no longer be trusted, a large number of citizens had become disenfranchised and begun to question every part of American life. Captain America was following the nation's lead and as a symbol of America he had begun to question not only the country but also himself.

The Disenfranchisement of Captain America

In early 1973, Captain America was fighting against himself and questioning his choices, motives, and desires. In the coming years, as Americans became more jaded and critical of their country, Captain America began to battle evils within the United States, including foes inside the American government. Beginning in July 1973, Captain America starred in a multi-part story in which he combats a mysterious organization known as the Secret Empire. The long storyline ran from *Captain America and the Falcon* #163–176 and follows the hero as he learns of the secret organization that operates within the U.S. government. Eventually Cap and his partner Falcon infiltrate the Secret Empire and learn that the group is attempting to take over the U.S. and even create a superhero named Moonstone to replace Captain America. At the story's conclusion, good ultimately triumphs over evil and Captain America defeats Moonstone in a battle on the White House lawn. The Secret Empire's leader, Number One, witnesses the fight and runs into the Oval Office, where Captain America captures and unmasks him. The reader never sees Number One's face but learns that he is a powerful government official who wants to take total control of the United States. Knowing that Captain America has stopped the domination plan, Number One shoots himself and dies.[25] Captain America has won again and good has triumphed over evil.

In the past this story would have ended with Captain America's victory and it would have emphasized the safety and dependability that he brings to the nation. Because this final part of the story was published in 1974 and reflected the nation's mood, it did not end on such a high note and instead left readers with deeper questions to ponder about their country and themselves.

From Captain to Nomad

Although Captain America defeated the villainous Secret Empire and watched their leader commit suicide in the White House, he had achieved a hollow victory at best. Writer Steve Engelhart was clearly basing Secret Empire members on people within the Nixon administration. The most obvious parallel is clearly that Number One is President Nixon, which Engelhart himself admitted in later interviews.[26] In this story, Captain America defeats a megalomaniacal madman bent on world domination. This is a seemingly monthly occurrence in comic books and would not normally warrant a second glance. What is unusual is that the evil organization was based on the then current administration and the main villain, who commits suicide, mirrors the president of the United States. In the past, creating a villain based upon the president would have been unthinkable, but the Vietnam conflict, Watergate, and a series of other social problems and complications had so badly disillusioned such a large number of American citizens that it had become acceptable to treat the commander in chief as First Villain.

Even more remarkable is what Captain America decides to do after destroying the Secret Empire and defeating Number One. In the past, the triumphant hero would have reveled in a job well done and would have moved on to his next battle; 1974's Captain America decided to quit. Learning the president of the United States is a supervillain drives Steve Rogers to discard his identity as Captain America. Instead he chooses to fight crime as Nomad, the man without a country. Captain America has lost his faith in himself and his country and chooses to no longer represent the United States. For the next six issues, the country-less Nomad/Steve Rogers attempts to understand American society. As Steve Rogers casts aside his Captain America identity in issue number 176, he notes, "The government created me in 1941—created me to act as their agent in protecting our country, and over the years I've done my best. I did things I'm not proud of, but I always tried to serve my country well. And I find the government serving itself.... I'm the one who's seen everything Captain America fought for become a cynical sham."[27]

Although Steve Rogers would regain his Captain America identity before too long, his quitting made a clear and powerful statement. Things were going terribly wrong in the United States and even the nation's protector and masked symbol could not ignore society's ills. Steve Rogers was so disillusioned with his country that he could no longer be Captain America, and unfortunately many Americans understood the feeling all too well.

The Day the Music Died

In June/July 1973, Marvel Comics published a Spider-Man story that gripped fans and expressed the era's hopelessness. The Gerry Conway–penned "The Night Gwen Stacy Died" and "The Green Goblin's Last Stand," published in *The Amazing Spider-Man* #121–122, contained a major event in Spider-Man's life that still resonates with many Spidey fans decades later. In the story, Spider-Man's arch enemy, the Green Goblin, attempts to make the web-head's life miserable by targeting those close to him. The Green Goblin kidnaps Spider-Man's girlfriend, Gwen Stacy, and throws her off a bridge tower, forcing Spider-Man to attempt to save her. Spider-Man shoots his webbing and uses it to catch Gwen's legs as she falls. Spidey yanks the web and pulls Gwen upward to him, believing that he has saved her life. He soon realizes that Gwen is dead and it is unclear whether it was the fall or Spider-Man's rescue attempt that killed her.[28]

This story marked one of the first times that a main character was permanently killed in a major superhero comic book. (Permanently killed sounds redundant, but it should be remembered that many comic book characters "die" and then are resurrected.) Spider-Man now has to mourn the loss of his lover and also carry the guilt of possibly having caused her death. This kind of gritty realism was new to superhero comic books and reflected the current dark period in American society. The story's writer, Gerry Conway, noted the connection between the U.S.'s social and political ills and the story's dark subject matter. In a 2009 interview Conway stated,

> We were in the midst of a real crisis of ideals. We were being disillusioned at every turn. There's a feeling of futility to life and yet you still had to go on.... Thousands of kids were being killed in Vietnam. People were dying in the streets in riots. We had a president who was being drummed out of office for committing illegal acts. You know, it was a horrific time and I think that story sort of reflected it. It was the first time that that particular fatalism, I guess, had been addressed in comics.[29]

When Gwen Stacy died in *The Amazing Spider-Man* #121 it signified the end of Spider-Man's innocence and reflected a society that also was becoming disillusioned and jaded. Many Americans felt that their core social and cultural ideals had been destroyed and they no longer knew what to believe or who to believe in. Comic book superheroes were also facing new and more troubling situations as their worlds became more threatening and bleak. Comic book heroes and villains were now forced to live in a darker, grittier world and many found themselves becoming unhappy, disenchanted, and cynical because of it.

Prez and Other Strange Ideas

While Marvel was creating stories that questioned American society and mirrored the nation's weary state, DC was attempting to appeal to younger readers but also wished to remain traditionally grounded. This odd mixture of progressive and traditional led to a variety of new concepts and stories — some good, some bad, and most very strange. While Marvel characters like Captain America and Iron Man battled against real life social menaces, few DC characters, besides the Green Lantern–Green Arrow team-up, took on social and political problems. Most DC stories focused on evil supervillains and imaginary problems, while many Marvel tales referenced real world troubles. Jack Kirby continued to create new comic book stories based on past ideas merged with futuristic visions. Kirby's Fourth World stories were coming to an end and he began working on his new creations, Kamandi and the Sandman. Kamandi, billed as the "last boy on Earth," premiered in his self-titled comic book in November 1972. The character, who was one of the last humans in a future world ruled by intelligent animals, was quite similar to a Kirby story from 1957's *Alarming Tales* #1 and the 1968 film *Planet of the Apes*.[30] Kirby's Sandman uses a 1940s hero's name but creates a new character that fights within dreams against a computerized menace in order to defend our fragile reality.

While Kirby's ideas were generally futuristic refashionings of older concepts, a non–Kirby DC series, written by the King's former *Captain America* partner Joe Simon, attempted to create something altogether new. In September 1973, *Prez* #1 featured 18-year-old Prez Rickard, "the first teenage President of the U.S.A."[31] Before the series was cancelled after four issues, the young president appointed his mother vice president, battled against crooked politicians, evil chess players, handicapped vampires, and a right-wing militia, while selecting a shirtless Native American who lived in a cave to be the new FBI director. Although Prez's plots seem laughable to current readers, the storylines were DC's misguided attempt to appeal to young readers. Much like most other Americans, DC creators and heroes were trying to understand the country and what was changing and going wrong. Unlike Marvel, DC appears to often have misjudged the nation's mood and created a number of comics that were out of step with American society. As the nation struggled against hard times, the major comic book companies attempted to reflect American society and provide heroes to help in the struggle. The stories they choose reveal much about the publishers and the country. While Marvel was creating comic books stories that focused on a villainous version of the real life president, DC was creating a campy teenaged leader.

Falling into a Malaise

On July 15, 1979, U.S. President Jimmy Carter delivered a soon to be famous speech in which he stated that Americans were "losing faith" in the country and had developed a "crisis of confidence." Carter stated, "It is a crisis that strikes at the very heart and soul and spirit of our national will. We can see this crisis in the growing doubt about the meaning of our own lives and in the loss of a unity of purpose for our nation."[32] President Carter's assessment of American society was sound, although it would prove to be a political liability in the 1980 presidential election. The nearly five years between Richard Nixon's August 1974 resignation and Carter's speech had produced numerous problems and challenges that left many Americans both weary and apathetic. While the 1970s began with many Americans questioning the 1960s liberal changes and rethinking society's direction, it ended with a beaten and bloodied nation reeling from a nightmarish decade — a decade that had seen a contentious conflict's end, witnessed a president's fall, and contained energy crises and economic hardships. It is little wonder that President Carter believed that Americans were battling a crisis of confidence. With all of the adversities that the nation had faced in the previous ten years, it would have been unusual if the people of the nation had not grown more cynical and jaded.

Difficult Times

Although Americans' crisis of confidence started before the Watergate scandal, Nixon's disreputable and possibly criminal activities debilitated many citizens' trust of and belief in the U.S. and its government. Many hoped that President Nixon's August 1974 resignation would allow the nation to move on from the protracted Watergate scandal. The new president, Gerald Ford, quickly pardoned Nixon of all crimes, in order to save Americans the distraction of watching their former leader being prosecuted. Although Ford and others wanted to move on, Watergate had deeply injured the American psyche in a manner that could not quickly be healed. Americans had lost faith in their government and this would not be easily restored. Coupled with the Watergate trauma was the more than decade-long conflict in Vietnam.[33] In April 1975, North Vietnamese forces captured the city of Saigon, following the evacuation of U.S. personnel from the area. North and South Vietnam were soon united under communist control. By the end of 1975, the Watergate Scandal and the U.S.'s military involvement in Vietnam were over, but these twin terrors would remind Americans of dreams lost and hopes dashed. Nonetheless other matters would soon take center stage. In 1976, Americans would commemorate the nation's bicentennial, but the country's ongoing crises dampened the celebration.[34]

Red, White, and Black and Blue

The United States entered 1976 as a nation scarred by old disappointments and fearful of new tribulations. As the shadow of Watergate and Vietnam hung over the country, Americans worried about energy crises, oil shortages, unemployment, crime, inflation, and the loss of identity. So, a wounded nation afraid of the future turned to the past and celebrated the two hundredth anniversary of the Declaration of Independence's signing. The Bicentennial, as the celebration was popularly known, focused on the U.S.'s mythologized past and presented a vividly sunny vision of both the nation's present and future. Many Americans reveled in the past and dreamed of a better future, while others just reflected on the increased misery around them. As the nation spent the year celebrating both its founding and its future, it also prepared to elect a new president. Gerald Ford had taken office after Richard Nixon's resignation and had captured neither the American public's hearts nor its imagination. Ford immediately upset much of the American populace when he quickly pardoned Nixon for any Watergate related crimes. The president rapidly became known for his ineptitude and was the butt of jokes, including Chevy Chase's scathing *Saturday Night Live* impressions. President Ford soon became a metaphor for the time, a bumbling, ineffectual leader for an incompetent nation that had lost its way.[35] By the end of the 1976, Jimmy

Carter was elected the 39th president of the United States and Americans hoped for a better four years than the ones before. Unfortunately, this wish would not come true and the nation would have to endure several more years of problems and sacrifices.

Mid-Decade Superheroes

As comic book superheroes entered the decade's middle years, Marvel continued to embrace socially significant stories that often featured a liberal message and DC attempted to reuse old ideas in new ways while providing mostly escapist fare. One the most visible examples of Marvel's growing liberalism was Iron Man and his alter ego, Tony Stark. Stark's early appearances (and even Iron Man's origin) presented him as a conservative businessman who was staunchly anti-communist and a great supporter of the U.S.'s involvement in Vietnam. In his first appearances in 1963, Stark was a wealthy American who firmly believed that the U.S. military must win the Vietnam conflict in order to protect the world from communist forces. Because Iron Man's origins were so decidedly right-wing, nationalistic, and pro–U.S. policy in Vietnam, his stories and his identity changed greatly during the late 1960s and early to mid 1970s. A 1975 Iron Man story showcases Tony Stark's growing disillusionment with U.S. foreign policy in Vietnam and displays massive changes in the industrialist's beliefs and character. The story in *Iron Man* #78 (September 1975) entitled "Long Time Gone" exhibits how much Stark has changed since his early pro-war days. In his Iron Man persona, Stark witnesses war atrocities and wonders how U.S. policymakers can allow these things to happen. Stark questions the military, the U.S. government, and American society itself. It is an amazing transformation for a hero who a few years earlier was a conservative hawk whose superheroing exploits mainly consisted of fighting communists and trumpeting the righteousness of the Vietnam war effort. In the "Long Time Gone" story Stark regrets the people who were killed with the weapons he manufactured and promises to "avenge those whose lives have been lost through the ignorance of men like the man I once was."[36]

Stark, the stereotypical Cold Warrior, dramatically changed his view of the Vietnam conflict and of the U.S.'s role in the world. Although he is only one of many Marvel heroes, his transformation is emblematic of changes within the publisher's stories. Marvel superheroes were becoming disillusioned and were questioning the very basis of American society, a trend that mirrored many Americans' experiences. In 1976, Marvel heroes, like a large number of Americans, celebrated the nation's bicentennial but many things had changed. It was no longer easy to blindly trust the nation's leaders and to believe that things would only get better. Americans and Marvel heroes were still proud of the U.S. but they were also angry and disillusioned with it, a potent mix that overlaid much misery and anguish.

DC Heroes — Keeping the Comic in Comic Books

As Marvel heroes were questioning the nation's leaders and policies while trying to define their relationship to the state, DC's heroes were attempting to entertain the masses and working to make readers forget about some of the nation's problems. Although DC heroes fought against many current problems and social ills, these characters did not have the same disillusionment and anger that permeated many of the Marvel heroes. A few DC stories, like those in the short-lived *Green Lantern/Green Arrow* series, presented heroes that questioned authority and expressed mistrust of the government, but most DC superheroes remained conservative guardians of the state. DC creators tried to make Superman hipper by giving him a new wardrobe and a television reporter job, but the Man of Steel remained a conservative symbol of authority. Batman became grittier and more hardcore but he still did not question the nation's leadership or its direction. While DC heroes worked hard to keep up with the times, at their very bases they were conservative, trusting agents of the state who could not bring themselves to question authority even if many others were.

After a paper shortage pushed DC to raise prices and cut the pages per comic book, the publisher introduced 16 new titles in 1975.[37] These titles included a re-envisioning of the Greek heroes Hercules and Atlas, a product of the martial arts craze named Richard Dragon, Kung-Fu Fighter, cavemen Tor and Kong the Untamed, sword and sorcery characters Claw the Unconquered, Stalker, and the Warlord, and a Marvel co-produced adaption of the *Wizard of Oz*. September 1975 witnessed the first issue of *Batman Family*, which featured a number of reprints and a new story in which Batgirl and Robin team up to battle the evil duo of Benedict Arnold and Satan. In the issue the team fights a revived Arnold for both their lives and their country.[38] This fantastical yet nationalistic law and order centered story could easily have been written in the 1950s and has little to connect it to the 1970s' social and political disillusionment. While Marvel was producing stories about the growing cultural backlash, DC was attempting to entertain its readers and make them forget about their troubles. At their cores Marvel was still the status quo-challenging outsider while DC was ever the conservative proponent of the status quo. Although both tried to adjust to the times, the two companies in many ways only remained what they always were.

The End Is Near

After their celebratory bicentennial year Americans had to return to business as usual in 1977. Unfortunately, business as usual depressed and disheartened many American citizens. The economy was struggling, people still suffered post–Watergate hostilities towards the government and political leaders, the Vietnam conflict continued to haunt Americans' minds, and for the first time in a long time a large number of citizens were not optimistic about the nation's future. President Carter attempted to restore the public's faith in the nation but had great difficulty changing hearts and minds. In January 1977, Carter pardoned most Vietnam draft evaders in hopes that the people of the nation could move on and no longer be constantly troubled by the conflict. This action resulted in a national debate regarding a citizen's responsibility and the country's commitment.[39]

In July 1977, New York City suffered a two day blackout that seemed to symbolize the problems facing the nation. The city was already nearly bankrupt due to the ongoing recession, causing the local government to cut numerous social services. These cutbacks also had hampered the city's efforts to fight crime and preserve New York's infrastructure. The blackout, along with street crime, economic hardships, and the serial killer David Berkowitz (known as the Son of Sam), greatly harmed New York's self-image and the city's reputation. It also forced already disillusioned Americans to rethink their understanding of themselves and their country. The U.S.'s largest and most prominent city seemed to be a lawless crime-ridden ghetto that had fallen into disrepair so badly that it could no longer govern itself.[40] If New York, arguably the nation's greatest city, had turned into a rotten shell of its former self then what would become of the country as a whole? A decade already filled with bad news seemed to consistently produce only more dreadful headlines. A beaten and battered American people continued to battle a nightmarish decade of which two years still remained.

The Malaise Intensifies

In 1978, the social and cultural malaise continued to burden the nation as unemployment rates rose, the dollar lost value, and relations with the Soviet Union deteriorated. Increased Cold War tensions forced many already weary Americans to add World War III and nuclear holocaust to their already lengthy laundry list of daily concerns. These fears and horrors only strengthened in 1979 as economic and political pressures blended to create a bitter and unstable social cocktail. In March 1979, citizens learned that an accident had occurred at the Three Mile Island Nuclear Generating Station in Pennsylvania. Due to mechanical failures, nuclear reactor coolant escaped from the station causing an emergency evacuation. Though officials declared that the accident posed no threat to the populace, Three Mile Island became a rallying cry for anti-nuclear activists and added yet another worry to many citizens' ever growing inventories.[41]

Citizens' attentions also turned to the Middle East as Iran was experiencing turmoil that affected not only its society, but also the U.S. and the entire world. During 1978 and 1979, demonstrators protested Iranian leader Shah Mohammad Reza Pahlavi, citing opposition to his domestic and foreign policies. This movement that would eventually become known as the Islamic Revolution ousted the Shah on January 16, 1979, and ushered in an Islamic state in which leaders like Ayatollah Khomeini and Iranian citizens expressed anti–American sentiments. By early 1979 television news was replete with images of Iranians burning American flags and labeling the U.S. as the "Great Satan."[42]

More importantly at home, the events in Iran and President Carter's reaction to them lowered the amount of Iranian oil exported to the U.S. and raised prices considerably. Panicked Americans began hoarding gasoline and the U.S. soon found itself in an energy crisis. The U.S. faced gasoline shortages, long lines at the pump, and the fear of a world without enough fuel.[43] By mid–1979, the U.S. had entered another period of high inflation and unemployment, increased energy prices and shortages burdened many, the threat of nuclear annihilation remained omnipresent, crime and violence seemed to run rampant, the government appeared to be corrupt and ineffectual, foreign citizens burned Old Glory while insulting Americans, and the future seemed as bleak as the present. No wonder President Carter believed that Americans had lost faith in the nation and themselves. A large number of citizens read the newspaper each day and wondered how things could possibly get worse. Unfortunately, a lot could and would happen before the decade's conclusion.

Ayatollah in Iran, Russians in Afghanistan

As the decade limped towards its finish line, it still offered several difficult challenges for the American people. On November 4, 1979, a group of radical students and militants seized the U.S. Embassy in Tehran, Iran, and took a number of American citizens hostage. The crisis would last well over a year and some of the Americans would not gain their freedom until January 1981.[44] After witnessing Vietnamese forces overrunning the U.S. Embassy in Saigon only a few years before, many Americans were disheartened and saddened by the tragic events in Tehran. Twice within the decade foreign forces had desecrated American embassies and mocked the United States. This time militants had taken numerous Americans hostage and there appeared to be little that the American government could do to help. Only a few years earlier, Americans would have thought it impossible that their nation could seem so helpless and impotent. Every night network television news programs like *Nightline* would remind viewers that the U.S. government and military was unable to free the hostages and thus were powerless to keep the nation safe.

As many Americans ruminated on the country's apparent weakness, the Soviet Union's leadership took steps to immediately increase Cold War tensions. On December 27, 1979, the U.S.S.R. invaded the Central Asian country of Afghanistan. Although most Americans knew little and cared even less about Afghanistan, the invasion showcased strong Soviet aggression, and to many the military action seemed to signal the start of an offensive aimed at spreading communism. American political and military leadership agreed with pundits and journalists in expressing outrage and fear at the Soviet hostility. The Soviet military would stay in Afghanistan for over nine years and the invasion would dramatically strain U.S.-Soviet relations for years to come.[45] This late December 1979 invasion dramatically capped the 1970s and provided yet another worry for an already stressed and overburdened American people.

Heroes Sandwiched

Marvel continued to focus on social themes and publish superhero stories that outsold their counterpart at DC. After falling behind Marvel in sales and creativity, DC's new publisher, Jenette Kahn, turned to a number of methods for reinvigorating the company. In 1977, DC increased a comic book's price to thirty-five cents an issue while shrinking the story content to 17 pages. The publisher also introduced 20 new titles in 1977, appearing to flood the market with new heroes and stories. During 1977 and 1978, one of DC's main strategies was to poach talent from Marvel and hire these artists and writers to create new Marvel-like adventures for DC heroes. Former Marvel creators Gerry Conway, Steve Ditko, and Steve Englehart added Marvel-style realism to titles such as *Detective Comics, Shade, the Changing Man, Justice League of America, Mister Miracle,* and *Steel, the Indestructible Man.*[46] As DC "Marvelized" a number of its titles, it also continued to produce more conservative fare in titles such as *Superman, Wonder Woman,* and *DC Comics Presents.* Additionally, DC undertook numerous new projects that incorporated changing social notions. In April 1977, DC introduced Black Lightning, the company's first major black hero.[47] Marvel had already the established the African hero Black Panther and black American heroes the Falcon and Luke Cage.[48] Writer Tony Isabella created Black Lightning and dissuaded DC editors from publishing a potentially offensive character known as the Black Bomber. (The Black Bomber was a white racist military veteran who had been exposed to chemical weapons while serving in Vietnam. As a result, during times of stress he turned into a black superhero.[49]) In an unusual move, in March 1978, DC published a story in which Superman and Muhammad Ali team up to save the Earth from warmonger space invaders. The two champions create an elaborate ruse involving an interstellar boxing match and eventually outsmart a tyrannical alien.[50] Much like the country as a whole, DC seemed willing to try anything to pull itself out of its malaise — old ideas, new ideas, and even strange ideas.

Unfortunately, just as the nation was facing an increasing number of problems, DC also had a catastrophe looming on the horizon. The DC Implosion was coming and there was little the publisher could do to prevent it.

The DC Implosion

During the summer of 1978, DC Comics suffered a catastrophic series of events that became known as the "DC Implosion." Between 1975 and 1978, DC created 57 new comic book titles in an effort to increase the publisher's market share. This expansion was advertised as the "DC Explosion," and the company coupled the line extension with a cover price increase from 35 to 50 cents and story volume enhancement from 17 to 25 pages.[51] In an editorial, publisher Jenette Kahn stated that the publisher was giving readers a chance to read more superheroes while getting "a 47% gain in story, for a 43% raise in price" and increasing distribution.[52]

The DC Explosion promptly blew up in DC's theoretical face. Unfortunately, the 1977–1978 winter was one of the worst in memory for the entire country and the East Coast in particular suffered through bitter cold and several blizzard-like storms. This bad weather played havoc with comic book shipping and sales. Several entire comic book shipments were never made and the comic books that were delivered suffered an enormous drop in sales as many people were stranded inside and worried about purchasing life's necessities instead of superhero tales.[53] Marvel also suffered greatly during this decline, but DC's large and rapid expansion left the company in a precarious position. DC executives ordered that the number of comic books be drastically cut and soon the company cancelled 65 comic book titles, giving the publisher eight fewer than before the start of the DC Explosion. For obvious reasons this publishing carnage became known as the DC Implosion and left DC beaten and battered. Much like the nation, the publisher had suffered greatly and was now unsure how to move forward. Both the country and the company were trying to regroup but it was unclear what the future would hold.

Decade's End

As the 1970s ended DC and Marvel's superheroes faced what Jimmy Carter had termed "a crisis of confidence." The events of the last few years had dramatically transformed the nation and most of these changes were less than positive. In 1979, DC published a vastly reduced number of comic books and most of what the company did print proved conservative and formulaic. DC had attempted to revamp and expand its lineup and had failed and in 1979 the publisher seemed content to mostly recreate old concepts and ideas. Although Marvel had also suffered setbacks and losses during the preceding years, the company continued to produce several fan favorite titles, including writer Chris Claremont and artist John Byrne's *X-Men*. Many of Marvel's stories kept featuring real world problems and socially relevant storylines. One important and well-remembered story from the period is the Iron Man tale "Demon in a Bottle." This storyline appeared in *The Invincible Iron Man* #120–128 from March to November 1979 and spotlighted Tony Stark's gradual disintegration that symbolically emulated the nation's plight. During this story, Tony Stark begins to lose control of his Iron Man armor as it suffers numerous apparent malfunctions, seemingly kills a foreign ambassador, is forced to resign as the leader of the Avengers, is required to relinquish the Iron Man armor to the police, is kidnapped by one of his foes, and develops a severe drinking problem. Stark, the wealthy industrialist who began his career as a conservative crime fighter, mirrored many of the nation's changes during the late 1960s and early 1970s. The patriotic traditionalist at the beginning of the decade was transformed into a weary citizen who questioned both himself and American society and watched much of what he once held dear slip away. Although Stark regains his armor and hero status by the end of the "Demon in a Bottle" storyline, it is apparent that he, like many Americans, can never return to his past life.[54] At decade's end Tony Stark and other Marvel heroes were symbols of what Americans once were and what they had become. The energetic, self-assured industrialist had become a depressed, self-loathing alcoholic just as a once confident nation had become a self-questioning society. The 1970s were concluding and most Americans, both superpowered and not, were happy to see the decade's end.

Iron Man's "Demon in a Bottle" storyline (1979) presents Tony Stark's battle with his alcohol addiction and other personal problems. Iron Man's struggles showcased a new level of superhero reality and mirrored the internal and external problems that many Americans faced. (© 1979 Marvel Comics. All Rights Reserved.)

Conclusion

The 1970s marked the end of the conservative values of the 1950s and the idealism of the 1960s. The decade started with many Americans trying to come to terms with the dramatic changes that had occurred during the 1960s. As the nation attempted to clarify its social and cultural organization and merge traditional values with new political and social institutions, unforeseen problems and challenges appeared. World-altering events literally changed how most citizens saw themselves and the world around them. The Vietnam War, the Kent State Massacre, Watergate, the energy crisis, stagflation, the Iranian hostage crisis, and many other events and situations soon turned the 1970s into a nightmarish decade.

Superheroes also suffered during the long decade. With a few noteworthy exceptions, DC's heroes mostly continued to star in reconditioned versions of standard conservative tales. Alternatively, Marvel heroes generally emulated the nation and became darker and more jaded. Both DC and Marvel produced superhero stories that were a product of the time. Many DC stories noted the confusion that a majority of Americans felt and showcased a lack of understanding about new social and cultural standards that pervaded American society. Marvel's heroes channeled the fear and anger that permeated society, and the creators crafted super humans that shared the same nightmares. The 1970s tested U.S. citizens' strength and resolve and proved to be a difficult decade for most. As the decade ended most Americans hoped for a brighter future but many, undoubtedly, feared the worst.

Chapter 7

SUPER-CONSERVATIVES AND
NEO-COWBOYS (1980–1989)

In Alan Moore and Dave Gibbons' 1986–1987 seminal comic book series *Watchmen*, a group of costumed heroes live in a dark and threatening world that is very different from the past sunny climes that had generally served as comic book environs. Although some DC and Marvel heroes had faced "real world" problems in the recent past, few heroes had before encountered such a psychologically and emotionally bleak landscape. During the course of the story, superheroes like Rorschach, Nite Owl, and Dr. Manhattan battle both internal problems and the dystopian American society's social ills, while attempting to learn how to exist in a world to which they no longer belong. Many Americans entered the 1980s feeling much like the *Watchmen* characters — people living in a place in which the established rules no longer make sense. Interestingly, many American citizens and comic book characters reacted in the same manner, they changed the rules. During the 1980s, Americans and superheroes alike altered their outlooks and their actions. Americans created a new national narrative and worked to regain some of their lost dignity and pride. Citizens turned both inward and outward and fashioned a decade excess, in which Americans were encouraged to simultaneously increase personal gain while reportedly helping the U.S. to grow and excel. American culture created a new understanding in which selfishness contributed to the greater good and personal overindulgence benefited society.

This re-creation of the American narrative is prominently featured in the decade's superhero stories as many comic book heroes mirrored American society and culture and embraced intemperance. Numerous comic book creators also welcomed the excess and refashioned a substantial number of superheroes to be far grittier and more violent. As Americans changed the nation's social and cultural narratives, comic book heroes followed suit. The 1980s would serve as a decade of re-creation and re-imagination. Historians and laypersons still argue about the validity of the decade's changes but few contest its importance. For good or ill, the United States transformed itself during the 1980s and the nation's heroes had little choice but to once again recreate themselves as well.

Livin' on a Prayer

After the severe problems of the 1970s, most Americans were happy to see the 1980s commence. Unfortunately, the decade's first year did not provide most citizens much relief, as the misery index continued to rise for much of the country. The year began with

Americans still being held hostage in Iran and Soviet troops attempting to capture territory in Afghanistan. It marked the last full year of Jimmy Carter's four year term and the president's chances for re-election seemed rather bleak. The unemployment rate in January 1980 was 6.3 percent and reached 7.8 percent by July, while the inflationary rate started the year at 13.9 percent and peaked in March at a staggering 14.76 percent.[1] These statistics showcase the country's poor economic conditions, which, coupled with the recent energy crisis, caused many Americans to despair. During the year, Carter launched a military attempt to rescue the American hostages in Iran (which failed miserably), ordered U.S. athletes to boycott the summer Olympics in Moscow to protest the Soviet invasion of Afghanistan, and suspended grain sales to the USSR as a further display of the U.S. government's displeasure with the Soviet leadership. Although Carter did take symbolic actions against the Soviet Union, he had gained the reputation of being weak and ineffectual and in November 1980 he lost a one-sided presidential election to Ronald Reagan. The new president-elect promised to repair the faltering economy and to restore the U.S. to its former position of prominence. After suffering through the last four years most Americans were ready for a change when Ronald Reagan took office on January 20, 1981. The Reagan Era had begun and Americans were anxious to see what was going to change.

Stranger in Town

Ronald Reagan's 1980 campaign emphasized a return to fiscal and military conservatism and stressed a break from the policies of the 1960s and 1970s. He stressed the notion of shrinking the federal government and increasing the importance of the private sector. Reagan believed that government was inefficient and that if tax rates were lowered business and industry would create more viable solutions than bureaucrats and politicians could. The new president promised to cut taxes and government spending, which would encourage economic growth and innovation. Likewise, Reagan intended to deregulate many industries, which he contended would allow the companies to thrive once freed from the unneeded government oversight. During his Republican National Convention speech Reagan stated, "Government is never more dangerous than when our desire to have it help us blinds us to its great power to harm us."[2]

While attempting to generally shrink the size of the rest of the U.S. government, the president also pushed to increase funding for and expand the size of the military. Reagan expressed the belief that a strong military would help the nation greatly at both home and abroad. The new leader coupled his desire to strengthen the military with a heightened anti-communist policy and a belief that U.S. policymakers should firmly oppose many of the Soviet Union's policies. Reagan believed that past politicians had appeased the U.S.S.R. instead of pressing for change. Many of Reagan's policies and initiatives were in stark contrast to President Carter's agenda and in truth Reagan was attempting to roll back many of the liberal gains that had been put into place since the New Deal era. Reagan was not only pressing for new laws and policies, but also a new way of viewing and understanding the nation. The new president envisioned a United States in which citizens created a greater good by looking out for their own best interests as individuals. Reagan believed that less government and fewer taxes would help Americans to help themselves and that a strong America is a good America.[3] These policies would set the tone for the decade to come and would have consequences that Reagan could never have foreseen.

New Attitude

When electing Ronald Reagan voters were not only seeking new policies and programs but also were looking for a new attitude. President Carter's low-key and high-brow style had alienated a large number of Americans and many citizens desired substantial change. The new leader provided a much different philosophy from Carter's often grey, dire, and intellectual persona. Reagan promised to use the presidential bully pulpit to remind Americans how great the country truly was. Even when situations were grim, the president would smile and proclaim that everything was going well, thus setting an example for citizens to believe in themselves and their country. Reagan was not only providing new political leadership but also emphasizing a sunny new outlook.[4] Americans did not have to wait very long for the sense of change that they were seeking from their new president.

Only a few minutes after Reagan took the oath of office, Iran released the 52 Americans that had been held hostage for over 14 months. Although reality was different from perception, many Americans saw this diplomatic breakthrough as proof that Reagan was a strong and capable leader who could succeed in situations where Jimmy Carter had failed. On March 30, a deranged assassin shot President Reagan in the chest and severely wounded Press Secretary James Brady. Reagan's quick recovery and his upbeat attitude only cemented his appeal for many Americans. A substantial number of citizens were yearning for a public figure to tell them how special and great they were as Americans and Reagan fulfilled this need, even when he himself was facing the aftermath of an assassin's bullet. Although the economy was still terrible, jobless rates continued to rise, inflation remained at absurd levels, tensions with the Soviet Union were elevated, and the American manufacturing sector was in crisis, many Americans began to believe that things would get better. In August, Reagan would fire over 11,000 striking air-traffic controllers, which would only strengthen his image as a tough-minded man of action. American voters had desired change and had replaced an intellectual with a cowboy. Although little of substance had changed during Reagan's first year, the world looked different for many Americans, but tough times were still ahead.

Don't Stop Believin'

While many Americans seemed to like and respect Ronald Reagan, the economy proved to be a consistent drag on his popularity and citizens' general outlooks. During Reagan's first year in office, 57 percent of Americans approved of the job he was doing but during 1982 his average approval rating had plummeted to 43 percent.[5] Much of this was undoubtedly due to the worsening economic recession; the unemployment rate continued to rise and by December 1982 the jobless rate was at 10.8 percent.[6] Although Reagan's public approval may have been relatively low and the economic news remained dismal, there was a sense that many citizens liked and trusted the man and thus would give him and his policies an opportunity before they passed judgment. The Gallup polling organization noted, "Surveys also indicate that the public has more confidence in Reagan than approval ratings of his performance would suggest. While only one third approve of the way he is handling the economy, close to half express some degree of confidence that he will do the right thing with regard to the economy."[7] Reagan projected a likeable personality and used his acting training to create a public persona that inspired trust and confidence. White House staffer David Gergen notes, "Reagan understood, better than anyone since de Gaulle, the dramatic and theatrical demands of national leadership."[8] As Reagan pressed for a number of tax cutting measures and conservative programs, he also stressed a renewed nationalism and an increased sense of individual and national importance. Many Americans had grown weary of the hardships and shame associated with the 1970s and wanted to feel good about themselves and their country again. Reagan presented a neo-conservative vision of a strong and prosperous United States with citizens that no longer had to be scared or embarrassed. Many Americans were ready to focus on themselves and thus supported Reagan's notions of strong individualism with less emphasis on the common good. Although the hard times were not over, Ronald Reagan was convincing many Americans to concentrate on themselves and worry less about the world around them.[9]

Do You Really Want to Hurt Me?

As the economy remained mired in a long-term recession and people continued to battle a crisis of confidence, the U.S. was still engaged in a heated Cold War rivalry with the Soviet Union and other communist countries. The U.S.S.R. was continuing to wage war in Afghanistan and many conservative Americans believed that communism was advancing across the globe. Ronald Reagan spoke forcefully about supporting freedom and democracy around the world and working to stop the perceived oppressive communist forces. This rhetoric combined with a large scale military build-up to create a sense of militarized nationalism. The Reagan administration encouraged ideas of American exceptionalism, while simultaneously stressing the horrific nature of the Soviet Union and other communistic countries. By perpetuating a dichotomy in which the U.S. was "good" and the Soviet Union was "bad," Reagan and his advisors attempted to revive many Americans' faltering sense of nationalism. In striving to return to a binary understanding of Cold War affairs and geopolitics, Reagan was reconstituting an enemy to rally many Americans against. This model would increase the power and desirability of the state and allow government officials to change longstanding social and political mores, an ironic notion for a president whose central political tenement was the desire for a smaller government.

As Reagan increased the military's size and publically took a tough stance against the Soviet Union, he supported anti-communistic groups and regimes in other places.[10] One of the most notable is the administration's support of anti-government forces known as the contras in Nicaragua and the invasion of Grenada in 1983. Reagan portrayed the Nicaraguan contras as freedom fighters that were battling for their basic liberties against a communistic government. The president did not involve U.S. troops in the Nicaraguan situation, but rather relied on strong rhetoric and questionable funding methods to back the contras.[11] This methodology was a prudent first step and was probably the only one available for a president who understood that many Americans were still reeling from the U.S. military's more than decade-long involvement in Vietnam.

In 1983, Reagan did send military service personnel to Grenada and Operation Urgent Fury quickly overwhelmed the tiny Caribbean island's defenders. Reagan ordered the U.S. military to invade Grenada to rescue numerous American medical students after a rebelled military coup overthrew the government. The president claimed that Grenada "was a Soviet-Cuban colony, being readied as a major military bastion to export terror and undermine democracy. We got there just in time."[12] Although this statement seems almost comical in retrospect, it does showcase Reagan's desire to spotlight and create enemies and to reinvigorate the military's image. If Reagan wanted to strengthen the military, he needed to emphasize outside threats, both real and perceived, and find ways to consistently present the military as strong and capable. The president believed that a vigilant nation with a capable military would be better prepared to grow and prosper, a policy that would have interesting political, social, and cultural consequences in the years to come.

Dream Warriors

As American society entered a transitional period during the early 1980s, comic book publishers and creators also strove to construct rejuvenated stories and ideas. Ronald Reagan was reformulating the American narrative and attempting to expand the ideals of individual self-importance, nationalism, and American exceptionalism. Reagan's notions of a smaller government and a larger military, and his use of strong words and actions in foreign affairs, would appear to be well-tailored for comic book stories. The president's cowboy-like characteristics are akin to the stereotypical superhero who believes that he understands better than the government how to create a stable and prosperous society. This clichéd superhero is the ultimate emblem of individualism that rarely chooses cooperation or diplomacy, but prefers to overpower his adversaries through a massive display of strength and physical superiority. These ostentatious superheroes are symbols of American exceptionalism and provide an enduring mythology that allows readers to bask in the nation's preeminence. Although many superheroes turned introspective and apologetic, like much of the nation's populace, during the 1960s and 1970s, the qualities of individualism, conflict resolution through strength and physical engagement, and American exceptionality remained at the characters' core. Reagan's America would seem to align with superheroes' historical characteristics and would allow many of those characters to return to their roots. The president, and many citizens, believed that the U.S. had lost its way during the 1970s and that the nation needed a new outlook based on traditional principles. If superheroes could follow this pattern then maybe the slumping comic book industry could bolster sales and increase reader interest. As the nation as a whole would soon learn, every change also produces a series of unintended consequences that transform ideas and understandings in unimagined ways. Many comic book heroes would return to their traditional roots during the 1980s, but in ways readers had never dreamed.

Closer to the Heart

Possibly the most important comic book related change during the 1980s did not take place in a story or even in a series of tales, but in the ways retailers bought and sold comic books. Since its earliest days, the medium had relied on newsstand sales as its primary method of distribution. On a magazine rack, comic books had to compete with a large variety of other print publications and more importantly, the proprietor probably had little interest in or understanding of comic books. Additionally, many retailers only stocked a small number of comic books because the profit margin for the higher priced magazines was much greater.[13] This meant that a seller likely did not have a complete stock of every comic book and probably did not carry many titles each month. Because of this, disappointed fans could not always get the comic books that they wanted, which drove sales down. High inflation and unemployment, the ongoing recession, the need to raise prices substantially during the 1970s, and inaccessibility caused comic book sales to plummet. The comic book industry was in trouble and needed a solution quickly.

An apparent resolution presented itself when Marvel and DC employees noticed that a number of stores devoted to selling comic books had opened in the last few years. These stores were generally owned by comic book fans who were knowledgeable retailers that stocked every title and catered to other comic book connoisseurs. This direct market distribution system allowed publishers to create an alternative business model in which fans could easily find the comic books that they were looking for. More importantly, this new system changed the general audience for which DC and Marvel created comics. As comic book publishers sold less of their wares at newsstands and more at direct market stores, editors no longer believed that the general reader was a ten-year-old boy reading his first issue, but rather an avid fan with a greater knowledge of the characters and past storylines. This audience transition greatly changed comic books storytelling and revolutionized the medium in ways that would have not been possible only a few years before.

Modern Day Cowboy

As direct market comic book stores opened across the United States, DC and Marvel began to slowly change the types of comic books that they produced. In the decade's early years most superheroes starred in customary stories in which they easily defeated villains and defended the status quo. The sales slump forced many creators to tell traditional tales in which good triumphs over evil and the American way of life prevails because these types of stories seemed recession proof. Most superhero stories, even Marvel tales, reinforced conservative values and understandings. These narratives were in touch with the Reagan agenda, even if the creators rarely attempted to stretch the medium's boundaries.

Interestingly, the industry began to change and grow not by becoming more liberal, as it had during the 1960s and 1970s, but by creating a new type of neo-conservative tale in which the superhero is the last force of good in an amoral and lawless society. In traditional narratives the hero stops criminals from damaging society's healthy status quo. In these new stories, society has become a den of immorality and criminal behavior and the superhero is the lone moral figure in a world that often does not want or respect him. In these modern pessimistically conservative stories, the criminals have already won and the superhero is often quixotically attempting to restore society to its perceived natural state. This negative social view spoke both to readers who believed that the liberal reforms of the 1960s and 1970s had damaged American society, and to citizens who distrusted Reagan's conservative changes and worried about their effects on the country. Comic book historian Bradford W. Wright notes the liberal viewpoint: "Once confident symbols of hope, superheroes now spoke to the paranoia and psychosis lurking behind the rosy veneer of Reagan's America."[14] After generally becoming more liberal during the 1960s and 1970s, superheroes were mostly growing more conservative during the 1980s. This was a new conservatism for a new era, though, one that could be a showcase of either liberal or conservative ideology depending on the creators and the storyline.

I Won't Back Down

One of the first and most powerful examples of the super-conservative hero surfaced in 1979 when writer Frank Miller and artist Klaus Janson revived the Marvel character Daredevil. The Man without Fear first appeared in 1964 and was revealed to be Matt Murdock, a visually impaired lawyer who gained super-sensory powers when radioactive waste blinded him. Miller's stories updated Daredevil and turned the hero into a deeply conflicted crime fighter who wages an external battle against crime while internally struggling to resolve his belief in the law with his unlawful crime fighting activities. Daredevil lives in a gritty, crime-ridden, amoral world in which his ultraviolent style of heroism is the only true form of justice. In Daredevil's New York City, the government fails to protect its citizens, average Americans no longer believe in law and justice, and only the enlightened individualist Daredevil can return society to its rightful state.

These ideas are closely related to Ronald Reagan's conservative agenda and present several elements of the super-conservative hero. Additionally, Miller's Daredevil stories typically featured extremely graphic and brutal violent acts. Violence had been a superhero staple since Superman's first appearance, but Miller ratcheted up the vicious content and often portrayed violence in a realistic manner rarely seen before in comic books. This intensified violence suggested the consequences of Reagan's strengthened military and toughened Cold War stance. In returning to traditional understandings and ideas but increasing the intensity, Miller followed one of the central tenets of 1980s cultural conservatism; the desire to amplify traditional values and create grotesquely configured new versions. Miller's Daredevil was one of the first of a series of 1980s super-conservative heroes that augmented and intensified long-established superhero tropes. These super-conservatives closely mirrored the changes in American society and showcased a nation quickly moving towards an extreme version of itself.

I'm Not the Man I Used to Be

Frank Miller's work on *Daredevil* created a new comic book industry standard of producing amplified traditional superheroes that other creators soon began to follow. In the stories, these super-conservative heroes were the last vestiges of justice and morality in a corrupt and immoral society (a view of post–1970s America with which many conservatives could identify). As Miller was producing *Daredevil*, the change from newsstand to direct market distribution was beginning to alter the industry and transform how creators told superhero tales.

One of the prototypes for this new understanding of comic books was *Camelot 3000*, a twelve issue DC series published from 1982 to 1985 in which King Arthur and his knights reawaken to battle aliens in the year 3000. Although the storyline at times now seems hokey and dated, *Camelot 3000* introduces many new concepts and ideas that changed comic books during the 1980s. The sword and sorcery-superhero-space adventure tale addresses political and social themes including racism, gay-lesbian-transgender issues, and the seemingly broken political system. The story's King Arthur and his knights are not the heightened super-conservatives that would soon become 1980s vogue, but the crusaders do act as moral and physical guardians in a corrupt and desperate society. What makes *Camelot 3000* exceptional is that it was one of the first comic books to fully suggest the medium's new potential. *Camelot 3000* was the first comic book published as a maxi-series, a limited series usually of eight to twelve issues. It was also one of the first DC comic books to be printed on high-quality paper, published without Comics Code Authority approval, produced and marketed for mature readers, and sold exclusively through comic book stores and not on newsstands.[15] The series was creator-owned, which meant that the writer and artist, Mike W. Barr and Brian Bolland, legally controlled what stories could be published in the future.[16]

This list of firsts displays changes that would take hold in the comic book industry within the coming decade. Historically comic book publishers had created ongoing juvenile stories, printed on cheap paper, hamstrung by the comics code, and owned entirely by the company. *Camelot 3000* allowed for the possibility that one day some comic books would be creator owned and controlled high quality literature published for adults. As superheroes were becoming more conservative, they also were becoming more serious and adult, a transition that would soon change not only the comic book industry but American society as a whole.

Super Freak

During the 1980s, Hollywood was producing extremely violent, conservative, successful action films and Ronald Reagan continued to press for amplified traditional values, while comic book publishers attempted to match both trends. Frank Miller's *Daredevil* had created a framework for a tortured ultra-violent hero and sales indicated that audiences clamored for super-conservative characters. Marvel embraced the era and gave fans not only a violent anti-hero, but also a killing machine. Wolverine first appeared in an issue of *The Incredible Hulk* in 1974 and had slowly gained popularity as a member of the X-Men and Alpha Flight. The anti-hero was a super-strong and agile mutant with a propensity for killing, who could quickly heal from almost any wound, and strongly disliked authority. Much of Wolverine/Logan's past was unknown, but what seemed to excite most fans was his ability to savagely kill scores of adversaries with his retractable claws. While most established superheroes embraced codes against killing, Wolverine shared no such moral qualms. The mutant showed little remorse or desire to work within the law as he violently judged and sentenced wrong-doers. The character's turning point came in 1982 when Chris Claremont wrote and Frank Miller drew a highly popular *Wolverine* four issue mini-series. In this storyline Wolverine is portrayed as a combination cowboy/samurai (although Logan is Canadian) who has a far different code of honor than most superheroes.

During the mini-series, Wolverine slaughters an extraordinary number of his enemies and the mutant displays that his primary superpower is killing. Wolverine does not like his amazing ability to kill but he accepts that it is his social role and that it is a necessary evil in a corrupt and amoral society. Like Reagan conservatives, Logan believes in individualism and strong action against criminals and one's adversaries. Wolverine displays many cowboyistic traits as the brooding loner and tough lawgiver, but in true Reagan era fashion the super-killing mutant intensifies these traditional qualities to become an extreme super-conservative. Over time, Wolverine would prove to be one of Marvel's most popular characters and a clear example of the 1980s Reagan era ideal of intensified conservatism.

Big Talk

After over a decade of trials and tribulations, 1984 finally marked the start of an apparent upturn in American society as inflation and unemployment rates dropped and Ronald Reagan convinced many citizens to feel better about the nation and themselves. During his re-election campaign, the president took credit for the country's new prosperity, declaring that "it's morning again in America and under the leadership of President Reagan our country is prouder and stronger and better. Why would we ever want to return to where we were less than four short years ago?"[17] By spotlighting the improving economy, Reagan easily defeated Walter Mondale in the 1984 election. Staying true to his individualistic ideology, the president asked citizens to focus on themselves and support him if they personally were doing better than four years ago socially and economically. Reagan continued to espouse the neo-conservative belief that extreme self-interest benefits society as a whole. According to the president, cutting taxes, de-regulating industry, shrinking government, and encouraging self-centeredness and heightened consumerism would foster economic and social growth. In this new paradigm, self-interest was, in fact, altruism and prosperity started with the wealthy and trickled down to all those below. As the economy was growing, many Americans embraced this ultra-individualism and ostentatious displays of wealth became desirable. The television series *Lifestyles of the Rich and Famous* showed Americans what they should work for and the 1987 film *Wall Street* expressed (albeit cynically) the widespread notion that "greed is good." Reagan's notion of self-centered individualism was changing the national dialogue and the 1984 election results showed that the majority of voters approved of the president's agenda. As Reagan encouraged Americans to focus on themselves, he also reminded them that the nation also had a fearsome and dangerous enemy that should never be forgotten.

Under Pressure

While Ronald Reagan encouraged Americans to work hard, spend money, push for a smaller government, and focus on themselves, he also warned them to not forget about the ever dangerous Soviet Union. After years of cooperation, Cold War tensions had heightened late in the Carter administration when the Soviet military invaded Afghanistan. Reagan's strong anti-communistic rhetoric only further strained relations between the two nations and had the seemingly desired effect of frightening many American citizens. Reagan expanded the military, increased production of certain types of missiles and nuclear weapons, began developing a strategy to create the Strategic Defense Initiative (a missile defense shield commonly known as Star Wars), and continually reminded Americans that the U.S.S.R. was a dangerous enemy. In a June 1982 speech to the British House of Commons, Reagan forecasted that "the march of freedom and democracy ... will leave Marxism-Leninism on the ash heap of history."[18] In a May 1983 speech to the National Association of Evangelicals when talking about the Soviet Union, the president warned Americans about "the aggressive impulses of an evil empire."[19] In August 1984, Reagan tested a microphone before the beginning of a radio program by joking, "I've signed legislation that will outlaw Russia forever. We begin bombing in five minutes."[20]

In May 1985 and October 1986, the president met with the Soviet leader Mikhail Gorbachev, but the two men achieved few results. At least partially because of Reagan's strong posturing and tough rhetoric and the nation's large scale military buildup, fear of the U.S.S.R. in general and nuclear war in particular seemed to greatly increase during this period. Many Americans worried as the two super powers continued to stockpile weapons, while seemingly agreeing on little. According to the president, the Soviet Union was an evil empire that wanted to do the U.S. harm, and many Americans were frightened. Cold War tensions remained high during the mid–1980s, but a change was coming quicker than all but few could imagine.

Breaking the Law

While the perceived Soviet threat vexed a large number of Americans, many people were also concerned about their daily safety at home and in their neighborhoods. In places like New York City, crime rates skyrocketed and troubled citizens worried about their personal well-being. This substantial increase in violent crime dated back to the mid–1960s and many Americans were apprehensive that a substantial number of places in society were no longer safe and livable. A popular social narrative stated that crime had become a social blight and lawmakers and government officials were ineffectual and cared more about criminals than victims. A growing number of Americans believed that because government officials and the police could no longer protect them, then personal action outside the law was often called for. Vigilantism had become a popular Hollywood topic and film series like *Death Wish* and *Dirty Harry* showcased strong individualism and violent extra-legal crime fighting methods.

A real life 1984 incident also highlights the anger and frustration that many citizens felt about seemingly losing control of their lives and their neighborhoods. On December 22, 1984, New York City resident Bernhard Goetz shot four would-be robbers aboard a Manhattan subway train. Accounts differ, but Goetz claims to have fired at the four teenagers with an unlicensed handgun after feeling threatened and fearing for his safety. Many Americans sympathized with Goetz and the incident became a source of widespread public debate. A jury acquitted Goetz, who became known as the "Subway Vigilante," of numerous crimes associated with the incident and found him guilty of only illegal firearms possession, for which he served less than a year in prison. To many, Goetz became a symbol of the individual taking control and providing order and justice in a chaotic and unjust world. This narrative worked well with Ronald Reagan's promotion of heightened individualism and the president's claims that the federal government had become cumbersome and ineffectual.[21]

Several early comic book superheroes were also vigilantes, although most, like Batman, became orderly state-maintainers during World War II and the 1950s. A new version of the super-conservative vigilante was becoming popular in comic books during the mid–1980s and they were much more violent than their New Deal era counterparts.

Upside Down

As much of American society began to embrace Ronald Reagan's heightened-conservative notions of extreme individualism, conspicuous signs of consumerism and prosperity, intensified nationalism, and mass fearfulness, new and recreated heroes mirrored the world around them. These ultra-conservative ideals combined with rising crime rates and the public's seeming acceptance of vigilantes like Bernhard Goetz pushed comic creators to publish

Opposite: **Although created in 1970s, the Punisher's exaggerated violence and lax moral code exemplified the 1980s era in superhero comic books. (© 1987 Marvel Comics. All Rights Reserved.)**

new and re-created superheroes. One character that exemplified the Reagan era was a vigilante named the Punisher. The ultra-violent anti-hero is Frank Castle, a former U.S. Marine who has dedicated himself to fighting crime after a mobster murdered his wife and two children. The murders cause Castle severe mental anguish and render him psychologically unstable while pushing him to become an obsessed loner. The Punisher debuted in 1974 as a Spider-Man adversary and reappeared numerous times during the 1970s. The vigilante often uses violently unconventional methods like kidnapping, torture, and even murder to bring criminals to justice. Although created in the 1970s, the Punisher became popular during the 1980s and appeared in his first self-titled mini-series in 1986, and *The Punisher* ongoing series debuted in 1987.

The ultra-violent and highly individualistic Punisher was one of the first comic book anti-heroes and a proto-super-conservative who gained prominence during the Reagan years. Comic book creator Mike Baron wrote in 1988 that the Punisher filled a social need for strong justice that the legal system was not meeting. He writes that the Punisher embodies "the voice of 'conservative' Americans who see their quality of life threatened by criminal behavior and the confused thinking of 'liberals.' ... This average citizen [is] concerned with getting through the day and protecting his family." He later adds, "The police and the courts may constantly disappoint us, but the Punisher never does. So read and enjoy — and don't let 'liberals' make you feel guilty. The Punisher knows what's right — it's really quite simple, when you think about it. Just don't forget to shower afterwards."[22] Popular culture scholar Cord Scott notes that in early adventures writers compared the Punisher to Captain America as a method of understanding the changing idea of heroism. Scott writes, "The character of the Punisher represents the antithesis of Captain America (Cap), but at the same time represents a dark part of the American psyche. He is the one willing to do almost anything necessary to rid the world of truly bad people."[23] When the two heroes meet in January 1980, Captain America lectures the Punisher not to kill, not to use guns, and to allow the justice system to give every criminal a fair trial.[24] Cap's words seem archaic, and this marks the former World War II soldier as a hero from another era who has lost touch with the current generation's needs and desires. Captain America represents the World War II era conservative ideals of individualism and self-sufficiency tempered with a respect for government and desire to work towards the common good. The Punisher's 1980s super-conservative outlook emphasizes extreme individualism and self-interest and makes few exceptions for compromise and cooperation. Captain America believes himself to be a part of a larger system of law, order, and justice, while the Punisher considers himself to be the lone force of justice in a society gone terribly wrong.

During the 1980s, after several years of governmental and social atrophy, many Americans began to empathize with the Punisher's worldview and started to embrace Reagan's hyper-conservatism. Captain America was still an American symbol to many, but to numerous readers he had become more nostalgic than relevant.

It's the End of the World as We Know It (And I Feel Fine)

As Ronald Reagan was attempting to recreate American society, writer Marv Wolfman and artist George Pèrez were trying to rebuild the DC universe. DC creators and editors believed that mistakes had been made in the DC universe that must be corrected. The problem was that historically most DC superheroes stories were not produced to create a decades-long narrative in which stories fit together to fashion one coherent timeline. For decades, DC creators assumed that its young readership was changing after only a few years and very few readers kept track of past stories. As comic books gained an increasingly older and more mature audience, many fans began to expect stories to connect in order to create a long running narrative. This idea, known as continuity, was extremely troublesome for DC writers and editors who often could not satisfactorily explain the universe's timeline. To make matters worse, in order to clarify how the original Golden Age (1938–1950) heroes existed alongside their new Silver Age (1956–1970) counterparts, DC creators decided that their comic book stories featured an infinite number of universes, each slightly different from the other.

In this reality, each universe had its own Earth populated by its own heroes. Many of these parallel Earths had heroes with the same names or origins but each was slightly (or greatly) different. In this multiverse, the heroes featured in most DC comic books lived on Earth 1, the Golden Age heroes lived on Earth 2, and the numerous other Earths contained multiple additional distinct characters. Besides frustrating many long-time readers with continuity gaffes, the multiverse was difficult for new readers to understand and likely contributed to the company's declining sales. Much like Ronald Regan, DC wanted to wash away decades of unhelpful changes while creating new versions of traditional values and narratives. While Reagan pressed for amplified conservative values, he was still forced to work within the American political and social structure, and often he had to encourage change in slow incremental steps. DC's creators, on the other hand, had the luxury of completely rebuilding their social structure from scratch because in 1985 Marv Wolfman destroyed DC's entire society.

Brave New World

Starting in April 1985, DC Comics published *Crisis on Infinite Earths*, a monthly 12 issue maxi-series that completely restructured the comic book publisher's fictional society. In the story, heroes from across multiple Earths and timelines band together to fight a villain, the Anti-Monitor, who threatens to destroy all of existence. The heroes eventually defeat the Anti-Monitor but not before an infinite number of living beings are not only destroyed, but many are erased from reality and deemed to have never existed. The end result is that history is altered and only one universe with one Earth survives. Heroes' backgrounds and origins are rewritten and DC's society is rebuilt completely anew. Writer Marv Wolfman was able to completely restructure society and not only change the present but also retroactively reshape the past. Although *Crisis on Infinite Earths* does not feature new super-conservative characters, the storyline does kill an uncountable number of sentient beings, a body count that will probably never be matched in a comic book story line.[25] *Comic Geek Speak* host Peter Rios astutely notes that much like historical events, important comic book stories define a generation of readers. He states that for young fans reading *Crisis on Infinite Earths*, the story forged a new long-term understanding of superheroes and, to a certain extent, the young readers' roles in society. Rios claims, "We survived the *Crisis* as readers. There's nothing you can throw at us that we shouldn't be able to survive."[26] This sentiment matches how many Americans who lived through the early and mid–1980s feel about that period of their lives.

Numerous well-known DC characters died in *Crisis*, including Supergirl and the Flash.

Although shocking at the time, such "deaths" would become a commonplace superhero trope in years to come. While comic book violence and death at first stunned and titillated, it soon became mundane, forcing creators to invent larger threats and growing body counts. More importantly, the massive social restructuring in *Crisis* mirrors the conservative fantasy of remaking society by retroactively changing the past. In such a scenario, methodical change through compromise and negotiation is replaced with the godlike ability to prevent society from ever adopting offensive social norms. *Crisis* showcases the conservative dream of retroactively turning a dense and confusing multi-layered society in a less complex and more easily understandable world that shares the same background and understandings. Comic book historian Adam Murdough notes, "The reductionist impulse that drove DC Comics to collapse its fabulously diverse storytelling milieu down to a single world and history in 1985–86 parallels that which drove 'mainstream' American society to seek strength, security and stability in a cultural 'melting pot.'"[27] As Ronald Reagan was attempting to recreate American society in a heightened conservative manner, the DC universe traded complexity and variety for safety and simplicity.

Here I Go Again

In *Crisis on Infinite Earths*, writer Marv Wolfman retroactively changed the DC universe's history and reinvented many famous superheroes' origins and backgrounds. One of the most noteworthy of these changes is the re-creation of Superman that appeared shortly after the end of *Crisis*. DC Comics editors asked long-time Marvel writer and artist John Byrne to revamp Superman and make the Man of Steel more relevant for modern audiences. Although numerous writers had attempted (and mostly failed) to update Superman in the past, *Crisis of Infinite Earths'* history-altering events allowed Byrne more freedom to redesign the founding father of superheroes. The results first appeared in the 1986 six part miniseries *The Man of Steel*. Byrne, known for his conservative worldview and his stories that reflected heightened traditional values, attempted to modernize Superman by highlighting the character's core components and discarding what he deemed to be unneeded baggage. The writer developed a version of Superman that he claimed was a return to the character's roots but in reality was an enhanced 1980s version of a 1940s and 1950s conservative ideal. As previously noted, Superman's original 1938 incarnation was a liberal New Deal avenger, who worried more about correcting social ills than fighting super-villains. Byrne's reimagining embraced and augmented the late 1940s and early 1950s agent of the state Superman who protected the status quo while operating as a lone avenger. The author erased many of Superman's friends and allies and returned the Man of Steel to his status as the sole survivor of a doomed planet. Gone were any other Kryptonians, but returning were Clark Kent's parents, Jonathan and Martha Kent, who now served as a support system for the adult Superman. No longer did aliens and other outsiders act as Superman's family, but instead his salt of the earth adoptive parents provided all of the family that he needed. The conservative notion of removing outside ties and influences and making Superman more "American" reverberates throughout Byrne's stories. It also allowed Superman to now gen-

Opposite: John Byrne's *The Man of Steel* (1986) reinterpreted Superman for a new generation of readers. Byrne claimed to have returned the Man of Steel to his roots but the new conservative 1980s Superman appeared to share little with the 1930s Great Depression social avenger Superman. (© 1986 DC Comics. Used with permission of DC Comics.)

erally fight crime alone, appealing to the heightened need for displays of individualism in 1980s America. Although Byrne himself was born in England and grew up in Canada, the writer portrayed Superman as the ultimate American immigrant who embraced conservative Midwestern American values and distanced himself from foreign influences.

As the Cold War was intensifying, Reagan's America was becoming increasingly insulated and nationalistic. After his new overhaul, Superman also embraced this new form of amplified conservative nationalism. John Byrne erased the Man of Steel's alien family and foreign influences and strengthened Superman's devotion to the United States while making him an symbol of individualism, giving the American hero impeccable conservative credentials. Byrne himself noted that his job was "to try to pare away some of the barnacles that have attached themselves to the company's flagship title. To try to make Superman of today as exciting in his own right as was the primal Superman of yesterday. To try to recreate Superman as a character more in tune with the needs of the modern comic book audience." The author later added, "We are doing classic Superman because we're taking him back to where he started."[28] While this was not actually where the character started, it was a super-conservative Reagan era view of Superman's true nature.

Midnight Maniac

While John Byrne was recreating Superman as a super-conservative, individualistic friend of the state, another famous comic book creator was redesigning Batman. By 1986, Frank Miller was one of the most popular comic book writers in the industry. His work on *Daredevil*, *Wolverine*, and the apocalyptic Samurai comic book series *Ronin* had showcased ultra-violent storytelling that often contained mature themes and ideas. From February to June 1986, DC Comics published Miller's *Batman: The Dark Knight Returns*, a critically acclaimed four part mini-series that introduced an extreme version of the Caped Crusader. Miller wanted to return Batman to his pulp era roots and create an obsessed vigilante who operates outside the law to enforce his own code of justice. Miller did not copy the 1930s tales, but imagined how a super-conservative Batman would react to 1980s America. Miller states, "It was the very angry late '70s, early '80s, the time of 'Dirty Harry' and 'Death Wish.' I started speculating how Batman would act, the kind of person he'd be in this world."[29] *Dark Knight* features a 50-something Batman who comes out of retirement to restore order to a Gotham City engulfed in chaos. The older Caped Crusader must battle against his aging body while attempting to impose his version of justice on a world he no longer understands or feels a part of. Miller's Gotham is a dystopic nightmare in which crime, violence, and vice are the norm and justice has ceased to exist. Batman himself appears to straddle the line between being an extremely driven crime fighter and being insane, as Miller explores the mental state of a superhero who is obsessed with enforcing a strict moral code. In *Dark Knight*, the super-conservative Batman is the only force of justice left in a society that has succumbed to voyeuristic, mindless media and a corrupt government that keep citizens happy by appealing to their patriotism and consumerism.

While Miller's *Dark Knight* is a super-conservative version of Batman, the author also criticizes the country for failing to live up to true American ideals. The story's president is a Ronald Reagan caricature who dispenses folksy wisdom, feel-good sound bites, and patriotic proclamations in order to keep Americans content. Although cities are crumbling, crime is rampant, and justice has been traded for pleasure, most citizens blindly accept the status quo and do little to change society. Interestingly, this Orwellian nightmare is a savage critique of a conservative president and nation who fail to live up to the super-conservative Batman's ideals. The Reagan-like president is conservative in words alone, while Batman is conservative in the actions that implement his violent type of justice. At one point during *Dark Knight* when the situation appears dire, Batman takes to the streets while the president only appears on television and proclaims, "Nothing we can't handle, folks. We're still America — And I'm still president."[30] Even Ronald Reagan's brand of hyper-conservatism was not pure enough for the super-conservative Batman.

I Want Action

A further extension of Frank Miller's *Batman: The Dark Knight Returns's* argument that Reagan's America is not a true conservative movement can be found in the comparison of how Superman and Batman are portrayed. In *Dark Knight*, Miller does not use the Reagan-like president as the major contrast point to showcase Batman's true super-conservatism; rather Superman is portrayed as the Caped Crusader's opposite number. In this story, the godlike Man of Steel serves as a governmental agent who protects the status quo by doing exactly what the president orders. Miller creates an extreme version of both characters and portrays Batman as an obsessed anarchical individualist, while Superman is the ultra-powerful instrument of the state. In Miller's world, Batman battle to impose his own vision of justice, while Superman strives to enforce the state sanctioned understanding of law and order. At the end of *Dark Knight*, Superman and Batman battle and the Caped Crusader internally monologues, "You sold us out, Clark. You gave them — the power — that should have been ours. Just like your parents taught you to do. My parents ... taught me a different lesson ... lying in the street — shaking in deep shock — dying for no reason at all — they showed me that the world only makes sense when you force it to."[31]

To Miller, Superman is the rule-following conservative who blindly adheres to every governmental law and mandate, while Batman understands that individualism lies at the center of true conservatism. Superman is merely a tool of the state, while Batman is an individualistic force for freedom and justice. This comparison of DC's most prominent superheroes (and two of the medium's founding fathers) illustrates not only Miller's view of Reagan era America, but also what comic tales were acceptable during the period. Miller's criticism of Ronald Reagan, the news media, and American society in general is striking, but even more remarkable is that the author rather unfavorably deconstructs two comic book icons to create his story. Miller simultaneously critiques 1980s American society and superheroes and comes to the conclusion that both suffer from the same flaws. Both are overly violent, self-righteous, and self-absorbed, and should not be praised for these qualities. In *Dark Knight*, Batman is not a hero as much as he is an obsessed vigilante who believes that he alone can impart truth and inflict justice on an immoral society, mirroring Miller's understanding of a super-conservative. Towards the end of *Dark Knight* chapter 3, Superman reflects on Batman's nature and opines, "When the noise started from the parents' groups and the sub-committee called us for questioning — you were the one who laughed — that scary laugh of yours. 'Sure we're criminals,' you said. 'We've always been criminals. We have to be criminals.'"[32]

While other authors had begun to recreate super-conservative heroes that reflected Ronald Reagan's understanding of American society, Miller re-imagined Superman and

Batman as critiques of America in general and superheroes specifically. In Miller's world the U.S. was suffocating under the weight of crime, corruption, and apathy, and few citizens, including Ronald Reagan, were more than conservative in name alone. Batman, the only true conservative, was not a hero, but rather a force of justice to be feared; unfortunately he and his super-conservative brethren may have been the only ones that could save society.

Fight the Power

As numerous superheroes amplified their traditional violent and individualistic characteristics in order to keep in step with 1980s American society, a large number of supervillains also intensified their criminal traits and developed much more evil personas. Many characters that had once been entertainingly silly foils became violent sociopaths and cold-blooded murderers. In 1985, the formerly harmless Professor Zoom seemingly murdered the Flash's wife, causing the Scarlet Speedster to retaliate and kill the criminal.[33] In the 1987 Spider-Man story "Fearful Symmetry," writer J.M. DeMatteis portrays the previously lackluster villain Kraven the Hunter as a psychopath who needs to best Spider-Man and steal his identify. After physically and psychologically brutalizing Spider-Man, Kraven commits suicide and dies, having won his battle against the hero.[34]

Arguably, the most maniacal, terrifying, and recreated villain of this time period was long time Batman arch-nemesis the Joker. The Crown Prince of Crime was first featured in *Batman* #1 (1940) and in this and other early appearances he is portrayed as a homicidal maniac who kills indiscriminately and with great pleasure. During the 1950s and 1960s, the Joker became a silly prankster who displayed none of his former overly violent and murderous tendencies. In the 1970s, the Joker once again turned violent and homicidal, especially in his own self-titled nine issue series, which often featured stories filled with murderous mayhem. During the 1980s, writers intensified the Joker's violent and murderous qualities, making him a dark and terrifying sociopath.

A prime example of the Joker's amplified villainy is the 1986 Alan Moore story, *Batman: The Killing Joke*, in which the villainous clown paralyzes Batgirl (Barbara Gordon) and tortures her father, Commissioner Gordon, by making him view photographs of his daughter's assault. The dual assaults are far more brutal and disturbing than any previously chronicled Joker attack. Although the Joker had committed heinous acts before, he had never perpetrated such a violently vile act in so graphic a manner. An anecdote from Alan Moore, the story's author, illustrates that the thought process behind the graphic story was also rather casually brutal. Moore claims that while scripting the tale he called DC editor Len Wein on the telephone to ask permission to paralyze Barbara Gordon/Batgirl. Wein consulted with Executive Editorial Director Dick Giordano and replied to Moore, "Yeah, okay, cripple the bitch."[35]

As superheroes were becoming excessively violent and individualistic super-conservatives, super-villains were also intensifying their traditional core traits. Reagan's America

Opposite: In Frank Miller's *Batman: The Dark Knight Returns* (1986), a super-conservative Batman and an ineffectual Superman battle. This clash mirrors many of the social and political conflicts present in American society during the 1980s. (© 1986 DC Comics. Used with permission of DC Comics.)

demanded a society filled with extreme versions of traditional ideals and values. Superheroes and super-villains were changing to mirror society but sometimes the results were rather disturbing.

Finish What Ya Started

The last two full years of Ronald Reagan's second and final presidential term were 1987 and 1988, and although many Americans supported the president, the Constitution mandated that he step down in January 1989. Economic recovery, low inflation, lower unemployment, and a renewed sense of nationalism now made many citizens feel quite differently than they had at the start of the 1980s. Reagan had been unable to decrease the size and the role of government on the scale that he wished, but several adjustments were made to the tax code, multiple industries were deregulated, and other regulations were changed or updated. More importantly, Reagan consistently reiterated that government was becoming smaller and more efficient, and thus many Americans believed him. The president convinced people that the country and their lives were improving and they should feel proud of their nation and themselves. He continuously pointed to the better economic conditions and increased national goodwill as proof that his belief in smaller government and individualism were the core principles that had "saved" the nation during its dark hours. Many historians debate whether changes made during the Reagan years helped average and low income Americans or if the wealthiest benefited at the expenses of other citizens. In fact, Reagan's variety of extreme individualism produced a disparity of wealth unseen since the Gilded Age.[36] Still, American society changed greatly during the Reagan years, and most Americans seemed to be happy with these changes.

The Way It Is

While many Americans embraced Reagan's ideals of ultra-conservativism and extreme individualism during the late 1980s, several incidents called these beliefs into question. In October 1987, the Dow Jones dropped over 600 points in a few days. This massive stock market loss suggested economic weakness and possible upcoming national problems.[37] During this time the Reagan administration was also embroiled in a scandal involving activities in Nicaragua. The administration had provided illegal aid to a group of Nicaraguan rebels, called the contras, and had violated numerous Congressional mandates and federal laws in doing so. Furthermore, officials sold missiles to Iran via Israel and used the money to support the contras, another illegal activity. The affair become known as the Iran-Contra Scandal and eventually led to a congressional investigation and subsequent hearings. Although the president's popularity dramatically dropped and many in the public believed that he had broken the law, it was never definitely proven that he knew about the illegal activities.

One of the most interesting officials associated with the Iran-Contra Scandal was Marine Lieutenant Colonel Oliver North, who had been instrumental in illegally funding the contras. During his congressional testimony, North claimed to have broken the law and violated congressional mandates for the good of the nation, thus embracing individualism above the law. North's willingness to commit criminal acts in order to fulfill his own understanding of justice and order displays both the positive and negative aspects of the Reagan era's ideal of heightened individualism. The solitary hero who acts alone as a force of justice is a longstanding American fantasy, while the loose-cannon who will not follow rules and thus harms society is a nightmare. In the Iran-Contra Scandal Lieutenant Colonel North and several other Reagan administration members showed how ultra-individualism can be taken too far and can cause more damage than good. Comic book superhero stories were also beginning to display this same insight.[38] As Oliver North was testifying before Congress about his criminal patriotism, DC and Marvel were publishing the fictional adventures of a new breed of ultra-individualists and super-conservatives.

Second Chance

By 1987, comic book characters were following social and cultural trends and transforming into super-conservatives. Although well-known 1980s stories like *Batman: The Dark Knight Returns* and *Daredevil* presented re-crafted ultra-conservative heroes and villains, many other lesser-known characters also made the transformation. The changes made to these less-popular heroes and villains reflect the growing acceptance of the super-conservative movement. While one could argue that creators produced "artistic" comic books like *Watchmen* or *Camelot 3000* for small elite audiences, it is clear DC and Marvel published these super-conservative lower-tier heroes' tales for a general audience. In the comic book industry's version of supply side economics, powerful and well-regarded heroes and stories first transformed into super-conservatives, and then slowly the changes trickled down to their less-lofty brethren.

Several examples of these more niche ultra-conservative re-creations include the 1985–1987 DC Comics series *Hex*, in which traditional cowboy Jonah Hex is transported from the nineteenth century American West to a *Mad Max*–like apocalyptic future. Although Jonah Hex had always been an aggressive fighter, the chronologically-displaced cowboy now embraced the heightened level of violence that the brutal new era demanded. In 1988, *The Incredible Hulk* writer Peter David turned the Hulk into a Las Vegas casino enforcer named Joe Fixit. While the Hulk had always been a violent and individualistic anti-hero who feared the government, he now was using his violent talents to contribute to the economy.

In 1987, DC writer John Ostrander re-created the Suicide Squad, transforming the team once consisting of a group of war heroes into a secret government black operations squad mostly comprised of super-villains working to gain pardons for their crimes. While heroes once performed government service in order to promote the common good, now the government employed criminals to carry out these same assignments. Perhaps the most unusual 1980s super-conservative re-creation was the formerly ultra-liberal hero Green Arrow. From his conception in 1941 until the 1970s, the Emerald Archer was the costumed identity of Oliver Queen, a clichéd conservative billionaire playboy industrialist. The Robin Hood–like hero often used gimmicky weapons such as the boxing glove arrow, handcuff arrow, and fountain pen arrow to protect the status quo and entertain readers. In the late 1960s and early 1970s, Green Arrow lost his fortune, became an outspoken liberal, and paired with the conservative space cop Green Arrow in numerous stories. During this era writer Denny O'Neil used the Battling Bowman to voice liberal opinions and concerns that were prevalent in American society. Green Arrow had transformed from a conservative industrialist to a vocal anarchist, and then during the 1980s he changed yet again.

In 1987, writer Mike Grell created a three part mini-series entitled *Green Arrow: The*

Longbow Hunters in which Emerald Archer becomes a super-conservative. In the mature themed mini-series, and the Grell penned ongoing series that would follow, Green Arrow abandons his trick arrows and instead resorts to injuring and sometimes murdering criminals with his now lethal arrows. The character, like many other 1980s superheroes, now embraced a violent and hyper-individualistic version of conservatism. By emulating American society, Green Arrow transformed from a postwar conservative to a 1960s liberal to a 1980s super-conservative — the same arduous path that many people followed during the late 20th century.[39]

The End of the Innocence

In 1986–1987, as Ronald Reagan extolled the individualistic and patriotic tenements of hyper-conservativism and numerous superheroes transformed into ultra-violent and uber-self-centered super-conservatives, a comic book masterpiece premiered. Alan Moore and Dave Gibbons created *Watchmen*, a deconstruction of the superhero genre that presented self-indulgent costumed characters that acted differently than any comic book heroes had before. Moore's characters illustrated the consequences of classic superhero traits like self-absorption, violently enforcing one's personal morality, and individualism. In other words, *Watchmen*'s heroes were not really heroes at all, but rather an intense critique of the genre's conservative attributes that had been amplified both in comic books and in society during the 1980s. As many superheroes transformed into super-conservatives, *Watchmen* served as a call for readers to rethink the role of the hero in society and to question the ultra-conservative methods that had become generally accepted.

The story revolves around a group of costumed avengers that battle their personal problems more than they fight criminals in a dystopian America. One of the main characters, Rorschach, is a brutal vigilante who attempts to impose his absolute morality on a world that he believes has no other force of justice. Rorschach was an abused child who slowly changed into a mentally disturbed moralist and now feels the obsessive need to enforce his own code of justice and order. Another hero, Adrian Veidt/Ozymandias, chooses to kill millions of people in order to avert a potential nuclear war and believes that he has followed the heroic code by saving society from itself. The U.S. government employs another hero, the Comedian, to keep order even though his methods often include murder and rape. The *Watchmen* characters are Moore's warning against society believing too much in heroes' abilities to solve our problems.

As leaders like Ronald Reagan pressed for less government oversight and more unchecked individualism, Moore worried that conservatism could morph into fascism or despotism. Comic book historian Bradford W. Wright states, "Rorschach and his ilk were Moore's admonition to those who trusted in 'heroes' and leaders to guard the world's fate. To place faith in such icons, he argued, was to give up responsibility for our lives and future to the Reagans, Thatchers, and other 'Watchmen' of the world who [were] supposed to 'rescue' us."[40] Moore had created these new super-conservatives to warn Americans about trusting too much in heroes and government. Although many readers and industry figures greatly

Opposite: Alan Moore and Dave Gibbons's *Watchmen* (1986–87) deconstructed comic book superheroes and attempted to demonstrate how masked avengers would act in the real world. (© 1987 DC Comics. Used with permission of DC Comics.)

admired *Watchmen*, few heeded Alan Moore's warnings, and the re-creation of super-conservative heroes continued.

Crumblin' Down

On January 20, 1989, George H.W. Bush took office as the 41st president of the United States of America. The former vice president inherited a country at the brink of a decade of great change and new challenges. Undoubtedly, the most important of these changes was the fall of the Soviet Union and the end of the European communist bloc. After taking office in 1985, Soviet leader Mikhail Gorbachev instituted numerous social, economic, and political changes (commonly known by the Russian words *perestroika* and *glasnost*) to strengthen the struggling superpower. As president, Ronald Reagan had originally refused to meet with Soviet leadership, but during his second term Reagan became quite close to Gorbachev. The two leaders helped to reduce Cold War tension and even signed a treaty to remove all the intermediate-range nuclear missiles from Europe. In 1988, the Soviet military began withdrawing from Afghanistan, ending the war that had escalated anxieties during the early 1980s. Finally, in 1989, political and economic weaknesses within the Soviet Bloc led to a series of protests and reforms in communist countries like Poland, Czechoslovakia, and Hungary that damaged the Soviet empire beyond repair. Sensing the Soviet Union's inherent weakness, numerous communist countries broke from the Eastern Bloc and created new more democratic governments. In November 1989, protesters and revelers destroyed the Berlin Wall, which to many Americans symbolically ended the Cold War.

In just over two years the Soviet Union would officially cease to exist, but for all intents and purposes the empire concluded at the end of 1989. For over forty years, the Soviet Union had served as the U.S.'s chief adversary and the basis for much of the country's political, economic, and military policy. Now the "evil empire" was no more and the U.S. had won the Cold War. The 1980s were ending much like a comic book story in which the hero finally defeats his arch enemy and saves all of those around him. Like the hero, Americans would have little time to celebrate or gloat, though, because a new story was beginning and new threats were on the horizon.

Conclusion

Like most decades, the 1980s were a time of great social and cultural change. The decade began with the U.S. in a social, economic, and political downturn and ended with a more prosperous and stable country that had recently won the Cold War. While the ten year period started with Jimmy Carter's presidency and ended with that of George H.W. Bush, Ronald Reagan is most associated with the decade's changes. Reagan strongly preached a doctrine of smaller government, lower taxes, fewer regulations and restrictions on business and industry, increased military spending and buildup, and action against communism. All of these things fit into the president's belief in an enhanced form of individualism in which citizens chiefly worry about their own self-interest and trust that this will produce the greatest possible good for society. Historians disagree if this self-centered individualism helped to create a more stable and livable society, or if it promoted a system in which the wealthy reaped an exorbitant amount of the nation's economic and social benefits. What is certain is that many Americans socially and culturally began to identify with Reagan's amplified conservative ideas in word at least if not in deed. Patriotism and individualism were mixed with a distrust of big government and a fear of crime and other social elements to create the idea of the wary ultra-conservative. Comic book creators soon incorporated these ideals into superhero stories, and before long copious amounts of super-conservative heroes were born and recreated. These characters differed from past conservative superheroes in both tone and intensity and were often overly violent and extreme versions of traditional heroes. Heroes such as the Punisher, Superman, and Daredevil changed how they viewed and interacted with the world and pressed for a clean break from the recent past while focusing on an enhanced version of traditional American ideals. In comic books, as in American society, individualism was extolled far above its conventional station, while social responsibility and a respect for the law were devalued. This led to a society that valued excess in numerous social and cultural arenas and comic book characters that became overly violent and extravagant parodies of the heroes they once were. The 1980s changed the U.S. and comic book superheroes forever and proved that no matter how good something seems, it can be overdone.

Chapter 8

Searching for a
New Direction (1990–1999)

During the 1950s, millions of American children tuned in to view the television series the *Adventures of Superman*. George Reeves's portrayal of the Man of Steel thrilled the young audience who returned each week to watch their favorite superhero. Each episode began with energetic music and a description of Superman being "faster than a speeding bullet, more powerful than a locomotive, able to leap tall buildings in a single bound." After ordering the viewer to "look up in the sky" and describing which animal and airborne mode of transportation the hero resembles, the narrative provides a quick summary of Superman's background and superpowers. The narration ended with the announcer's exclamation that Superman "fights a never ending battle for truth, justice, and the American way."[1]

Comic book superheroes do, in fact, fight never ending battles against crime, misery, and super-villainy. Without an arch nemesis or opposing forces to battle against, a comic book hero would have little to do and almost no way to characterize him or herself. Like many nations, superheroes are defined as much by what they battle against as by what they stand for. What happens when the battle is over and the war is won, though? How do heroes, and nations, define themselves when their enemies have been vanquished and the never ending battle is over? This is the chief problem that the government and citizens of the United States faced during the 1990s. The U.S. had won the Cold War and the Soviet threat was ended, but on what should Americans now concentrate? The U.S.S.R. had been a threatening and stable adversary for over four decades that had provided a consistent "them" as a mirror to better clarify the American "us." Now that the Soviet Union no longer existed, how would the U.S. define itself and what would be its new mission?

Picking Up the Pieces

When the Soviet empire began to disintegrate in late 1989 much of the world was joyful. In 1989 and 1990, citizens in several Eastern Bloc states overthrew authoritarian governments and soon voters in numerous countries (in theory) elected representative governments. Freedom and democracy were seemingly sweeping through Eastern Europe and parts of Central Asia as places like Czechoslovakia and Poland were experiencing revolutions and social restructurings. Politicians, such as former president Ronald Reagan and current president George H.W. Bush, took credit for the international political and social changes and many Americans basked in the country's apparent triumph.

The celebrations quickly subsided though, as most Americans realized that life had not only changed abroad in the former communist countries, but at home as well. Almost overnight the U.S. had become the world's only superpower and the country now possessed expanded authority and responsibility. A new era had begun and few in the U.S. had anticipated how quickly and completely these changes would occur. As former Warsaw Pact countries struggled to create new political and social institutions, the U.S. and its citizens also attempted to redefine much of the nation's policies and understandings. The threat of communism had dominated American life for over two generations and many Americans did not remember a world in which the specter of the Soviet Union did not haunt their daily lives. Although Americans now needed to worry about rogue elements gaining control of former Soviet nuclear weapons and violent conflicts in former communist countries, most experts and laypersons alike agreed that the world had gotten better.[2] Democracy and capitalism had triumphed and tens of millions of people were now freer than they had been in generations. What did this mean for Americans though? The U.S. was now seemingly stronger and safer than it had been in decades, but what happened next? The world had dramatically changed and the U.S. needed a new purpose. It was not readily apparent what that would be.

Sun City

As Americans were adjusting to the rapid changes in Central and Eastern Europe, many citizens were also delighted to hear of massive political transformations in South Africa. The political system had long been racially segregated in a manner in which a small minority of people of European descent limited the rights of and imposed restrictions upon the Africans who formed the country's majority. People throughout the world had protested this system, known as apartheid (Afrikaans for "separateness"), for decades. Much like the collapse of communism in Europe, few expected amazing changes to happen in South Africa so quickly. In February 1990, authorities freed long time political dissident and international symbol of apartheid opposition Nelson Mandela after he had served 27 years in prison. South African President F.W. de Klerk also legalized several anti-apartheid groups, including the African National Congress, paving the way for more changes to come. Mandela's release was the symbolic beginning of the end of South African segregation. Negotiations would take place in the coming years that would lead to universal suffrage in 1994 and apartheid's complete abolition in 1996.

These rapid changes helped fuel the increasing notion that the world was entering an astonishing new age and the planet's citizens must embrace a new understanding of the present and the future.[3] Philosopher Francis Fukuyama declared that the Cold War's end may have signaled "the end of history" and started the "end point of mankind's ideological evolution and the universalization of Western liberal democracy as the final form of human government."[4] Although Fukuyama was only referring to changes in former communist European countries, South Africa's transformation only added to the prevalent perception that fundamental aspects of life had changed for the better and a new social, political, and historical dawn had broken. The beginning of the 1990s was a heady time in which the world seemed ripe with new challenges and possibilities. Conversely, old models and reference points were no longer the sage guides they once had been. The world had changed and citizens had to decide what to do next.

Short Hot Wars

In the coming years, part of the U.S.'s mission would be to help stabilize the former communist nations and attempt to prevent the former U.S.S.R. from falling into chaos. U.S. officials focused on political, economic, and social assistance rather than relying on military force. Although many Americans did not like the U.S.'s expanded nation building and sustaining role, most accepted its necessity. While working primarily as a pacifying and stabilizing force in Europe, the U.S. also turned to traditional military intervention in a number of places in the early 1990s.

In December 1989, President Bush ordered the U.S. to invade the Central American country of Panama. This military action, known as Operation Just Cause, attempted to oust Panamanian leader General Manuel Noriega, who White House officials claimed was threatening U.S. citizens in Panama, trafficking drugs, and mismanaging the Panama Canal. General Noriega had worked with the CIA during the 1970s and 1980s but Ronald Reagan had deemed the Panamanian leader a U.S. enemy after the general's role in the Iran-Contra Scandal became public. The 1989–1990 invasion swiftly concluded and the U.S. military captured Noriega on January 3, 1990. The general eventually stood trial in the U.S. and served time in U.S. prisons until 2007. After the initial military action, the U.S. quickly withdrew from Panama seemingly gaining a speedy victory.[5] Much like Ronald Reagan's short invasion of Grenada, the Panamanian action appeared to be more style than substance, a quick and easy U.S. victory that reassured worried Americans that the U.S. was still militarily and politically strong. Many Americans still grappled to define the country's place in the world. Other problems loomed on the horizon that would bring greater challenges to a nation still working to define itself.

Old Friends and New Enemies

After the brief military intervention into Panama, the U.S. soon faced another challenge when on August 6, 1990, Iraqi forces invaded the country of Kuwait. The United Nations Security Council quickly imposed economic sanctions against Iraq and the U.S. began to create a multinational coalition to liberate Kuwait and invade Iraq. While the majority of the troops were from the U.S., other nations joined the military coalition for what become known as the Persian Gulf War. Aerial bombing began on January 17, 1991, and ground warfare followed starting on February 23, 1991. Coalition forces soon ousted Iraqi troops from Kuwait, destroyed much of Iraq's infrastructure, and imposed heavy sanctions on the country. The coalition also enforced severe restrictions on Iraq's leader, Saddam Hussein, although the international force did not overthrow him. The U.S. led coalition achieved a resounding military victory, although the political ramifications would continue to plague the U.S. for decades to come.

The Persian Gulf War signaled an interesting new foreign affairs paradigm as the international community expected U.S. government officials to take a military leadership role in world affairs.[6] Since the end of World War II, the U.S. had been a world leader, but the Soviet Union often contested and attempted to prevent American interventionist efforts. With the U.S.S.R. no longer acting as a world power, the U.S. now had the opportunity and the necessity of taking on the role of global policeman. As Americans and the rest of the world adjusted to the new reality, they may have thought of the famous Spider-Man mantra, "With great power there must also come great responsibility." What the U.S. government, military, and American citizens in general would do with this power in the coming decade remained to be seen.

Yet Another Dark and Stormy Knight

As America was coming to grips with its place in the new world order, comic book superheroes also began to explore their strange and changing worlds. While many 1980s characters had transformed into super-conservatives in an effort to mirror and mold American social needs and desires, as the decade ended some superheroes began to change in new and exciting ways. Some of these new types of stories and novel approaches to superheroes were published just as the 1980s were ending, which meant they were not influenced by the new post–Cold War paradigm. These early stories seem to have embraced themes of newness, discovery, and change before most in American society began to make this leap.

One example of this is *Arkham Asylum*, a November 1989 story written by Grant Morrison and illustrated by Dave McKean. DC Comics published this mature-readers-only tale as a hardcover edition in which Morrison's dark and disturbing themes and McKean's jarring painted images give multiple meanings to the term "graphic novel." *Arkham Asylum* takes the simple sounding story of Batman entering a criminal asylum to quell a super-villain riot and explores numerous underlying themes and comic book conventions. *Arkham Asylum* is Morrison's reaction to the super-conservative Batman in stories such as Frank Miller's *Batman: The Dark Knight Returns*. Morrison stated, "The intention was to create something that was more like a piece of music or an experimental film than a typical adventure comic. I wanted to approach Batman from the point of view of the dreamlike, emotional and irrational hemisphere, as a response to the very literal, 'realistic,' 'left brain' treatment of superheroes which was in vogue at that time." Morrison later added that the story's Batman was "repressed, armored, uncertain, and sexually frozen."[7] This is something seemingly new to superhero comics, a deeply introspective tale that explores comic book characters as Jungian archetypes. In Morrison and McKean's hands, Batman becomes a psychologically tormented man with a mother fixation, while the Joker is a no longer insane but rather his aberrant behavior is now viewed as super-sane, "a brilliant new modification for human perception, more suited to urban life at the end of the twentieth century."[8]

If the super-conservative heroes of the 1980s were byproducts of the decade's amplified traditionalism, then *Arkham Asylum* signals a break from the past and the willingness to embrace new ideas and understandings. On the cusp of the new decade some proto–1990s stories were already abandoning traditional notions and exploring new realities, much as many U.S. citizens would soon be forced to do.

Deus Ex Machina

While Grant Morrison was exploring new perspectives and understandings in *Arkham Asylum*, he also was questioning the very nature of traditional comic book reality in the superhero series *Animal Man* from 1988 to 1990. As many superheroes were embracing the remaining months of the Cold War era dialectic and basking in hyper-conservatism, Morrison began questioning the very notion of comic book reality. Before this series, Animal

Man was a generic 1960s superhero with a standard origin and run of the mill superpowers. Morrison used the character to explore philosophical questions regarding the meaning of life, the true nature of existence, and basis of reality. As Morrison's stories come to an end, Animal Man learns that he is a comic book character and journeys to find his "creator." Eventually the superhero speaks with Morrison and, in a scene reminiscent of Job's meeting with God, the (comic book) creator explains the meaning of (comic book) life.

As most 1980s superheroes were embracing new found power and authority, Morrison rendered Animal Man powerless and subservient. Metatextualism was not new in comic books; numerous examples exist including when Stan Lee and Jack Kirby were kept out of Sue Storm and Reed Richards's wedding in *Fantastic Four Annual* #3 in the 1960s and DC editor Julius Schwartz met his alternate Earth doppelganger in a 1980s story.[9] This was one of the first times that a mainstream superhero learned that he was merely a comic book character though.[10] In Morrison's final *Animal Man* issue, the writer informs the fictional character, "I can make you say and do anything. I can make you hate your wife and children. I can make you forget you were ever married. It's all here, this is where I write the wrongs of the world."[11] Like many Americans at the end of the 1980s, Animal Man discovered that his reality was not what he had previously thought it to be. While Morrison reset Animal Man's reality at the end of the story and made the hero forget what he had learned, Americans had little choice but to confront their new reality and imagine a post–Cold War world.

X Marks the Spot

As writers like Grant Morrison were exploring new and exciting superhero ideas, other creators were producing more traditional comic books that thrilled readers and sold millions of copies. Two of the most popular comic books of the era were 1990's *Spider-Man* #1 and 1991's *X-Men* #1, which were created by three of the most admired writers and artists of the time, Todd McFarlane, Chris Claremont, and Jim Lee. The McFarlane-helmed Spider-Man title reportedly sold 2.5 million copies, while the Claremont-Lee X-Men book sold an astonishing 8 million issues.[12] These *Spider-Man* and *X-Men* comic book titles combined exciting new versions of classic superhero tropes with stunning art and bright and flashy packaging. Although the stories were not ground breaking or inventive, they were a reflection of the unencumbered energy and enthusiasm that was released when the Cold War ended. Much of this exuberance was present during the Reagan years and became enhanced after the Soviet Union's collapse. At the beginning of the 1990s, Americans had to move forward while also retaining the country's defining characteristics. Almost everyone understood this in theory but few could understand what it meant in practice. In comic books, creators like Grant Morrison's novel ideas and Jim Lee and Todd McFarlane's traditional stories exemplify this challenge.

Annus Mirabilis and Annus Horribilis

The issues of 1991 spilled into 1992. Challenges in Iraq continued while former communist states moved toward greater political, economic, and social autonomy. Other international situations clamored for the U.S.'s attention. The former communist country Yugoslavia had split into several new states and ethnic and religious conflicts were igniting old prejudices and previously buried hatreds. The government generally held these problems in check during the communist era, and now old notions of bigotry and cultural, racial, and religious superiority resurfaced.

Conflicts also arose in the African country of Somalia. In 1991, a civil war broke out in the east African nation and thousands of citizens were brutally killed as the country became unstable and in places unlivable. Starting in January 1992, the United Nations Security Council adopted a series of resolutions that condemned human rights abuses in Somalia. At first, no member nations wanted to get involved in the civil war because of financial, social, and security concerns. The Bush administration originally expressed apprehension of being embroiled in a long-term conflict with no clear strategy or objective and endeavored to avoid a military quagmire. As the situation continued to deteriorate in Somalia, U.N. members passed a resolution in December 1992 to send in peacekeeping troops. American military personnel staffed a large portion of the operation and the U.S. once again served as an international policeman. Ultimately, U.N. peacekeepers were unable to halt the civil war or restore social order, and after several high profile military setbacks the operation ended in March 1995 when troops withdrew from the country.[13]

Americans may still have been adjusting to the new international framework but problems remained that demanded the country's attention. The U.S. was learning to be the world's only superpower and was deciding what kind of authority it wanted to assert.

Internal Conflicts

As the government and citizens of the United States were attempting to define the country's new international status, domestic issues also demanded the nation's attention. Besides the U.S.'s economy and the country's role as a world power, social issues such as crime and poverty also received significant concern from the press and the public. One of the most significant domestic events of the early 1990s was the Rodney King beating and the Los Angeles riots that would follow. In March 1991, a group of Los Angeles police officers attempted to subdue Rodney King, a paroled felon, who had led California Highway Patrol officers on a high speed chase after refusing to pull over during a traffic stop. The Los Angeles police officers tasered King then kicked him in the head and beat him repeatedly with batons as he attempted to crawl away. A local man videotaped the incident and the footage soon became a national sensation. King's beating forced Americans to discuss the issues of race, crime, police brutality, and law and order in general. Unsurprisingly, blacks viewed these issues quite differently from their white counterparts and it became clear that black and white citizens often disagreed on how society did and should function.

In April 1992, a predominantly white criminal court jury failed to convict the four police officers of assault and excessive force. The evening of the verdict, riots began in South Central Los Angeles and continued for several days. Rioters and looters, who were mostly black, attacked a number of Caucasian, Hispanic and Asian citizens, and destroyed numerous shops and other businesses. More than fifty people died during the riots and over 2000 were injured. It is estimated that rioters destroyed more than 1,500 buildings and caused roughly 1 billion dollars in damage. Nationally, the riots alarmed many Americans.[14] The events forced citizens to question their understanding of American society and life. Although the U.S. had won the Cold War, part of a major American city was in flames and much of the nation was still divided along racial and class lines. Many of these problems, along with a major economic recession, weighed on voters' minds in November 1992 when President Bush lost his re-election battle against Arkansas Governor Bill Clinton. As President Clinton took office in January 1993, Americans still looked to the future with optimism, but it was clear that much work needed to be completed both at home and abroad.

New Image

In 1992, the comic book industry also experienced a breakdown of traditional publishing roles. Since the early 1960s, Marvel and DC had been the two superpowers of superhero publishing. While other smaller companies existed, Marvel and DC dominated the market and mostly controlled what kind of stories would be published. Unlike the Soviet Union, neither Marvel nor DC went out of business during the 1990s (although Marvel did file for bankruptcy at one point), but a new entity debuted that would change superhero stories for a generation. In 1991, a group of popular comic book artists asked Marvel to give them creative control and ownership of the work they produced. Although both Marvel and DC had recently begun providing their creators a limited amount of creative control, the industry had a long history of publishers paying writers and artists little while keeping control of the characters and stories. The creator rights movement had been growing since the 1970s but little had been done to overhaul the tightly controlled industry.

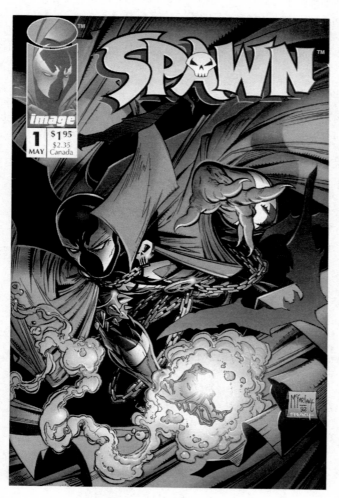

Image Comics was founded in the early 1990s when several comic book creators wanted to own and manage their characters. This move towards creator owned properties changed the comic book industry not long after the end of the Cold War. One of Image's most popular heroes is Todd McFarlane's Spawn. (Spawn, its logo and its symbol are registered trademarks © 2011 Todd McFarlane Productions, Inc.)

After Marvel refused to expand creator rights, eight popular artists left the publisher and started a comic book company named Image Comics. The new company's charter included two important stipulations: "Image would not own any creator's work; the creator would," and "No Image partner would interfere — creatively or financially with any other partner's work."[15] Image Comics quickly became a success and for awhile the publisher sold more comics than DC.[16] Although shipping delays, art-centered comic books with subpar writing, and partnership squabbles would eventually hamper Image, the company proved to be a powerful force during the 1990s and continues to publish numerous well received titles in the twenty-first century. More importantly, Image offered creators another venue for their ideas and changed the comic book industry for better and for worse. Much like the people of the United States, Marvel and DC's editors were witnessing unsettling change.

Death of a Hero

As Image was creating popular comic books in 1992, DC Comics also was producing several well-received storylines. DC's best selling event of the year was a series of stories in which Superman is killed and eventually returns. The stories that were originally intended to introduce a new cast of supporting characters soon became a phenomenon. Newspaper headlines and television reports announced that the American icon was dead. Comic book fans and other interested parties bought millions of copies of *Superman* #75 in which the hero dies after a titanic battle with the murderous Doomsday.[17] The story's creators had introduced Doomsday to fulfill the sole purpose of killing the Man of Steel in a battle that apparently pitted the 1980s style ultra-violent villain verses the traditional hero Superman. The Man of Steel's death created a void that needed to be filled with new heroes and villains. As many Americans were searching for a new way forward after the Cold War, DC Comics ostensibly began auditions for a new Superman.

With the original Man of Steel dead and buried, four new supermen stepped forward to take his place. This new storyline, entitled "Reign of the Supermen," introduced four supermen to seemingly vie for the Man of Steel's mantle. The new characters are Superboy, a young and naïve clone of the deceased Superman; The Eradicator, a piece of Kryptonian technology in superhuman form that often employs brutal methods to fight crime; Cyborg-Superman, an evil machine-human combination that poses as the Man of Steel before eventually revealing his villainous intentions; and Steel, a technological genius who builds a superpowered armored suit and fights crime as a tribute to Superman. Each of these characters explores the new era's fears and promises and offers a different possibility of what the new Superman could be. Eventually, none of the candidates are selected and the original Superman returns from the dead to claim his true place in American culture.[18]

"The Death of Superman" and the "Reign of the Supermen" storylines provide an interesting understanding of what was happening in American society. After Superman's death, the DC universe ostensibly had a number of new and exciting possible alternatives to the Man of Steel that had never been considered before. Briefly, there was a possibility that one of these new supermen could have met society's needs better than the original had. Eventually though, the storytellers discarded or marginalized each of these new candidates and the more traditional Superman returned. U.S. citizens were also facing a world with new and exciting possibilities, many of which had previously seemed impossible. Would the nation choose a radical new path or select a more traditional way forward? If Superman's death was any indication, lasting change would be harder than most Americans realized.

The Death of Superman storyline in 1992 was extremely popular with both comic book fans and the public at large. The story was one of numerous changes that occurred at DC and Marvel during the 1990s. Much like American society in general, the two most popular comic book publishers were attempting to find a new way forward after the Cold War's end. (© 1992 DC Comics. Used with permission of DC Comics.)

Fallen Knight

Not long after Superman's death and return, comic book creators also fashioned a Batman storyline in which the original Dark Knight is decommissioned, replaced, and eventually reinstated to his former role. Unlike Superman, Batman did not die, but rather Bruce Wayne was injured and unable to perform his superhero duties. In the storyline, entitled "Knightfall," which appeared in several Batman titles from April 1993 until August 1994, a new villain named Bane paralyzes Batman by breaking the Caped Crusader's back and forces the original Dark Knight to retire and recuperate. Bane's co-creator, Graham Nolan, noted in an interview that writer Chuck Dixon designed Bane to be an evil version of the pulp hero Doc Savage.[19] It is fitting that a villain based on a pulp hero would defeat and physically incapacitate Batman, a superhero originally designed with many pulp fiction elements. The ultra-intelligent and super-strong Bane both out-thinks and out fights Batman and seems to prove the Dark Knight to be too antiquated to be useful in the new era. With the original Batman no longer able to fight crime, a new hero named Jean-Paul Valley takes over the storied cape and cowl. The new Batman wears a highly-armored costume and employs more violent methods than Bruce Wayne had utilized. Eventually, Valley becomes mentally disturbed and even more violent as he allows villains to die and attacks and almost kills Robin. Ultimately, Bruce Wayne returns and physically battles and defeats Jean-Paul Valley in order to reclaim his identity as Batman.[20]

Much like Superman's recent storyline, events forced the original Batman to depart and a new more modern Dark Knight to take his place. This at first seems like the beginning of a new era that will permanently change the character's identity and purpose, but, like the Man of Steel, eventually the elder Caped Crusader returned and things continued much as they had before. Many Americans were also thinking about the country changing its identity and purpose after the end of the Cold War, but it was unclear what these changes should be and how long they could last. Although the U.S. had almost reached the 1990s' midpoint, many Americans were still searching for their new purpose.

If Scientists Can Clone Sheep Then Why Not Spiders?

As DC's creators dramatically (yet briefly) changed Superman and Batman in the early and mid–1990s, Marvel also attempted to revamp several of their most prominent heroes during this period. The most notorious of these storylines is the 1994–1996 Spider-Man Clone Saga. After witnessing the extremely popular death of Superman and the Knightfall Batman stories, Marvel editors reportedly wanted to create major changes for their characters as well. In the story, Peter Parker, Spider-Man's secret identity, encounters several clones that he had battled in a previous tale during the mid–1970s. Through a series of convoluted events it is revealed that one of the clones, Ben Reilly, is actually the real Spider-Man and Peter Parker is Reilly's clone. During the story, Peter Parker loses his powers, retires from being Spider-Man, and leaves to start a family with his pregnant wife. Eventually, all of the story elements revert to their traditional positions and it becomes clear that Peter Parker is the true Spider-Man and the previous changes were the result of a villain's manipulation.

This storyline lasted for over two years, and apparently Marvel management initially intended to make Ben Reilly the new Spider-Man and only changed directions after creators and fans complained. Former Marvel editor and writer Glenn Greenberg remembers that Spider-Man writer Dan Jurgens convinced Spider-Man Group Editor in Chief Bob Budiansky to restore Peter Parker as the true webslinger, even though Marvel had developed long term story plans for a Ben Reilly Spider-Man. Greenberg states, "Dan explained to Bob that he did not and could not accept Ben as Spider-Man, and he believed that readers felt the same way. Twenty years of continuity and significant character development — including the marriage to Mary Jane — could not simply be shunted aside and forgotten. Longtime readers could not be asked to accept that the character they followed for so long wasn't the 'real' guy."[21] Although Marvel editors and creators had originally wanted to construct a new Spider-Man, they eventually relented and settled for the traditional version. In both comic book and real world American society, numerous changes were being contemplated and tested but few seemed to take root.

The Boom and the Bust

As comic book characters like Superman, Batman, and Spider-Man confronted powerful new foes and faced life threatening battles, comic books were experiencing a massive sales growth across the country. By 1993, nearly 11,000 comic book shops sold tens of millions of comic books, totaling $800 million to $850 million in sales that year alone.[22] Though some of these sales can be attributed to collectors interested in new storylines in comic books like *Superman*, *Batman*, *Spawn*, and the *X-Men*, most were the product of an increasing collectors' mindset that meant millions of these comic books were bought by customers who never read them. Many non-comic book readers were treating comic books as a mini stock market–type investment and were purchasing "important" issues in hopes that the funny books would soon rise in value. Several early comic books were beginning to sell at auction for astronomical prices and numerous investors theorized that in a few years the current issues would also greatly rise in value. Comic book publishers quickly began to take advantage of this new mindset and introduced gimmicks and additional covers, so that collectors often felt compelled to buy several slightly different copies of each issue. Publishers added brightly colored eye-candy to the comic books in the form of foil covers, polybagged issues, or different cover art to entice buyers. These attention-grabbing alternates, variants, and extras provided a short-term windfall that ironically seemingly propelled the industry forward while actually creating a speculator bubble that threatened comic book publishing's very foundation.

Like most industries or sectors caught in a boom and bust cycle, the 1990s comic book industry grew because investors greatly overvalued the product. Non-comic book readers believed that they understood the hobby's market reality while in fact they were ignorant of several basic facts. The few comic books that are highly-valued and prized, like most other expensive resources, are in demand because they are scarce. This was generally not true of new comic books because to meet demand, publishers printed million of copies of some popular titles, almost guaranteeing that the issues would retain little or no value. These increased sales enticed publishers to often focus more on style than substance and thus began to alienate legions of longtime readers. By the start of 1994, many investors began to realize that their comic books would probably never be valuable and a large number of comic book fans were no longer happy with the stories that most creators were producing. By the end of 1994, the comic book market bubble had burst and sales were plummeting.[23]

While the comic books industry had been riding high only a year before, now it was forced to wonder how it would pick up the pieces.

Strange Fruit

As the comic book industry was entering a period of market re-evaluation and restructuring, much of American society was still adjusting to its post–Cold War status. Without the Soviet Union to serve as an accepted adversary, Americans of all walks of life continued to adjust to the new social order throughout 1994 and 1995. News outlets reported rumors of ethnic cleansing in the former Yugoslavia that soon required NATO actions, including repeated aerial bombing. The Bosnian War ended in 1995 and the U.S. took on a leadership role in the NATO operation and hosted the conflict ending peace conference. Arguably, these socially important events of 1994–1995 pushed Americans to focus on the issues of race, class, and government.[24] While the U.S. was acting as an international peacekeeper in places like the former Yugoslavia, Americans were also re-evaluating many of the nation's fundamental understandings.

The Rodney King beating of 1991 and the subsequent Los Angeles riots the following year showcased an unattractive part of American society that many citizens had believed did not exist. In 1994, Americans were again forced to focus on the issue of race, but this time the matter was coupled with class and celebrity. On June 12, 1994, Nicole Brown Simpson and Ronald Goldman were murdered in Brown Simpson's condominium, and the police soon focused on former football player O.J. Simpson as their main suspect. When O.J. Simpson, who was Brown Simpson's ex-husband, failed to turn himself in to police custody after being charged with murder, the authorities were forced to arrest him after a highly publicized low speed automobile chase. The subsequent trial became a media sensation that often polarized American society along racial and class lines. Simpson's trial was televised nationally and regularly served as the predominant water cooler subject for many across the country. When a jury of Simpson's peers eventually found the former football star not guilty of murder in 1995, millions of Americans were outraged while others believed that the state had not proven its case.[25] In retrospect, the Simpson murder trial appears to have served as a vehicle for debating parts of the country's underlying social structure while providing the kind of distraction that only a true crime story can. As Americans contemplated the changing world around them, for over a year the O.J. Simpson trial furnished many of them a titillating view of their nation. Unfortunately, other problems faced the country and some were much more horrifying.

Terror in the Heartland

Few Americans were prepared for the news when on April 19, 1995, a terrorist attacked the Alfred P. Murrah Federal Building in Oklahoma City, Oklahoma. It was later determined that Timothy McVeigh, an anti-government militia member, detonated a truck bomb that killed 168 and injured scores more. McVeigh and his associates, Terry Nichols and Michael Fortier, were later convicted of orchestrating and perpetrating the bombing. The state executed McVeigh for his crimes in June 2001.

McVeigh claimed that the bombing was a political statement against a federal government run amok and retribution for law enforcement's recent mishandling of highly publicized standoffs in Waco, Texas, and Ruby Ridge, Idaho.[26] Almost every American was shocked and saddened by the Oklahoma City bombing. While the role of the government in citizens' lives had been an ongoing question since before the nation's founding, most Americans envisioned this debate in a politically non-violent manner. People could scarcely believe that an American citizen would commit terrorism against his countrymen. Although American history is replete with politically violent acts, many believed such vicious protests to be incompatible with the U.S.'s post–Cold War reality.

In February 1993, a group of foreign terrorists had attacked the World Trade Center in New York City with a truck bomb. This coupled with the Oklahoma City bombing forced many Americans to question their daily safety. No longer could Americans assume that bombings and attacks only happened in other countries to other people. By the mid–1990s, everyday American life felt a little less safe and citizens felt a little less secure. The Soviet nemesis had been defeated but now Americans had to worry about their daily safety. Unfortunately, this was only the beginning of a new kind of terror in American society.

A House Divided

As Americans were witnessing violent and terrorist actions against the U.S. government, much of the country remained divided politically as well. In 1996, Bill Clinton was decisively elected to a second term. The youthful president easily defeated his Republican challenger, Kansas senator and World War II veteran Bob Dole. At election time Clinton benefited from a strong U.S. economy that had recovered from the early 1990s' recession and his progressive appeal to create a stronger country for the twenty-first century. Although Clinton was experiencing some bad press based on a questionable past real estate deal known as Whitewater, the president had few apparent negatives of which opponents could take advantage.

In contrast, the 1994 Congressional elections had not gone as well for Clinton and fellow Democrats. The Republicans took control of both the House of Representatives and the Senate for the first time since 1952. Many Republican candidates signed a document called the "Contract with America" in which they promised to introduce legislation to institute governmental reform, fight crime, weaken United Nations peacekeeping operations, balance the budget, reform Social Security and welfare, and advance numerous other conservative ideas. Most of these legislative items were promised rollbacks of 1960s and 1970s era liberal reforms. The new speaker of the House of Representatives, Newt Gingrich, became the face of Congressional Republicans, who pressed for a far different agenda than the more liberal President Clinton. Over the next few years the Congressional Republicans and the Clinton White House would battle over the country's direction and its future. Twice during 1995 and 1996 non-essential federal services were shut down and governmental employees were furloughed because the two sides could not agree on a spending bill.[27] These political ideological conflicts showcased the deepening divisions in American society. Many Americans were still trying to decide the country's direction even more than a half a decade since the Cold War's end. Although President Clinton was decisively elected to a second term in 1996, he was still the leader of a nation in transition.

A Hero's Role

As America clashed over the nation's social and political direction, a similar debate was also taking place within the comic book industry. Comic book creators and fans alike were at odds over the social and cultural roles of superheroes at the end of the twentieth century. Many comic book readers and creators asked if a superhero should be a positive moral and ethical symbol of good citizenship or should the hero adopt a new more relativist ethical viewpoint? Should heroes serve as an example of what readers could strive for or should these supermen and women provide violent wish fulfillment to readers burdened by an often dangerous and discouraging world? This debate was not new, and excessively violent and less traditional heroes had become increasingly popular in the 1970s and 1980s.

During these years, DC refashioned some of its heroes into more aggressive and violent vigilantes, but most of the publisher's more popular characters retained their traditional agents of the state outlook. By the mid–1990s, DC was searching for a new direction and was unsure how to proceed. New, more modern versions of Superman and Batman had briefly replaced the traditional heroes, but before long those two icons had returned with only a few minor changes, while other heroes like Green Arrow and Aquaman embraced a new, more aggressive ethos over a longer period time. In other words, DC was proceeding as it generally had for decades, testing new ideas in a limited way while continuing to embrace its core conservative values.

Marvel also embraced its core beliefs and created heroes that attempted to mirror society rather than mold it. During the 1970s and 1980s, many signature Marvel characters developed moral codes that greatly broke with traditional superhero beliefs. Heroes like Wolverine and the Punisher unrepentantly tortured and killed opponents and acted in a manner that would have been unacceptable only a few years before. Although Marvel had many heroes that operated in a more traditional heroic way, creators generally accentuated the characters' numerous flaws and built a grittier and less historically conventional universe. In the mid–1990s, Marvel, like DC, also had to decide on what new direction to follow. Many of the publisher's best known creators had left to form Image Comics, and the comic book company was facing financial and creative problems. Much like the nation, both DC and Marvel were struggling to move into the future while respecting the past — an objective that is far more difficult than it sounds.

Not Such a Marvel

As Americans were attempting to readjust their expectations to the nation's outlook and purpose, Marvel Comics was struggling to ensure that the company indeed had a future. The country's most popular comic book publisher experienced financial problems due to poor investment strategies and the comic book market's collapse. In 1996, Marvel filed for bankruptcy and was perilously close to going out of business.[28] While Marvel was enduring financial turmoil, the company continued to publish comic books, although most lacked the creativity and zest that had made Marvel a fan favorite. In 1996–1997, Marvel attempted to recapture some of this lost inspiration by outsourcing several of its most popular titles to creators Jim Lee and Rob Liefeld, former employees who had left to co-found Image Comics. Lee and Liefeld were very well respected among comic book fans and Marvel hoped the company could recapture the success of the late 1980s and early 1990s.

The new stories, entitled *Heroes Reborn*, created a new universe and redesigned heroes like the Fantastic Four, Iron Man, and Captain America to be more relevant to young readers. Heroes' origins were updated and linked to events closer to the present day rather than the 1960s, while artists redesigned costumes to display a more modern look.[29] However, these revamps lasted for just over a year before the heroes reverted to their previous incarnations. *Heroes Reborn* was yet another failed comic book superhero change during the 1990s. Much like many Americans, comic book readers seemingly enjoyed the idea of new and improved ways of life but in reality wanted to retain tradition.

Trying Anything

As Marvel was experiencing financial and creative problems during the mid–1990s, DC Comics was also having difficulty finding an inspired and consistent company-wide voice. One of the publisher's main concerns was that many of DC's superheroes seemed like outdated representatives of a bygone time. As the U.S. searched for a novel way forward in a post–Cold War world, DC struggled to understand what readers desired in this new era. In 1994, creators and editors decided to once again revamp the DC universe in order to make it more inviting for new readers and to fix continuity errors that bothered many long-time fans. The 1994 mini-series *Zero Hour* featured an epic battle that restructured the existing timeline and streamlined the DC universe, which allowed writers and artists to have a semi-fresh start with many long established characters. Creators produced new stories that attempted to redefine classic comic book characters for a new generation of readers. One often-used type of story involved an established hero losing his or her position and a new younger hero donning the costume and mantle. Seemingly, this was DC management's chance to create novel versions of recognized heroes for a new, younger audience.

The comic book publisher had previously experienced high sales by killing or injuring Superman and Batman and introducing new characters, although the traditional characters soon returned. In 1994–1995, creators turned the Silver Age Green Lantern, Hal Jordan, into the villain Parallax, killed Jordan, and introduced the new, younger Green Lantern, Kyle Rainer. In 1995, DC killed the original Green Arrow, Oliver Queen, which allowed his recently discovered son, Connor Hawke, to become the new Emerald Archer. In January 1995, Diana lost her position as Wonder Woman and was forced to fight crime under another persona as the young Artemis became the updated Amazing Amazon. Additionally, in July 1994, a new and younger speeder named Impulse was introduced, and in September 1994 a reinvented version of the 1940s hero Starman premiered. While almost all of the older heroes would later return, during the mid–1990s DC Comics was attempting to redefine itself in much the same manner as the nation.

New Revelation

The comic book story that best exemplifies the debate regarding a superhero's role in mid–1990s America is the 1996 four part mini-series *Kingdom Come*. The story is set in a possible future in which Superman has retired after seeing the public embrace superheroes that employee ultra-violent methods and advocate murdering supervillains. The Man of Steel returns to duty after a superhero battle turns disastrous and a large nuclear blast irradiates much of Kansas, killing millions. Without Superman's guidance, heroes and villains have become nearly identical, and both now resemble superpowered gang members fighting over minor squabbles with no concern for the damage they cause or the people they harm. The brash, reckless, and extreme new young heroes/villains horrify the Man of Steel, who creates a society-army of likeminded heroes who attempt to regulate superheroic activity and punish those that will not follow the new super-social norms. Superman imprisons a large number of the superhumans who do not fall in line with his new guidelines. Eventually, the metahumans escape, a grand battle ensues, and several supervillains are revealed to have orchestrated many of the events. The United Nations launches three nuclear warheads that ultimately kill a large number of heroes and give Superman a new perspective. Superman and the other surviving superhumans decide to now lead by example rather than imposing their will on citizens. The former heroes integrate into society instead of standing apart in the traditional manner. At the story's end Superman becomes a farmer and Batman a doctor, both choosing the careers of their fathers.[30]

At the heart of the narrative are the questions of what is acceptable superhero behavior and does the American public still desire old-fashioned moralistic superheroes. Writer Mark Waid and artist Alex Ross conceive of a new path that rejects traditional superheroic actions and yet embraces superheroes' moral guidance. Waid and Ross opine that 1990s society did not require distant otherworldly protectors, but rather needed moral examples who integrated themselves into normal society. Comic book writer Elliot S! Maggin notes, "It is a conclusion to which our new bards lead us as elegantly and precisely as Socrates led us through an argument or Pythagoras led us through a geometric proof. Even super-heroes need to grow. We know that now."[31] *Kingdom Come* outlines a novel role for superheroes in a society coping with rapid changes. Unfortunately, society can rarely implement new ideas quickly or painlessly either in comic books or in real life.

New Ways, Old Desires

As Marvel and DC were attempting to create new, more vibrant fictional societies that followed a traditional template while heading in a new direction, the country also was continuing to slowly change. During the first part of Bill Clinton's second term, the Congress enacted and the president signed numerous pieces of new legislation that curbed 1960s era reforms and continued the nation's move in a more conservative direction. The government also began to downsize several aspects of the U.S. military in order to better meet the country's post–Cold War needs. Additionally, the U.S. took on an expanded new international role as the world's lone superpower attempting to provide stability and leadership. In 2004, the U.S., Canada, and Mexico created the North American Free Trade Agreement (NAFTA) which eliminated barriers to free trade among the three nations. While NAFTA proved to be controversial, the agreement showcased the U.S.'s growing desire to create a more international economy.[32] Partially because of expanding global markets, the country once again experienced a period of economic growth and prosperity during the mid and late 1990s. While this looked bright for many Americans, the nation also appeared to be searching for tangible goals or challenges in which to engage. The Soviet Union's collapse had left a void in American life that had never been filled. With no external enemy to battle, many Americans turned inward and instead focused on domestic crimes and scandals. By 1998, a political sexual scandal would engage the nation and disrupt the country for well over a year.

Sometimes a Cigar Is Just a Cigar

In early 1998, rumors began to circulate that while he was president Bill Clinton had engaged in a sexual relationship with White House intern Monica Lewinsky. Kenneth Starr, serving as independent counsel, was already investigating President Clinton for possible past ethics and legal violations, and news reports often carried ongoing details of this probe. At a January 26, 1998, White House press conference, President Clinton denied having "sexual relations with that woman, Miss Lewinsky," but after more evidence was uncovered Clinton was forced to admit an "improper physical relationship" during grand jury testimony on August 17, 1998. In December 1998, the U.S. House of Representatives voted to issue the articles of impeachment against Clinton because the president apparently denied his relationship with Lewinsky while testifying in court regarding another matter. Members of the House of Representatives believed that Clinton had not only committed perjury but also was guilty of obstruction of justice by influencing Lewinsky's testimony. This was only the second time in American history that the House of Representatives had impeached a president. The Senate conducted a twenty-one day trial but ultimately voted to acquit the president of any wrongdoing.

The Lewinsky scandal polarized much of the nation and became the lead news story and most popular American conversation topic for well over a year. Citizens' opinions regarding the allegations and the impeachment proceedings often served as a Rorschach test of a person's social and political views. During this time the country remained divided on numerous important issues and the Lewinsky scandal highlighted many of those political, social, and cultural disagreements.[33] Unfortunately, the country's intense concentration on the scandal and subsequent impeachment proceeding also prevented numerous people from focusing on the nation's direction. While the scandal served as a way for many Americans to voice their opinions and concerns about the nation's present and future, it did not provide a mechanism to addresses these issues and subsequently stopped Americans from finding other outlets for social and political change. Because of this, little change or reform took place in the remaining months of the 1990s. A decade that had begun with such grand possibilities and great expectations had become bogged down in partisan politics and sexual scandal.

Bipartisan Superheroes

As the Clinton scandal and impeachment divided much of the country and many politicians fiercely battled along party lines, DC and Marvel created a unique literary compromise that literally merged their two universes for a short time. The process had started as a crossover in 1996 when the two companies co-published *DC versus Marvel*. During this four part series DC and Marvel superheroes battled and fans voted to determine the victors.

At the center of the conflict are two godlike cosmic beings known as the Brothers who war against each other because they do not want the other to continue to exist. Eventually,

Mark Waid and Alex Ross's *Kingdom Come* (1996) questioned superheroes' social and political roles while many Americans were attempting to understand American society's new post–Cold War direction. (© 1996 DC Comics. Used with permission of DC Comics.)

the fighting forces the two universes to merge and create a single universe which shares traits from both Marvel and DC stories. A fictitious comic book company (actually a combination of the two companies) named Amalgam Comic published stories containing the new Marvel and DC combined characters. Numerous amalgamated characters populate the new universe, including Dark Claw (a combination of Batman and Wolverine), Super-Soldier (Superman and Captain America merged), and Spider-Boy (the amalgamation of Spider-Man and Superboy). Eventually both universes are restored to their original realities but the stories demonstrated that even adversaries such as DC and Marvel could put aside their differences and work towards the common good.[34]

The two comic book publishers may have been attempting to mold public opinion and press for more compromise in American society in general and in the political arena in particular. Unfortunately, these changes did not take root in society at large and individuals seemed to rarely compromise their conflicting ideologies to reach a unified view. While comic book characters had often been predictors or creators of public opinion, even the nation's mythological heroes could do little to change the political schism of the time.

Super Changes

As the Clinton scandal and impeachment titillated and enraptured many Americans and DC and Marvel completed their historic and brief amalgamation, both major comic book publishers continued to search for a new way forward. Throughout the decade both DC and Marvel had tried to revitalize their stories in numerous ways, including killing or retiring old characters, introducing new heroes, and changing their universes' histories. As the decade neared its end the companies continued to experiment with a plethora of ideas, many of which appear comically bizarre in retrospect. The symbol of this desire to create change no matter how out of place it may seem is Superman. The Man of Steel began the decade as a new version of his classic self. In 1993, Superman died, was replaced by four usurpers, and then resurrected from the dead. In 1996, Clark Kent, Superman's secret identity, married his long time love interest Lois Lane and revealed to her that he was secretly the Man of Steel. It appears that death, resurrection, and matrimony were not groundbreaking enough changes, though, so in 1997 Superman gained different powers and a new costume. He now had blue skin, was a being composed entirely of energy, and had a containment suit to keep his body intact. Superman's new powers were electricity-based and he could now fly at much faster speeds than before.

Although most readers expected Superman to quickly revert to his traditional power set and appearance, creators and editors actually made even more drastic short term changes to the character. In 1998, the new pure energy powered Superman split into two separate entities, one red and one blue. This story, which was based on an imaginary tale from the early 1960s, created an aggressive and hot headed red Superman and a more laid back and cerebral blue Man of Steel. This storyline finished before the end of 1998, and soon Superman returned to his more traditional state.[35] In this period Superman symbolizes the comic book industry and in some ways American society in general. Both superheroes and Americans attempted to create lasting change during the decade but often only reverted to traditional practices. Although some changes remained (Superman would continue to be married to Lois Lane in the comic books until 2011), many attempted modifications merely returned to previous norms.

Conclusion

In many ways the 1990s seemed to adhere to the old saying regarding March, that if it arrives like a lion it exits like a lamb. The 1990s began with much fanfare and anticipation as the nation (and the world) breathlessly awaited a new post–Cold War era. The Soviet Union had fallen and the United States stood as the world's lone superpower. U.S. citizens gazed towards a seemingly limitless future in which a strong and prosperous America enjoyed the fruits of its Cold War victory. First, citizens and politicians alike had to determine how to move forward and what changes were best for the country. Although almost every American understood that some changes were necessary, few were able to agree on how the country should function both internationally and domestically. Problems in places such as Iraq, Somalia, and the Balkans forced Americans to question the role of the United States in world affairs. Political pressure and infighting between liberals and conservatives stalled many domestic changes and pushed the country into political and often social gridlock. While some social reforms were agreed upon and many were discussed, the country never adopted a grand vision for moving forward and instead settled for a handful of piecemeal changes that in reality failed to revolutionize the United States. Americans choose to focus on tradition and scandal rather than the social and political transformations that seemed possible at the decade's beginning.

As is historically the case, comic book superheroes mirrored the hopes and fears of the decade and focused on creating change. Like the country as a whole, few of these changes lasted and before long most superheroes returned to their traditional statuses. Superman died, Spider-Man and Batman quit, and a plethora of new characters took over long established superhero identities. New universes were created, merged, and destroyed. In the end, almost none of these changes survived and instead both DC and Marvel returned to their traditional cores. Although the comic book publishers often seriously attempted to create lasting change, in the long term little came of their efforts. Both the country as a whole and the two largest comic book publishers ended the decade without creating a lasting plan for significant change. Although change would come quickly at the start of the next decade, it would not be the kind that Americans wanted.

Chapter 9

DECADE OF FEAR (2000–2009)

During the lead-up to DC Comics' maxi-series *Crisis on Infinite Earths*, many super-heroes noticed the sky over their cities turning red. Although these changes meant little to the heroes, to the readers they foreshadowed the coming crisis. While comic book denizens were unassumingly enjoying their peaceful lives, evil forces were gathering on the horizon. In situations like this comic book creators often build suspense and move a story forward by foretelling an upcoming crisis or emergency. The crisis is frequently in contrast to the peaceful life that presently seems to surround the hero. As an evil madman plots revenge, only the reader can wince and worry, while the heroes are oblivious to the impending danger. This "calm before the storm" style of storytelling has the desired unsettling effect on the reader but the writer allows the fictional hero the opportunity to enjoy a few days of well-deserved, unencumbered tranquility. In retrospect, the end of the 1990s and the beginning of the 2000s were a relative collective calm before a decade of destructive social storms. While no one knew it at the time, the United States was transitioning from a decade of relative peace and prosperity to a decade of terror.

The 1990s ended much as they had begun, with a mixture of hope and fear and a general lack of direction. As a new millennium dawned, many Americans began to take stock in their lives and to think about the future.[1] Although President Bill Clinton often had spoken of building a bridge to the twenty-first century, a great number of Americans were unsure in which direction the nation should be headed. The Cold War had ended over a decade before, but the country still appeared to be lacking a national purpose. While the economy was seemingly booming, many citizens turned their attention to issues like the aftermath of the president's impeachment. In many ways the 1990s had been a transitional decade in which Americans grappled with uneasy questions about change and the nation's future, but few citizens seemed to embrace a positive attitude towards the new century. Turn of the century trepidations are not unusual; many societies have experienced mass fear and paranoia as new centuries approached. These fears generally disappear once the century debuts and are scarcely seen again. In the U.S., twenty-first century fears started early with the Y2K paranoia, quickly turned to terror after the September 11, 2001, terrorist attacks, and continued to grow and change throughout the decade. The transitional 1990s gave way to the terror-filled 2000s.

Comic book superheroes also quickly transitioned during the aughts. While the 1990s proved frustrating for creators that seemingly needed societal conflict to supply a motivation for superheroes, the 2000s provided excessive negative stimuli for new terrifying storylines. In other words, superhero narratives during the first years of the twenty-first century closely mirrored society's new fears. Just as they had in previous decades, comic book superheroes embraced the social zeitgeist as writers and artists created ever darkening worlds. The decade of the 2000s would bring terror to many parts of most Americans' lives and superheroes were not exempt. Terror had come and not even society's colorful avengers could escape it.

Maybe the Luddites Were Right

The twenty-first century's fearful attitude began even before the new decade started, as people worldwide worried about a technological glitch causing international havoc. Many technology experts and social forecasters believed that at the stroke of midnight on January 1, 2000, computer systems across the world would cease to function due to a software programming problem. Insiders dubbed this potential catastrophe "Y2K," shorthand for the "Year 2000." Media sources publicized the possible social and infrastructural breakdown and stories about the coming unrest abounded. On January 18, 1999, almost an entire year before the perceived digital disaster, *Time* magazine published an article about Y2K worries entitled, "The End of the World As We Know It?" In this text, numerous authors discuss the growing Y2K paranoia and link the social uneasiness to millennial fears.[2] A December 30, 1999, *New York Times* article prognosticated that "years from now, historians will be fascinated by the combination of arduous planning, breathless hype and stubborn indifference that have gone into preparations for the computer glitch known as the Y2K bug."[3] This introspective self-assessment fails to mention the underlying fear, but ends by forecasting:

> At the stroke of midnight, amid fears of terrorism and computer breakdowns, we will listen expectantly to the news, hoping for the best. Even those of us who have not filled the bathtub with emergency water, withdrawn extra cash from the bank and stocked up on food will be entering the new millennium sobered by the awareness that unknown problems of our own making are an enduring part of existence.[4]

Although most of the Y2K fears were unfounded or the potential problems were corrected in time, the episode provided a fitting starting point for the first decade of the twenty-first century. Y2K paranoia had swept through American society and many citizens believed the worst. Most of these fears seem quaint in retrospect, and when remembering the aughts many Americans forget about Y2K altogether. The majority of the fears that existed at the start of the year 2000 went unrealized, but the year 2001 would bring new all too real horrors. First, Americans had to come to terms with one of the most unsettling presidential elections in decades.

Bush v. Gore

Americans entered the year 2000 with the Y2K problem behind them, and the future was rosy. There was no clear mandate regarding the nation's future and the U.S. seemingly lacked a purpose both internationally and domestically. This social apathy seemed of little consequence as the nation nearly sleepwalked through President Clinton's last year in office. Presidential candidates Al Gore and George W. Bush did little to inspire many voters and much of the country seemed uninterested in the upcoming election. Low voter turnout, third party candidates, and increased political polarization helped to create one of the most unusual elections in U.S. history, though. After voting ended on November 7, 2000, Vice President Gore and former Texas Governor Bush found themselves in a virtual deadlock. The election results were so close that officials were initially unable to determine a victor. A sequence of legal actions, including a Supreme Court ruling, ultimately laid the groundwork to declare George W. Bush the new president. Although Gore won the popular vote in early November, the Electoral College results were in question until almost mid–December. The exceptionally long and uncertain election proved both bewildering and frightening to many Americans. People expected the electoral process to be tiresome and annoying, but most had never considered a scenario that did not provide a quick and conclusive outcome. The 2000 elections showcased what happens when the American political system fails to work as expected. Although the system ultimately produced a winner, in the interim millions of Americans lost faith in something they had trusted their entire lives. By the time Supreme Court Chief Justice William Rehnquist swore in George W. Bush as the 43rd president of the United States on January 20, 2001, the nation had been questioning the American electoral system for months. Numerous states enacted measures to strengthen the voting process, but many Americans were angered and confused about the 2000 election. While there was no widespread social upheaval, voters had grown uncertain about the U.S. political system and what the future may hold. This uncertainty set the stage for the upcoming events in which seemingly stable institutions would become unnervingly vulnerable.[5]

The Coming Terror

If the Y2K fear and paranoia served as the aughts' cornerstone and the 2000 election continued to lay a foundation of uneasiness, then the September 11 terrorist attacks cemented widespread national feelings of terror. On September 11, 2001, terrorists hijacked four commercial airlines on the United States' East Coast. The hijackers flew two of the aircraft into the World Trade Center twin towers in New York City, one airplane severely damaged the Pentagon, and the other plane crashed in a Pennsylvania field. The 9/11 attacks galvanized the nation while also pushing many Americans towards base feelings of fear and paranoia. Citizens quickly began to worry about unseen enemies and unknown conspiracies. Many believed that a terrorist could be anyone hiding anywhere just waiting to do harm. As Americans mourned, many asked how this could happen in the U.S. and what would be the terrorists' next target. Only a week later, on September 18, as the nation was still reeling from the 9/11 attacks, an unknown terrorist mailed the first of a series of letters containing deadly anthrax spores.[6] During the next month and a half, 22 people would become ill and five would die due to contact with the anthrax pathogen contained in the letters.[7] Suddenly, nothing, not even the most mundane activities, seemed safe anymore. Terror had come to the United States and many Americans wondered if they would ever feel safe again.

We Have Nothing to Fear but Everything

After the September 11 terrorist attacks, the Patriot Act and other federal legislation curtailed civil rights, and airports and other public places instituted strict search policies that changed longstanding ideas of mobility and personal freedom. These standards became even more stringent when, only a few weeks later, Richard Reed tried to detonate a so-called "shoe bomb" on a commercial flight. Soon Americans were being frisked in line for sporting events and told to protect themselves from possible chemical and biological weapons. President Bush declared war on terror and U.S. troops quickly invaded Afghanistan, but domestically terror appeared to be winning. Many were frightened and this fear did not appear to subside as the decade progressed. In 2003, the U.S. armed forces also invaded Iraq, forcing the nation to militarily fight terror on two separate fronts. The Bush administration began holding political prisoners at Guantanamo Bay, Cuba, and opening secret prisons in various places across the globe all in the name of combating terror and quelling American fear. The decade continued with talk of the U.S. military conducting torture and ever depressing wars in Iraq and Afghanistan. Declarations like "they hate us for our freedom" and the "axis of evil" only served to heighten feelings of fear and push Americans towards increased terror and paranoia. The U.S. had become a place where the government and news media encouraged fear and many believed that being afraid was the only acceptable option in a world that appeared to many to have gone insane.

This is the world in which comic book creators wrote the decade's superhero stories, a world in which nearly all societal outlets were not only encouraging but demanding that citizens be afraid. Although comic book superheroes carry the potential to inspire great hope and courage, during the first decade of the twenty-first century most of our spandex-clad champions followed society's drummer and instead preached fear and paranoia.[8]

Fearful Heroes

The 9/11 attacks shocked and frightened comic book superheroes just as they had terrorized the rest of the nation. Fictional characters like Spider-Man and Superman appeared grief-stricken and ultimately unusually powerless. In *Amazing Spider-Man* #36, writer J. Michael Straczynski and artist John Romita, Jr., chronicle how Peter Parker deals with the September 11 aftermath. The single issue story reveals that many Marvel universe luminaries are as saddened, terrified, and frustrated as their real world counterparts. In one scene, supervillain and would-be world conqueror Dr. Doom is shown crying because of the September 11 tragedy.[9] Much as the heroes could do little during the titanic battles of World War II, they also were helpless against the 9/11 attackers. Both DC and Marvel published special editions in which firemen and policemen were declared true heroes and superheroes displayed their support for the nation. The DC edition showcases an Alex Ross painted cover in which Superman and his superdog Krypto stare in wonder and disbelief at a poster featuring brave policemen and firemen. This cover is an homage to 1944's *Big All-American Comic Book* #1, in which a boy and his dog are overwhelmed at the sight of a superhero poster.[10]

Unlike comic books published during World War II, DC and Marvel did not send their heroes to war or express racial or cultural stereotypes in their comic books. Virtually no major superheroes fought terrorists at home or abroad. America's new enemy was much too nebulous and ill-defined for superheroic battles. At first, comic book writers and artists appeared unsure how to fight against the nation's new foe. For the first few years following the September 11 tragedy, most superhero comic books continued much as they had before and the majority of the stories remained relatively the same. What comic book creators eventually did was construct a decade long nightmare for heroes and villains alike. Although comic books had been becoming darker during the 1980s and 1990s, those changes generally

reflected individual characters adopting more aggressive methods of fighting crime and corruption. While some may see these 2000s stories as mere extensions of earlier dark tales, the new stories created entire universes seemingly governed by fear. Comic book stories had been getting darker and more violent for decades, but the 2000s shifted into a realm of overwhelming fear and forced readers to question who could be trusted. Much like their real world counterpart, fear soon controlled the DC and Marvel universes.

A Short Pause

Although DC and Marvel both reacted quickly to the September 11 attacks, each company soon returned to its previous storylines. Superman, Spider-Man, Batman, Captain America, and a host of other characters battled supervillains and continued much the same as they had in the previous years. Safe stories like *Batman: Hush*, a classic Caped Crusader tale, *Marvel 1602*, a reimagining of Marvel characters in Elizabethan England, and a Justice League of America and Avengers team-up dominated the sales charts.[11] Superheroes, like many Americans, seemed to be attempting to understand their new reality and chose to continue to act the same until they understood what to do. It is not unusual for comic books to lag a few years behind social and cultural transformations, especially when these changes are quick and unexpected. As the U.S. invaded Afghanistan, upgraded security, curtailed civil liberties, and moved towards war with Iraq, comic book heroes remained an oasis of pre–9/11 life. Slowly, this began to change, and the terror that filled many Americans' lives invaded the fictional super-universes. It took superheroes several years to mirror the terror that had engulfed the U.S., but soon costumed heroes became as terrified as most Americans were.

The Wolves Are at the Door

In the months following the September 11 attacks, Americans labored to remake their society while comic book heroes attempted to find their place in the new order. After making very few story changes for over two years, comic creators seemed to catch up in 2004. By this point terror had become an everyday part of American society and voices from across the spectrum encouraged citizens to be afraid. Government officials, news media spokespersons, and even popular culture outlets consistently informed Americans to remain afraid. One of the most memorable of these fearful appeals was a 2004 presidential campaign television advertisement supporting George W. Bush's re-election. The commercial showcases a pack of wolves that appear ready to attack nearby prey. As the wolf pack menacingly paces, a narrator informs viewers that, if elected president, Bush's opponent, John Kerry, cannot and will not keep the U.S. safe. The narrator warns viewers that weakness is not an option because there are forces which wish to do the U.S. harm. This is only one example of how many people and organizations, both public and private, had embraced feelings of panic and terror.[12] During this period the news media continued to run sensationalized stories,

Opposite: This scene from a special story in *Amazing Spider-Man* #36 displays how scared and emotional even comic book heroes were in the wake of the September 11 terrorist attacks. (© 2001 Marvel Comics. All Rights Reserved.)

and the Department of Homeland Security prompted Americans to check the color-coded Homeland Security Advisory System so that citizens could determine how afraid they should feel throughout their day. The U.S. news media often referred to the colorful scale as the "terror alert level" and reporters frequently reminded Americans of what the daily fear level was.

The September 11 attacks were shocking, disturbing, and utterly terrifying, and almost all Americans were understandably afraid and uncertain about how to proceed with their lives. At the start of 2004, this fear and uneasiness had become institutionalized, and many Americans accepted uncertainty as a necessarily part of their daily affairs. By August 2004, this fear had also reached the Marvel universe, and soon superheroes would become as terrorized as most real life citizens.

Disassembled

As the Marvel universe became a more fearful and frightening place, one of the first comic books to change was one of Marvel's oldest and most successful supergroups. The Avengers first appeared in 1963 when the Incredible Hulk, Iron Man, Thor, Ant-Man, and Wasp teamed up to battle threats too powerful to tackle alone.[13] The Avengers soon became Marvel's première superteam as fans thrilled at the rotating cast and the group's extraordinary exploits. The 2004 Avengers Disassembled mini-series brought terror to the beloved supergroup, while killing members and destroying the existing team. Although comic books are replete with stories in which popular characters are killed and special places destroyed, Avengers Disassembled was the first in a new series of stories that created modern havoc and terror in the Marvel universe. The series' writer, Brian Michael Bendis, noted that this story was different from other events because things would permanently change the heroes' lives.[14] In fact, Avengers Disassembled is the initial tale in a new Marvel canon that would begin to question twenty-first century America's frightening foundation.

In the main story, a series of foes attack the Avengers, kill a number of members, and destroy the team's headquarters. After several lengthy and destructive battles, the Avengers learn that one of their own colleagues, the Scarlett Witch, caused each of the attacks. Unknown to the readers and the Avengers, the Scarlett Witch had slowly been going insane for years and had come to blame her super-teammates for the loss of her children. The Scarlett Witch uses her powerful abilities to alter reality in an effort to punish the Avengers and terrorize her former friends and teammates. The series ends with the Avengers disbanding and leaving a void within the Marvel universe.[15] Part of the reason that Marvel published Avengers Disassembled was undoubtedly so the comic book company could create a new Avengers team consisting of more popular members like Spider-Man and Wolverine. The series paved the way for the new Avengers by turning a long-time team member into a mentally disturbed murderer who cruelly and calculatingly slaughters her fellow heroes. The Scarlett Witch does so by changing the universe's very essence and recreating a new warped reality. This new reality creates a terrifying state of existence in which random attacks kill, maim, and destroy without warning and seemingly for little or no reason. No one can really ever feel safe because an enemy may attack at any moment in any way. Although this is the underlying plot of a superhero story, it sounds suspiciously similar to the way that many Americans were feeling in 2004.

Another Crisis

Like Marvel, DC also began creating unsettling comic book stories in 2004 that mirrored the uneasiness and vulnerability that many Americans felt. While Marvel terrorized the Avengers until they disbanded, DC assaulted its superteam, the Justice League of America (JLA), in thoroughly disturbing ways. The 2004 mini-series *Identity Crisis* contains a story which forces the reader to question both superheroes and the world itself. The series begins with longtime character Sue Dibny's murder and the investigation and terror that it causes. The slain Mrs. Dibny is a B/C level character best known for being both stretchy-superhero Elongated Man's wife and his professional partner. As the heroes attempt to determine who killed Sue, their prime suspect becomes Dr. Light, a villain that writer Brad Meltzer reveals once attacked and raped Sue in the past. After the rape, as both punishment and precaution, several members of the JLA agreed to magically wipe Dr. Light's memory and to change his personality, effectively lobotomizing him. These past events shock several younger heroes, who also learn that later other villains received mindwipes, and as did the hero Batman when he protested Dr. Light's treatment/punishment. During the course of the mini-series, the killer orchestrates the deaths of Robin's father, Jack Drake, and the villain Captain Boomerang, while also threatening superheroes' spouses such as Lois Lane. The series ends when the heroes discover that the murderer is the Atom's ex-wife, Jean Loring, who planned the crimes in order to win back her former spouse.[16]

Identity Crisis's storyline clearly states that neither friend nor family members can be trusted. Jean Loring kills and threatens both friends and colleagues in order to get what she wants. Numerous superheroes trade their morals and values for safety and violate the rights of other heroes and villains that disagree. No one is safe and no one can be trusted. Our heroes and their families are not who or what we thought they were and now everyone must be seen with fear and suspicion. As many Americans began to distrust those around them, so did their heroes. No one, either real or fictional, could be viewed outside a fear-filled lens.

Creating Terror

By 2004 both Marvel and DC seemingly felt the need to produce gritty, hard-edged comic books that mirrored American society's fear and frustration. Each company turned long established characters into murderers and recreated worlds in which no one could be trusted. The Scarlett Witch and Jean Loring both killed their friends and colleagues and each helped to destroy or weaken highly regarded and important organizations. DC and Marvel appeared to be repositioning themselves as more representative of American society and embracing the terror that many Americans felt. Former DC editor Valerie D'Orazio confirms the publisher's wish to create darker stories when she codedly writes about DC's motivation for publishing *Identity Crisis* in her internet blog, *Occasional Superheroine*. In several 2006 blog entries, D'Orazio describes working for a fictional comic book company that publishes a story in which a character is raped. It seems obvious that D'Orazio is describing *Identity Crisis* and is changing names and identities in order to avoid legal action. D'Orazio claims that the comic book company she worked for wanted to become more socially relevant and increase sales by producing heightenedly aggressive stories. D'Orazio asserts that editors decided, "They needed a rape. Because there's nothing quite so badass as rape, let's face it."[17] The former DC editor states that her company determined that sales were low because stories were "too good-natured and nice."[18] The publisher created what one can assume is *Identity Crisis* and "our books changed. There was rape, and murder, torture, death, and mutilation. Superheroes did amoral or outright evil things and the line between good and bad was blurred."[19]

This was not the first time that a comic book company produced sensationalized stories to sell more issues. What is important about this change is how much it mirrored American society. In Valerie D'Orazio's last quotation a few sentences ago, replace the word "books" with "society" and change "superheroes" to any abstract group that you believe committed violent acts during the aughts (terrorists, the government, the military, etc.). This passage could easily describe twenty-first century American society and its many perceived changes. Superheroes were coming to resemble other American groups and organizations, at least the way citizens perceived them. Society had changed and comic books were changing with it.

War and Disaster

As George W. Bush won the 2004 presidential election, he promised to keep Americans safe and reminded the electorate that enemies wanted to harm the nation. The U.S. was still embroiled militarily in Iraq and Afghanistan, and domestically Americans worried about possible terrorist attacks. A June 2005 CNN/USA Today/ Gallop poll found that 59 percent of Americans were opposed to the war in Iraq.[20] While most Americans had once supported the military action, many citizens' opinions changed when the U.S. military found no weapons of mass destruction and the war continued to drag on. Possibly even more damaging were the allegations that U.S. Army personnel tortured, abused, and humiliated detainees at Abu Ghraib prison in Iraq. An investigation produced numerous shocking photos and eventually led to the military charging a number of service personnel with misconduct and court-martialing several others.[21] By 2005 many were concerned about the military's capability and morality. President Bush's popularity would also begin to drop by the year's end as a growing number of Americans questioned his handling of the Iraq and Afghanistan wars and his reaction to Hurricane Katrina. As the national disaster devastated the Gulf Coast and destroyed much of the city of New Orleans, governmental reaction was both slow and inadequate. As over a thousand people died in New Orleans and thousands more were trapped in the city, the emergency response effort was ill prepared and lacking. The nation observed as President Bush commended the head of the disaster agency, Michael Brown, by stating, "Brownie, you're doing a heck of a job."[22]

No More Terrorists

As America neared the decade's mid-point, superhero comic books no longer served as a refuge. Stories that had once provided escape from many of society's problems now mirrored American culture. *Avengers Disassembled* and *Identity Crisis* in 2004 marked the start of new stories that would emphasize fear and uncertainty among heroes and villains alike. Marvel continued this new direction with the 2005 mini-series *House of M*, written by *Avengers Disassembled* author Brian Michael Bendis. In this new limited-series, the ultra-powerful mutant and villain of *Avengers Disassembled*, the Scarlett Witch, Wanda Maximoff, alters reality and creates a world in which formerly despised mutants control every aspect of society. In this new existence humans are legally and socially inferior to mutants, a reversal of the "normal" Marvel universe. Mutants, and a select number of human superheroes, live much better lives, as Wanda has created a society that now appreciates mutants at the expense of humans. In short, the Scarlett Witch becomes a terrorist and uses her mental weapons to remake society for the betterment of her people. Although Wanda does not appear to hate human society for its freedom, she does dislike the perceived political and social injustices humans inflicted on mutants.

Wanda's attempts to reshape society ultimately fail and the original reality is restored. After this happens the Scarlett Witch vastly reduces the number of mutants to less than two hundred. Not only does Wanda's terrorist plot fail, but it backfires and harms her cause. (The Scarlett Witch herself cleaves the mutant population when she begins to feel disenchanted with her fellow mutants.) The series ends with most former mutants no longer possessing superpowers and everything else returning to normal.[23] Although the terrorist plot had been extremely frightening, it in the end is unsuccessful. The Marvel universe is an ever terrifying place but even in a fictional world the terrorists cannot be allowed to win.

A World in Crisis

As Marvel stories were exploring issues of social terror, DC was continuing to create a darker and more frightening universe. If 2004's *Identity Crisis* showcased the idea that everyone must be viewed with fear and suspicion, then 2005's *Infinite Crisis* asks if we could even trust ourselves and the very world around us.

The storyline begins in a special countdown issue in which former Justice League leader Maxwell Lord murders his past teammate, Ted Kord, the Blue Beetle. Both of these characters are best remembered for their appearances in the light-hearted Justice League stories of the late 1980s. When the formerly buffoonish Max Lord brutally shoots the often silly Blue Beetle in the head, the reader understands that no one, no matter how seemingly unassuming, can be trusted. Soon the reader learns that Lord has used his mental powers to take control of Superman, leaving the Man of Steel defenseless and untrustworthy. Superman, the ultimate American weapon, has fallen into the hands of the enemy and has literally been brainwashed to do evil. As the series ends, Wonder Woman chooses to kill Maxwell Lord by snapping his neck and thus frees Superman from his mental imprisonment. The episode forces the reader to wonder: if we cannot trust Superman can anyone ever really be trustworthy again?[24]

Possibly the most damning part of the *Infinite Crisis* storyline is the return of the Golden Age Superman who had been living in a paradise dimension since the end of 1985's *Crisis on Infinite Earths*. This Earth 2 hero was the original Superman who appeared in *Action Comics* #1 but had seemingly been removed from continuity in the 1980s. This Superman had been secretly watching the events of the last twenty years and now returns to express his displeasure. He believes that the new DC universe is inherently broken and is a far cry from the idealized world that he inhabited. Although it is later revealed that several of his comrades duped him into many of his actions, the Golden Age Superman's core belief still resonates. The first superhero returned to Earth from heaven and declared that he was disappointed in how we lived and acted. He told us that he did not trust any of us and we in turn should not even trust ourselves or the world around. An icon had come back to life and declared that society had not taken the wrong path but rather it had been built in a flawed and shoddy manner and thus was inherently defective. According to the Golden Age Superman, Max

Lord's mental control of Superman and Wonder Woman's act of murder were not individual acts but rather symptoms of a universe that was rotten to its core. Citizens of such a place not only had to fear everyone around them but also themselves, because no one is safe from the dark forces that surround them. This message seems to especially connect to an American society that had grown accustomed to terrorism, war, the threat of biological attacks, torture, and senseless violence in the previous few years. Seemingly, no one was secure and few could be trusted. In a 2005 *New York Times* article entitled "Recalibrating DC Heroes for a Grittier Century," several DC writers and executives noted that the company's stories were evolving with a bleaker and more sophisticated society.[25] The world had gotten darker and far more terrifying and not even the original Superman could save us.

Weekly Comics Action

After the events of *Infinite Crisis*, the DC universe seemingly entered a state of grieving and rebuilding. This process very much resembled American society after the September 11 tragedy. Heroes and villains alike tried to adjust to the world's new rules. In 2006, the U.S. was also still trying to cope with the 9/11 aftermath, as the nation began to question and discuss many of the choices that citizens and elected officials had made. Many Americans were still frightened and apprehensive, but some were also becoming distressed at the nation's direction. Americans were rebuilding their society as they came to terms with the way that they lived. In DC Comics' 2006 limited series *52*, fictional citizens also began to reconstruct their society from the literal and figurative rubble of another crisis.

Published weekly for an entire year, *52* focused on a number of characters' attempts to remake their lives and their world. These individuals had to accomplish their goals without the help of Superman, Batman, and Wonder Woman who, for different reasons, were not involved in the DC universe for the entire year. Instead of seeing DC's trinity save the world again, readers followed heroes such as Animal Man, the Question, Adam Strange, and Starfire. One story centers around Ralph Dibny, the Elongated Man, as he endeavors to cope with the death of his wife Sue, whom Jean Loring killed in *Identity Crisis*. Another ongoing tale showcases the hero Steel's efforts to thwart the villainous Lex Luthor's plans to create and control a team of superpowered employees. Although each of the stories focuses on someone's attempts to adjust to their new existence or to create a better one, things do not work out well for many of the heroes and for society as a whole. Elongated Man ultimately dies (although he is reunited with his wife in the afterlife). Black Adam tries to become a benevolent ruler and family man only to have all that he cherishes destroyed. Booster Gold discovers that an evil mastermind has corrupted his former partner and robotic friend Skeets. To make matters worse, during week 50, Black Adam goes insane with grief and starts World War III. The *52* series showcases the trials and tribulations of "average" superheroes and reveals how society adjusts to an epic tragedy.[26] Unfortunately, Americans had become experienced at rebounding from catastrophes and once again a comic book series was emulating real world experiences.

The Fear Continues

The arrival of 2007 brought with it not only old anxieties but also new previously underappreciated fears and apprehensions. While many Americans still worried about terrorist attacks and the wars in Iraq and Afghanistan, other concerns captured many citizens' attention. In October 2006, North Korea announced that it had conducted a successful nuclear test.[27] The idea of a rogue state like North Korea possessing a nuclear bomb caused panic among many members of the U.S. government and public alike.[28] In March 2007, the U.S. sub-prime housing mortgage industry crashed and several sub-prime lenders were forced to declare bankruptcy.[29] This and other factors pushed housing prices downward and many Americans' homes were soon worth far less than before. As the housing bubble burst, fear began to spread throughout the financial sector and the general population that an economic downturn had commenced and soon the collapsing real estate market would create a recession. An April 2007, a Bloomberg/*Los Angeles Times* poll found that 60 percent of Americans believed that the U.S. would go into a recession within the next twelve months.[30]

While citizens worried about the U.S. economy, they also closely watched China's economic and political growth. The Chinese government estimated that its economy would grow at an astounding 11.9 percent in 2007 and China would thus pass Germany as the world's third largest economy.[31] Many Americans were buying Chinese made goods, and the U.S./China trade deficit increased by 10.2 percent in 2007. American consumers bought $256.3 billion more of goods from China than the U.S. sold to the Chinese.[32] This growing economic imbalance brought greater concerns to abundant existing economic woes.

On April 16, 2007, Seung Hui Cho shot and killed 32 other students and himself while wounding 25 others at Virginia Polytechnic Institute and State University, better known as Virginia Tech.[33] The massacre deeply disturbed many Americans who had witnessed too many acts of violence in the last few years and who worried about the nation's future. It was one of many events adding to an already bleak picture.

A House Divided

American society's undercurrent of fear continued to find its way into mainstream comic book stories. In 2007, Marvel produced *Civil War*, a company-wide crossover event written by Mark Millar. *Civil War*, built on plotlines from several earlier mini-series, including the previously discussed *Avengers Disassembled* and *House of M*. The battle that ensues when the U.S. government attempts to regulate superhero conduct is the focus of *Civil War*. Unlike the Keene Act in the 1980s' *Watchmen*, *Civil War*'s Superhuman Registration Act does not ban costumed heroes but rather requires all superhumans to register with and work for the U.S. government. This legislation divides the superhero community and pits current heroes and former allies against each other. The series creators ask the reader to question how freedom is often traded for security and what is lost in the process. As Iron Man leads the pro-registration camp and Captain America heads the opposition, the reader is presented with the unsettling fact that neither society as a whole nor their fellow costumed avengers actually trusts superheroes. These brightly colored heroes once inspired awe and reverence but now often bring terror. This is displayed in one of *Civil War*'s opening scenes in which several superheroes unwittingly destroy parts of Stamford, Connecticut.[34] Writer Mark Millar shows these heroes to be weapons of mass destruction, which many denizens of the Marvel universe believe need to be regulated.

Civil War ends with Captain America capitulating because the battle is physically and figuratively destroying the United States. Cap surrenders, and as Millar states, *Civil War*

becomes "a story where a guy wrapped in the American flag is in chains as the people swap freedom for security."[35] At its heart, *Civil War* is a story about fear and distrust. As the Bush administration declared that unseen threats surrounded the nation, Marvel creators emphasized the country's differences and its growing and continuing fears.

The Short Death of a Legend

As many U.S. citizens battled the fears and frustrations that came with the new millennium, in 2007 a murder shocked the nation and caused numerous Americans to mourn. Terrorists had assassinated an American icon and the U.S. populace would have to face yet another terrible loss. At least that is how many of the media sources of the day portrayed the story. Villains had seemingly killed Captain America in a comic book story, but many news sources were taking the superhero's death very seriously and most were concerned about what it symbolically meant for the United States. In March 2007, Captain America/Steve Rogers was killed in *Captain America* #25.

The story takes place shortly after the events of *Civil War*. Authorities have arrested the fugitive Captain America and are leading him through the streets in handcuffs.[36] As protestors pelt the costumed hero with fruits and vegetables an assassin guns him down. The Ed Brubaker penned tale was popular among fans and critics alike, but the story also struck a chord with many in the non–comic book media. In a March 8, 2007, *New York Times* story entitled "Captain America Is Dead; National Hero Since 1941," writer George Gene Gustines exclaims, "The assassination ends the sentinel of liberty's fight for right, which began in 1941."[37] A Bryan Robinson article for *ABC News* expressed the author's strong opinion in the title "What the Death of Captain America Really Means. Bullets Killed Him, but the War on Terror Really Did Cap In." Robinson opines, "Bullets took the life of the Sentinel of Liberty, but he was really a victim — and product — of the times."[38] Robinson later writes, "You're not crazy if you think Captain America's struggle parallels the debates over the Iraq War, the Patriot Act, the Bush domestic surveillance program and other controversial programs in the post–Sept. 11 world."[39] *American Chronicle* author Daniel Taverne believed that Captain America's death marked the end of the American Dream, and "In many ways I'm not surprised that Captain America died, but after thinking about this for a while, I'm surprised he didn't already commit suicide."[40] Syndicated columnist Leonard Pitts, Jr., stated, "Captain America's death ... has more to do with what's going on in our world than his. Meaning terrorism, war and this creeping sense some of us have that our country is being stolen."[41]

On July 1, 2007, Colleen Long reported on Captain America's funeral for the Associated Press. She notes, "With the story line so relevant to present-day politics, and the timing of the latest issue so precise, it's hard not to think the whole thing is one big slam on the government."[42] Long also quotes writer Jeph Loeb, who explains the story by saying, "Part of it grew out of the fact that we are a country that's at war, we are being perceived differently

Opposite: At the end of Marvel's *Civil War* #7 (2007) Captain America surrenders in order to keep the United States safe. Writer Mark Millar described the comic book as "a story where a guy wrapped in the American flag is in chains as the people swap freedom for security." The narrative reflected the fears of many Americans of this era who were also questioning the line between freedom and security. (© 2007 Marvel Comics. All Rights Reserved.)

in the world. He wears the flag and he is assassinated — it's impossible not to have it at least be a metaphor for the complications of the present day."[43] Even satirist Stephen Colbert commented on Captain America's death when Marvel editor-in-chief Joe Quesada revealed that the slain hero had bequeathed his battle shield to the comedy host. Colbert accepted the shield, thanked Captain America for the honor, and declared, "Cap, I hope I can make you proud."[44] Writers, fans, bloggers, and even serious news sources treated Captain America's death as a significant event. To many, the superhero's death became an analogy for all the things that were wrong with the United States. Although Captain America death was "only" a comic book story, it somehow tapped into the nation's collective fear and apprehension. Many Americans saw Cap's death as a metaphor for the despair that filled their daily lives.

A Not So Secret War

If 2007's *Civil War* and the death of Captain America are ultimately tales about the growing fear and discord in the United States, then Marvel's 2008 *Secret Invasion* is about unrestrained terror. The mini-series' tagline "Who do you trust?" is not only an explanation of the comic's main theme, but also could serve as the decade's one sentence motto. *Secret Invasion* is a basic alien invasion shape-shifter tale in which the characters are unsure who is friend and who is foe. Even old allies could be enemy alien Skrulls in disguise and our heroes are never certain who is should be trusted and who should be feared. This type of story is certainly not unique to the 2000s. In many ways it resembles the *Invasion of the Body Snatcher*–type narrative that surfaced during the McCarthy-inspired fear of the 1950s. What makes *Secret Invasion* distinctive is not only the continuing thought that our super-protectors may be enemies in disguise, but also the understanding that citizens are never safe from unknown enemies.

If *Civil War* declared that superheroes are weapons of mass destruction, then *Secret Invasion* questions what citizens know about these super-weapons. *Secret Invasion* asked the reader to question who he or she trusts and ultimately the answer was clearly no one. Just as many Americans feared undercover terrorists in their midst, Marvel heroes were also now suspect. *Secret Invasion*'s ending reinforces this fear when Tony Stark is disgraced and loses control of the superpowered community to Norman Osborne, the Green Goblin. When the citizens of the Marvel universe villainize hero Tony Stark after he helps to save the world and lionize mentally unstable and true villain Norman Osborne, the reader understands that no one can truly be trusted. No longer can it be assumed that the good guy wins in the end.[45] Instead we are left with a world in which we can never truly know who is hero and who is villain, an idea that mirrors many Americans' understanding of the world at the start of the twenty-first century.

Brand New Day

As 2007 turned into 2008, the nation began to prepare to elect a new president. George W. Bush was completing his second term and was constitutionally prohibited from seeking another four years as president. Partially because of the upcoming election, many Americans began to evaluate the Bush years, which coincided with most of the twenty-first century.

A number of Americans had been questioning Bush-era policies for years, but the 2008 election forced the nation to evaluate the last seven plus years. Both Republicans and Democrats alike judged President Bush's record and often the man himself. Barack Obama defeated John McCain in November 2008 to become the 44th president of the United States.

Much of the year leading up to the election was a heated battle between numerous candidates vying for the presidency. As President Bush's ratings sank, even Republican candidates tried to distance themselves from their national and party leader.[46] Republican Party nominee Arizona Senator John McCain represented himself as a maverick and stressed how many times he had disagreed with President Bush.[47] Obama won the 2008 election on a platform of change but the American public was deeply divided. Many Americans disagreed with Barack Obama's proposed policies and feared that as president he would make the U.S. more vulnerable to terrorist attacks and would increase the size of the federal government. While tens of millions of Americans were upset with and afraid of Bush era policies, an almost equal number were fearful of President Obama. Many Americans were worried that they would lose much of their freedom during Obama's tenure, while millions of other citizens claimed that this had already happened during the Bush years. Americans were re-evaluating the nation's past and present but the fear still remained. The U.S. was changing, but these changes brought about their own frightening consequences.

Teenage Wasteland

While attitudes within the U.S. were seemingly changing, comic book stories were not. Just as it had taken a few years for superheroes to adjust to the post–9/11 reality, comic book creators were still following an apparently older paradigm and creating stories based on fear. Although many Americans were debating the merits of change, the nation was seemingly changing nonetheless. Superheroes were either behind the times or were tapping into a deeper fear that lay under the whitewash of apparent hope. DC Comics further embraced fear-based stories in 2007–2008 when the company published a six issue story reuniting Superman and his boyhood pals, the Legion of Super-Heroes. The Legion first appeared in April 1958 and originally the group served as a superhero club with which Superboy could adventure. The Legion is based one thousand years in the future, and for decades provided an optimistic view of what will come in the next millennium. Although like many comics, the Legion's 30th century society became darker in the 1970s and 1980s, most stories assured readers that the future would be a better place to live.

In this 2007–2008 Superman and the Legion of Super-Heroes tale, writer Geoff Johns transports the Man of Steel to a xenophobic and intolerant 31st century Earth filled with denizens that fear the citizens of other worlds. Trust and cooperation between species had always been a hallmark of Legion stories, but Johns created an Earth ruled by isolationists that wanted to expel outsiders from society. Johns opens the story by focusing on a farming couple that happens upon a young alien child that has crash landed on this future Earth. This scene is an homage to Ma and Pa Kent rescuing and raising the young Kryptonian orphan that would one day become Superman. (This seminal event lies at the heart of Superman's mythos and is arguably the most important episode in the hero's fictional life. Jonathan and Martha Kent's care and devotion allowed the young alien to become a well-adjusted American citizen. Had they acted differently, Superman may have never existed, or worse, the young alien may have used his powers for evil purposes.) In Johns' future

Earth the young farming couple do not rescue the baby but instead kill it because of its alien origins.[48] In this story, many of Earth's citizens have become afraid of outside influences and social and political leaders have re-written history to extinguish any mention of alien influence. This new history teaches that Superman was born on Earth and that all aliens should be feared and hated.

Johns' Superman and the Legion of Superheroes story mirrors Americans' post–September 11 social fears and the nation's isolationist and sometimes xenophobic tendencies. While fears of terrorism appeared to be subsiding by 2008, Americans still had much to worry about and faced many reminders of outside dangers. American society as a whole became more closed-off and reactionary after the 9/11 attacks, but internal and external social and political issues continued to demand attention, including illegal immigration, legalizing gay marriage, and nationalizing health care. Just as future Earth citizens attempted to understand their society in Geoff Johns' Superman and the Legion story, twenty-first century Americans also struggled to define who they were and what they believed. Most of the issues that engaged the nation were of the "us vs. them" variety, in which American citizens had to classify which behaviors were normal and which were deviant.

Many Americans needed to create an "other" in order to solidify the "us" and thus make the decade's social, political, and economic problems more understandable. The decade's anti-terrorist mantra, "they hate us for our freedom," famously attempted to create a binary geopolitical understanding. Other political and social issues forced Americans to define what were "normal" working practices, lifestyles, living conditions, and personal liberties. Similarly to how Geoff Johns' future citizens confronted their fears by categorizing themselves and others, twenty-first century Americans classified themselves and everyone else in order to better cope with the new social, political, economic, and culture paradigms. Although the nation was changing, many fears still remained, and Americans were attempting to better understand both themselves and the world around.

Remaining and Changing Fears

The end of 2008 saw Barack Obama elected as U.S. president, and by January 2009 he had taken the reins as the nation's leader. This move marked the start of a new era, but fears and doubts about both international and domestic problems persisted. To add to these political and social fears, the U.S. had entered into a massive economic downturn that left millions unemployed and the economy reeling. As banks and other economic institutions began to fail at a staggering rate and housing prices dropped dramatically, Americans had yet another thing to worry about. In late 2008 and into 2009, DC and Marvel continued to embrace the undercurrent of fear that still seemed to permeate American culture. Both comic book companies published major storylines in which villains took control of society. As many Americans were forced to confront both new and old fears, comic book superheroes were living in worlds where evil won.

Yet Another Crisis and a Dark Reign

In July 2008, DC Comics began publishing *Final Crisis*, a seven issue mini-series written by superstar Scottish author Grant Morrison. The tale is an often dark and disturbing look at a world in which the good guys have seemingly lost their never ending battle against the evil tyrannical god Darkseid. DC's one sentence promotional description of the story was "The Day Evil Won."[49] In a 2008 interview, Morrison described *Final Crisis*: "The war between Good and Evil has been won by the wrong side and Evil is now in control of the DC Universe." He later adds, ""The Gods are here to destroy everything that we hold dear, everything that has meaning to us, everything that has value for us. They want to utterly crush the human species and reduce us all to slavery and that's as big a threat as it gets."[50] DC had certainly published dark stories in the past in which villains do terrible things (that is what villains do after all). *Final Crisis* seems different, though, because it presents a situation in which the superheroes no longer are sure that it is their birthright to win. In past stories it was assumed that the universe was rigged so that good would always eventually triumph. Comic book superheroes were expected to defeat evil no matter how long the odds. *Final Crisis* attempts to strip away this bias and asks the reader to consider a world in which good and evil are on equal footing.

In the series' first issue the villain Libra explains the story's premise, "Strikes me that your enemies fight and win again and again because they truly believe their actions are in accordance with a higher moral order. But what happens in a world where good has lost its perpetual struggle against evil?"[51] This newly perceived balance of power and its psychological ramifications mirror post–September 11 changes in the United States. To many Americans, the events of 9/11 and the aftermath violated numerous understood but unwritten laws. People believed that terrorist attacks could not happen in the United States because some force of good protected the nation. These Americans were forced to come to terms with a society in which the rules, as they understood them, had changed. In their minds, evil had beaten good and now anything was possible. Much like the villainous Darkseid defeating the heroes of the DC universe, nothing was impossible because the old rules no longer applied.

By *Final Crisis'* end, the old defunct rules give way to a new understanding of society and life. In issue #5 Darkseid has brainwashed most of humanity and only a few unaffected humans still possess free will. Just as all seems hopeless, a group of Darkseid's prisoners discuss the situation and an unidentified person states, "If your superheroes can't save you, maybe it's time to think of something that can. If it doesn't exist, think it up. Then make it real."[52] Although things look dire, citizens of this fictional world have to recreate hope and idealism in order to survive. In many ways, this is a mirror of American society in late 2008 and early 2009. The nation was faced with a slew of seemingly insurmountable problems that violated the understood social structure. Many people believed that troubles like this were not supposed to happen to the United States and its citizens. A majority of Americans attempted to create a new social and political understanding by electing Barack Obama and embracing change. Just as in the DC universe, American society had seen many of its most cherished beliefs destroyed, but both places were attempting to rebuild their trust and hope again.

As an evil god was enslaving the DC universe, a villainous madman with the help of an evil god was presiding over the Marvel universe. While Darkseid mentally imprisoned most of humanity in *Final Crisis*, Norman Osborne and his advisor the Norse god Loki politically manipulated the U.S. in Marvel's 2009 companywide crossover *Dark Reign*. After the events of *Civil War*, the Marvel universe is thrown into chaos and Norman Osborne, who is secretly the villainous Green Goblin, is credited with defeating the Skrull queen. Most Americans treat him as a hero and the U.S. president appoints him as the superhero community's supervisor. This happens while the true hero, Iron Man, is blamed for the Skrull invasion and is forced out of his leadership position in shame. This political transformation mirrors real world events and writer Brian Michael Bendis also noted a connection to the modern day U.S.:

> Think about Katrina, think about any wars — immediately, people are thrown under the bus and ruined without even an investigation, and it's very politically motivated. It's very damning. And people kind of eat it up because they want it. They want someone to blame. They want to feel safe immediately. You know, there's an argument that people want to watch TV and not feel panicked. And some politicians use that fear to punish.[53]

The newly powerful Osborne quickly creates his own Avengers team made up mostly of villains. Many of Osborne's Avengers are even given the heroic identities of former heroes. Spider-Man's nemesis Venom takes over the hero's identity. Mass murderer Bullseye seizes Hawkeye's heroic mantle and Norman Osborne creates an identity known as the Iron Patriot that mixes Captain America and Iron Man. Osborne attempts to use his team and his influence to remake society and to complete a list of items, including killing Spider-Man. Although Osborne ultimately fails and the heroes retake their rightful places and identities, the damage cannot be easily wiped away. The American public gave control of the superhero community to a villainous madman who replaced hero with villain and attempted to evilly recreate society. How can anyone feel safe when the American public can never know who are the true heroes and villains? *Dark Reign* showcased a Marvel universe in which the unwritten rules had changed and citizens could never trust things to be "normal" again. Society had seemingly transformed for the worse and the public no longer knew who to fear and who to trust. This story closely mirrored the real world U.S. where many Americans were facing these same unresolved issues.

Conclusion

Many DC and Marvel stories from the first decade of the twenty-first century mirrored the fear and isolation and that flourished in American society. As the leaders and marketers of the war on terror encouraged Americans to be afraid, comic book superheroes advised readers to trust no one, not even themselves. Once again, superheroes became a product of the society that created them and presented a mirror for Americans to view themselves. Often what they saw was truly terrifying. Like many citizens, superheroes entered the decade unsure of the future and uncertain how to proceed. This lackadaisical attitude soon gave way to full scale terror following the horrific events of September 11, 2001. Both corporeal and fictional Americans reacted with sadness, anger, and fear, and many loudly wondered if life would ever be the same again. Each American, both real and imaginary, changed as terror shaped every aspect of the nation. Unfortunately, comic book superheroes could provide little assistance or guidance; the nation's protectors were as unsure and afraid as everyone else.

CONCLUSION

Neil Gaiman once described the plot of his wondrous comic book series *The Sandman* as "The king of dreams learns that one must change or die and then makes his decision."[1] In the storyline, eventually Morpheus, the dream king, chooses to die and a new incarnation of dream takes his place. Since Morpheus was more of a concept than a person, his passing was not the death of an individual but rather the demise of an idea or a perspective. After Morpheus's death when the new lord of the dreaming assumes the throne, he brings with him a change of era and viewpoint.

Comic book superhero stories have proven to be exceptional outlets for showcasing changes in American society. From not long after Superman's first appearance in 1938 until the present day, superheroes have often changed in order to fulfill society's wishes and needs. Supermen and superwomen have adjusted to be better compatible within an ever evolving American society. Costumed heroes like Superman and Batman began their existences as Great Depression social avengers but soon transformed into patriotic World War II citizens and then again to postwar super-company men. These radical changes matched the real life progression of American society and throughout the 1960s until the present superheroes have continued to follow American political, social, and cultural changes.

In the proceeding nine chapters, I have attempted to document and analyze how changes within superhero comic books from 1938 to 2009 have both mirrored and molded American society. By the first few years of the twenty-first century, superheroes have become the dominant form of American mythology. While many Americans would contend that they have never read a comic book or have not read one in many years, superheroes nonetheless surround them. Superman's "S" symbol and Batman's Dark Knight oval have become ubiquitous parts of American culture and can be seen everywhere from t-shirts to body art to professional basketball players' custom made swimming pools. Films, television, or advertising often use superheroes or employ storytelling methods derived from comic books. Most Americans know that Peter Parker is Spider-Man's secret identity and that Batman's sidekick is Robin. Superheroes have become a part of the American social fabric, and although many Americans have not read the heroes' comic book adventures, these stories determine how the characters will be presented in films, television, and other media. America's superheroes often represent the nation and comic book creators work hard to develop stories that illustrate important current political, social, and cultural situations and understandings.

Comic book superheroes are important because their tales demonstrate what has been, what is, and what can be. Because they are generally published monthly, superhero stories can capture the nation's changing zeitgeist in ways novels, films, and other storytelling forms cannot. Superhero tales create a working class narrative that skillfully interweaves adventure and heroics with the prevailing national mood to produce something unique and special. No other medium so regularly offers complex social analysis in such a simple monthly brightly-colored package. Comic books were created as inexpensive populist entertainment that gave young Americans an outlet in which to address complex social and political issues in straightforward ways. Although comic books have become more sophisticated (and expensive), they still often serve the same purpose. Every month tens of thousands of readers invest their time and energy as their favorite heroes attempt to save the world and rescue us from our problems. Superheroes continue to exist because we continue to need them. We need them to show us who we are and who we could be. We need them to save us from our enemies and from ourselves. For over seventy years, superheroes have served as our guides and our protectors. They are the Virgils that guide our through our infernos and the Atlases that take the world's problems on their backs. If history is any guide, then we can safely assume that they will continue in these static yet ever changing roles for many years to come, because in the coming days we will undoubtedly need them more than ever.

NOTES

Chapter 1

1. DC Comics was known as National Periodical Comics for several decades, and Marvel Comics used the names Timely Comics and Atlas Comics in its early years. To avoid confusion, throughout this text I refer to the two companies by their most identifiable names, DC Comics and Marvel Comics.

2. Jerome Siegel and Joe Shuster, "Superman," *Action Comics* #1 (New York: DC Comics, 1938).

3. Siegel and Shuster in *Superman: The Dailies, Part I* (New York: Sterling, 2006), 13–174.

4. Siegel and Shuster, "Superman," *Action Comics* #1.

5. Gerald Jones, *Men of Tomorrow: Geeks, Gangsters, and the Birth of the Comic Book* (New York: Basic Books, 2004), 109–111.

6. Mike Benton, *Superhero Comics of the Golden Age: The Illustrated History* (Dallas: Taylor, 1992), 7–16.

7. "The Presidency," *Time*, July 11, 1932, Vol. 20.2, http://www.time.com/time/magazine/article/0,9171,743953,00.html. Accessed on 2 July 2009.

8. William E. Leuchtenburg, *Franklin D. Roosevelt and the New Deal, 1932–1940* (New York: Harper & Row, 1963), 35.

9. Ibid., 100–102.

10. Ibid., 115–116.

11. Leila Sussmann, "FDR and the White House Mail," *The Public Opinion Quarterly*, Vol. 20.1, Spring 1956, 5.

12. Dixon Wecter, *The Age of the Great Depression: 1929–1941* (New York: Macmillan, 1948), 61–75.

13. Benton, 12–13.

14. Jones, 78–82.

15. Quoted in Benton, 17.

16. Jones, 141.

17. Ron Goulart, *Comic Book Culture: An Illustrated History* (Portland: Collectors Press, 2007), 44.

18. Harvey A. Zorbaugh, "The Comics — There They Stand!" *Journal of Educational Sociology*, December 1944, Vol. 18, 197–199.

19. Michael Chabon, "Secret Skin: An Essay in Unitard Theory," *The New Yorker*, March 10, 2008, http://www.newyorker.com/reporting/2008/03/10/080310fa_fact_chabon/?currentPage=all. Accessed 8 December 2009.

20. Jules Feiffer, *The Great Comic Book Heroes* (Seattle: Fantagraphic Books, 2003), 9.

21. Grant Morrison, *Supergods: What Masked Vigilantes, Miraculous Mutants, and a Sun God from Smallville Can Teach Us About Being Human* (New York: Spiegel and Grau, 2001), 6.

22. Benton, 8–12.

23. Jones, 124–125.

24. Siegel and Shuster, "Superman."

25. Ibid.

26. Ibid.

27. Studs Terkel, *Hard Times: An Oral History of the Great Depression* (New York: Pantheon, 1970), 426.

28. Brad Meltzer, *The Book of Lies* (New York: Grand Central, 2008), 433–435.

29. Siegel and Shuster, *Superman: Sunday Classics 1939–1943* (New York: Sterling, 2006), 189.

30. Ibid., 190.

31. Siegel and Shuster, "Superman."

32. Ibid.

33. Siegel and Shuster, *Superman: The Dailies, Part 1*, 72–73.

34. Jones, 125.

35. Larry David and Jerry Seinfeld, "The Stock Tip," *Seinfeld Lists*, http://www.seinfeldscripts.com/The StockTip.htm. Accessed on 9 July 2009.

36. Les Daniels, *A Celebration of the World's Favorite Comic Book Heroes* (New York: Billboard Books, 2003), 32.

37. Bob Kane, *Batman Archives*, Vol. 1 (New York: DC Comics), 1990.

38. Rick Marschall, "Foreword" in *Batman Archives* Vol. 1 (New York: DC Comics, 1990), 6.

39. David M. Ewalt, "Becoming Batman," *Forbes.com*, June 20, 2005, http://www.forbes.com/2005/06/20/batman-movies-superheroes-cx_de_0620batman.html. Accessed on 15 July 2009.

40. E. Paul Zehr, *Becoming Batman: The Possibility of a Superhero* (Baltimore: Johns Hopkins University Press), 2008.

41. "Tomorrow's Legacy," *The 1939–40 New York World's Fair*. http://xroads.virginia.edu/~1930s/DISPLAY/39wf/frame.htm. Accessed on 16 July 2009.

42. Kane, 23–27.

43. Ibid., 46, 50.

44. Ibid., 75–77.

45. Ibid., 8–114.

46. George Washington, "Farewell Address to the People of the United States," *Archiving Early America*, http://www.earlyamerica.com/earlyamerica/milestones/farewell/text.html. Accessed 19 July 2009.

47. Benton, 65.

48. "Man of Steal," *Time Bullet*, http://timebulleteer.wordpress.com/2011/01/10/the-man-of-steal/. Accessed on 22 July 2011.

49. Bill Parker and Jon Smalle, *Nickel Comics* #1 (New York: Fawcett Comics, 1940).

50. *Bulletman* #1 (New York: Fawcett Comics, 1940).

Chapter 2

1. Gerhard L. Weinberg, *A World at Arms: A Global History of World War II* (New York: Cambridge University Press, 2005), 7–10.

2. Robert James Maddox, *The United States and World War II* (Boulder, CO: Westview Press, 1992), 9–12.

3. Philip Warner, *World War II: The Untold Story* (London: Bodley Head, 1988), 8.

4. John Keegan, *The Second World War* (New York: Viking, 1990), 31–35.

5. Ibid.; *The Library of Congress World War II Companion*, ed. David M. Kennedy (New York: Simon & Schuster, 2007), 17–19.

6. Henry Steele Commager, *The Story of the Second World War* (Washington, D.C.: Brassey's, 1991), 2–8; B.H. Liddell Hart, *History of the Second World War* (New York: Putnam's, 1970), 6–11; Louis L. Snyder, *The War: A Concise History, 1939–1945* (New York: Simon & Schuster, 1960), 57–61.

7. Snyder, 24–27; *The Library of Congress World War II Companion*, 19–22; Keegan, 241–244.

8. *Rebel Without a Cause*, motion picture, director Nicholas Ray, Warner Bros., 1955.

9. Warner, 27–29; Maddox, 86–90.

10. Joe Simon and Jack Kirby, *Captain America* #1 (New York: Marvel Comics, 1941).

11. *The Library of Congress World War II Companion*, 63, 671.

12. Ronin Ro, *Tales to Astonish: Jack Kirby, Stan Lee, and the American Comic Book Revolution* (New York: Bloomsbury, 2004), 21.

13. Joe Simon and Jim Simon, *The Comic Book Makers* (Lebanon, NJ: Vanguard, 2003), 43.

14. "The Most Famous Poster," Library of Congress, http://www.loc.gov/exhibits/treasures/trm015.html. Accessed on 10 December 2009.

15. "Private Joe Lewis Says," print advertisement, date unknown, *Powers of Persuasion: Poster Art from World War II: The National Archives*, http://www.archives.gov/exhibits/powers_of_persuasion/united_we_win/images_html/private_joe_louis_says.html. Accessed on 21 August 2009.

16. McClelland Barclay, "Man the Guns — Join the Navy," print advertisement, 1942, *Powers of Persuasion: Poster Art from World War II: The National Archives*, http://www.archives.gov/exhibits/powers_of_persuasion/man_the_guns/man_the_guns.html. Accessed on 21 August 2009.

17. Jules Feiffer, *The Great Comic Book Heroes* (Seattle: Fantagraphic Books, 2003), 57.

18. Franklin Roosevelt, December 9, 1941, Radio Address, http://www.mtholyoke.edu/acad/intrel/World War2/radio.htm. Accessed on 9 December 2009.

19. C.C. Beall, "Don't Let Him Down," print advertisement, 1941, Northwestern University Library Collection, http://digital.library.northwestern.edu/otcgi/digilib/llscgi60.exe?DB=0&ACTION=View&QUERY=home%20efforts&RGN=M653&OP=and&SUBSET=SUBSET&FROM=1&SIZE=10&ITEM=5. Accessed on 19 August 2011.

20. Herbert Roese, "Kinda give it your personal attention, will you? More Production," print advertisement,

1942, University of North Texas Digital Library, http://digital.library.unt.edu/ark:/67531/metadc210/. Accessed on 19 August 2011.

21. Wright, 43.

22. "I gave a man! Will you give at least 10% of your pay in war bonds?" print advertisement, 1942, *Butterfunk.com*, http://www.butterfunk.com/image-109/northwestern+university.html. Accessed on 19 August 2011.

23. *The Library of Congress World War II Companion*, 150.

24. *Action Comics* #58 (New York: DC Comics, 1943).

25. *Action Comics* #59 (New York: DC Comics, 1943).

26. *Batman* #12 (New York: DC Comics, 1942).

27. *Batman* #15 (New York: DC Comics, 1943).

28. *Batman* #17 (New York: DC Comics, 1943).

29. "Defense needs rubber : Save your tires," print advertisement, 1941, Northwestern University Library Collection, http://digital.library.northwestern.edu/otcgi/digilib/llscgi60.exe?DB=0&ACTION=View&QUERY=%43%6F%6E%73%65%72%76%65%20%6D%61%74%65%72%69%61%6C%73&RGN=%4D%36%35%33&OP=and&SUBSET=SUBSET&FROM=1&SIZE=10&ITEM=3. Accessed on 6 December 2009.

30. Walter DuBois Richards, "They've Got More Important Places to Go Than You! Save Rubber. Check Your Tires Now," print advertisement, 1942, Northwestern University Library Collection. http://digital.library.northwestern.edu/otcgi/digilib/llscgi60.exe?DB=0&ACTION=View&QUERY=Conserve%20materials&RGN=M653&OP=and&SUBSET=SUBSET&FROM=11&SIZE=10&ITEM=11. Accessed on 12 August 2009.

31. "I'll carry mine too! Trucks and tires must last till victory," print advertisement, 1943. Militarywives.com, http://www.militarywives.com/index.php?option=com_content&view=article&id=311:ill-carry-mine-too&catid=38:conserve-materials&Itemid=254. Accessed on 18 August 2011.

32. Roy Schatt, "Scrap," print advertisement, 1942, Northwestern University Library Collection, http://digital.library.northwestern.edu/otcgi/digilib/llscgi60.exe?DB=0&ACTION=View&QUERY=Conserve%20materials&RGN=M653&OP=and&SUBSET=SUBSET&FROM=1&SIZE=10&ITEM=2. Accessed on 19 August 2011.

33. "Farm Scrap Builds Destroyers: 900 Tons of Scrap Metal Goes into a Destroyer," print advertisement, 1942, Northwestern University Library Collection, http://digital.library.northwestern.edu/otcgi/digilib/llscgi60.exe?DB=0&ACTION=View&QUERY=%43%6F%6E%73%65%72%76%65%20%6D%61%74%65%72%69%61%6C%73&RGN=%4D%36%35%33&OP=and&SUBSET=SUBSET&FROM=1&SIZE=10&ITEM=6. Accessed on 19 August 2011.

34. "Share the Meat," print advertisement, 1942, Northwestern University Library Collection, http://digital.library.northwestern.edu/wwii-posters/img/ww1645-33.jpg. Accessed on 19 August 2011.

35. Weimer Pursell, "When you ride ALONE you ride with Hitler! Join a Car-Sharing Club Today!" print advertisement, 1943, *Powers of Persuasion: Poster Art from World War II: The National Archives*, http://www.archives.gov/exhibits/powers_of_persuasion/use_it_up/images_html/ride_with_hitler.html. Accessed on 5 August 2009.

36. Henry Koerner, "Save waste fats for explosives. Take them to your meat dealer," print advertisement, 1943, *Powers of Persuasion: Poster Art from World War II: The National Archives*, http://www.archives.gov/exhibits/powers_of_persuasion/use_it_up/images_html/save_waste_fats.html. Accessed on 6 August 2009.

37. The United States Constitution, First Amendment, 1787.

38. "Loose Lips Sink Ships," Ad Council advertising campaign, 1942–1945, http://www.adcouncil.org/default.aspx?id=127. Accessed on 10 December 2009.

39. "Someone Talked!" print advertisement, 1942, Northwestern University Library Collection, http://www.library.northwestern.edu/govinfo/collections/wwii-posters/img/ww0207-04.jpg. Accessed on 11 August 2009.

40. Eric Ericson, "The sound that kills: Don't murder men with idle words," print advertisement, 1942, Northwestern University Library Collection, http://digital.library.northwestern.edu/wwii-posters/img/ww1646-71.jpg. Accessed on 19 August 2011.

41. Valentino Sarra, "If you talk too much," print advertisement, 1942, University of North Texas Digital Library, http://digital.library.unt.edu/ark:/67531/metadc517/m1/1/. Accessed on 9 July 2011.

42. Anton Fischer, "A careless word — A needless loss," print advertisement, 1943, Northwestern University Library Collection, http://digital.library.northwestern.edu/otcgi/digilib/llscgi60.exe?DB=0&SORTBY=%4D%32%34%35&ACTION=View&QUERY=%6A%70%65%67&RGN=%4D%38%35%36%31%5A&OP=and&SUBSET=SUBSET&FROM=1&SIZE=10&ITEM=5. Accessed on 19 August 2011.

43. Albert Dorne, "Less dangerous than careless talk: don't discuss troop movements, ship sailings, war equipment," print advertisement, 1944, Northwestern University Library Collection, http://digital.library.northwestern.edu/otcgi/digilib/llscgi60.exe?DB=0&ACTION=View&QUERY=%74%61%6C%6B&OP=and&SUBSET=SUBSET&FROM=1&SIZE=20&ITEM=7. Accessed on 19 August 2011.

44. "Wanted!" print advertisement, 1944, Northwestern University Library Collection, http://digital.library.northwestern.edu/otcgi/digilib/llscgi60.exe?DB=0&ACTION=View&QUERY=%77%61%6E%74%65%64&OP=and&SUBSET=SUBSET&FROM=1&SIZE=20&ITEM=1. Accessed on 19 August 2011.

45. *Captain Marvel Adventures* #14 (New York: Fawcett, 1942).

46. *Master Comics* #29 (New York: Fawcett, 1942).

47. *Marvel Mystery Comics* #32 (New York: Marvel Comics, 1942).

48. *Superman* #17 (New York: DC Comics, 1942).

49. "Women in War Jobs: Rosie the Riveter (1942–1945)," Ad Council advertising campaign, 1942–1945, http://www.adcouncil.org/default.aspx?id=128. Accessed on 11 August 2009.

50. Tracie Dungan, "BENTONVILLE: Crystal Bridges museum obtains Rosie the Riveter," *Arkansas Democrat Gazette,* June 9, 2009, http://www.rosietheriveter.org/painting.htm. Accessed 2 August 2009.

51. Mike Madrid, *The Supergirls: Fashion, Feminism, Fantasy, and the History of Comic Book Heroines* (New York: Exterminating Angel Press, 2009), 20.

52. Ibid., 16–22; Donald D. Markstein, "Don Markstein's Toonopedia," http://www.toonopedia.com/index.htm. Accessed on 13 December 2009.

53. Bradford W. Wright, *Comic Book Nation: The Transformation of Youth Culture in America* (Baltimore: Johns Hopkins University Press, 2003), 31.

54. Robert Lee Beerbohm, "The Mainline Comics Story: An Initial Examination," *The Jack Kirby Collector* #25, http://www.twomorrows.com/kirby/articles/25mainline.html. Accessed on 11 December 2009.

Chapter 3

1. Tom Brevoort, "No Prize!" *Marvel.com,* 22 March 2007, http://marvel.com/blogs/Tom%20Brevoort/entry/361. Accessed on 14 December 2009.

2. Margot A. Henriksen, *Dr. Strangelove's America: Society and Culture in the Atomic Age* (Berkeley: University of California Press, 1997), 4–7.

3. Francisco Silva, "284. Artists and Models (1955)," *1001 Flicks,* August 22, 2008, http://1001flicks.blogspot.com/2008_08_01_archive.html. Accessed on 15 December 2009.

4. C.C. Beck, "Captain Marvel and the Atomic War," *DC's Greatest Imaginary Stories* (New York: DC Comics, 2005), 17.

5. Brian Cronin, "Comic Book Urban Legends Revealed #7!" *Comic Book Resources,* July 14, 2005.

6. "Atomic Toys — Comics," *Oak Ridge Associated Universities,* http://www.orau.org/ptp/collection/atomictoys/atomictoys.htm. Accessed on 11 October 2009.

7. George Gallup, *The Gallup Poll: Public Opinion 1935–1971,* Vol. 1 (New York: Random House, 1972), 527.

8. Diana Steele, "America's Reaction to the Atomic Bombings of Hiroshima and Nagasaki," http://users.dickinson.edu/~history/product/steele/seniorthesis.htm. Accessed 14 December 2009.

9. Paul Boyer, *By the Bomb's Early Light: American Thought and Culture at the Dawn of the Atomic Age* (Chapel Hill: University of North Carolina Press, 1994), 137.

10. Henriksen, 8–9.

11. Boyer, 10–12.

12. "Uranium Rush Board Game," Oak Ridge Associated Universities, http://www.orau.org/ptp/collection/atomictoys/uraniumrush.htm. Accessed on 19 September 2009.

13. "Atomic Style," *Atom-A,* http://www.atom-a.com/atomic.html. Accessed 19 September 2009.

14. Boyer, 11.

15. "Bikini 60 Years Old and Still Turning Heads," 17 August 2006, *The Paramus Post,* http://www.paramuspost.com/article.php/20060816162140460. Accessed on 19 August 2011.

16. Steve Rushin, "Bikini Waxing: From Bardot to Graf, from Ground Zero to Grass, Here's the Skinny on the Two Piece," 21 February 1997, *Sports Illustrated,* Online Edition, http://sportsillustrated.cnn.com/vault/article/magazine/MAG1009487/index.htm, Accessed 22 on September 2009.

17. "Operation Crossroads," *Radiochemistry Society U.S. Nuclear Tests: Info Gallery, 1945–1962,* http://www.radiochemistry.org/history/nuke_tests/crossroads/index.html. Accessed on 6 September 2009.

18. Mike Benton, *Superhero Comics of the Golden Age: The Illustrated History* (Dallas: Taylor, 1992), 58.

19. Griffin Fariello, *Red Scare: Memories of the American Inquisition* (New York: W.W. Norton, 1995).

20. "Bomb Shelters," http://www.lilesnet.com/memories/past/bomb_shelters.htm. Accessed 14 December 2009.

21. "The End: Nuclear Nostalgia," *FLYP,* Issue 28, April 27–May 9, 2009, http://www.flypmedia.com/content/end-nuclear-nostalgia. Accessed 14 December 2009; B. Wayne Blanchard, "American Civil Defense, 1945–1985: The Evolution of Programs and Policies," Emmitsburg, MD, 1985, 2–7, http://www.orau.org/ptp/pdf/cdhistory.pdf. Accessed 16 June 2011.

22. David Obst, *Too Good to Be Forgotten: Changing America in the '60s and '70s* (New York: John Wiley, 1998), 13–15.

23. "Duck and Cover: The Citizen Kane of Civil Defense," *Conelrad.com,* http://www.conelrad.com/duckandcover/cover.php?turtle=01. Accessed 14 December 2009.

24. Don Thompson, "OK, Axis, Here We Come," *All in Color for a Dime* (New York: Krause Publishing, 1997), 122–123.

25. *Captain America* #77 and 78 (New York: Marvel Comics, 1954).

26. An example of this is December 1952's *Captain Marvel* #139 in which "Captain Marvel Battles the Vicious Red Crusher." The title was cancelled less than a year later after issue #150.

27. "Oldest Baby Boomers Turn 60!" *U.S. Census Bureau.* January 3, 2006, http://www.census.gov/news room/releases/pdf/cb06-ffse01-2.pdf. Accessed 19 August 2011.

28. Tom Engelhardt, *The End of Victory Culture: Cold War America and the Disillusioning of a Generation* (New York: Basic Books, 1995), 168–170.

29. Herbert S. Dinerstein, *The Making of a Missile Crisis: October 1962* (Baltimore: Johns Hopkins University Press, 1976), 150–229; Nestor T. Carbonell, *And the Russians Stayed: The Sovietization of Cuba* (New York: William Morrow, 1989), 211–258.

30. Pierre Comtois, *Marvel Comics in the 1960s: An Issue by Issue Field Guide to a Pop Culture Phenomenon* (Raleigh, NC: TwoMorrows, 2009), 6–7; Matthew J. Costello, *Secret Identity Crisis: Comic Books and the Unmasking of Cold War America* (New York: Continuum, 2009), 58–61.

31. Stan Lee and George Mair, *Excelsior! The Amazing Life of Stan Lee* (New York: Fireside, 2002), 112.

32. Stan Lee and Jack Kirby, *Fantastic Four* #1 (New York: Marvel Comics, 1961).

33. The Hulk's creator, Stan Lee, claims that he only used gamma radiation because "the name had a nice ring to it" in *Excelsior! The Amazing Life of Stan Lee,* 121. While the claim is undoubtedly true it is impossible to fully understand how much of Lee's thinking was influenced by societal attitudes towards nuclear energy.

34. Lois Gresh and Robert Weinberg, *The Science of Superheroes* (Hoboken, NJ: John Wiley, 2002), 27.

35. Adam Capitanio, "'The Jekyll and Hyde of the Atomic Age': The Incredible Hulk at the Ambiguous Embodiment of Nuclear Power," *The Journal of Popular Culture,* Vol. 43.2, 2010, 251–258.

36. Stan Lee and Bill Everett, *Daredevil* #1 (New York: Marvel Comics, 1964).

37. Stan Lee and Steve Ditko, *Amazing Fantasy* #15 (New York: Marvel Comics, 1962).

38. Gerry Conway, "A Conversation with Gerry Conway," audio interview, *Comic Geek Speak,* Episode 701, October 6, 2009, 34:10. Accessed 19 August 2011.

39. Philip Jenkins, *Decade of Nightmares: The End of the Sixties and the Making of Eighties America* (New York: Oxford University Press, 2006), 155–156.

40. Gerry Conway and Al Milgrom, *Firestorm, the Nuclear Man* #1 (New York: DC Comics, 1978).

41. Cary Bates and Dave Cockrum, *Superboy and the Legion of Super-Heroes* #195 (New York: DC Comics, 1973).

42. Costello, 115–119; Wright, 241–243.

43. Bill Mantlo and George Tuska, *Invincible Iron Man* #78 (New York: Marvel Comics, 1975).

44. Costello, 115–119; Wright, 241–243.

45. Richard Pipes, "Ash Heap of History: President Reagan's Westminster Address 20 Years Later," *Ronald Reagan: The Heritage Foundation Remembers,* 3 June 2002, http://www.reagansheritage.org/reagan/html/reagan_panel_pipes.shtml. Accessed on 29 December 2009.

46. Jake Sunderland, "Cannon: It's About Objective Facts," *The Donald W. Reynolds School of Journalism,* 8 November 2006, http://www.unr.edu/journalism/content/061108/061108page2.htm. Accessed 29 December 2009.

47. Jenkins, 221.

48. Alan Moore and Dave Gibbons, *Watchmen* #1 (New York: DC Comics, 1986).

Chapter 4

1. *Stand By Me,* Rob Reiner, director, Sony Pictures, 1986.

2. National Archives, "World War II Causalities," http://www.archives.gov/research/arc/ww2/. Accessed on December 13, 2009.

3. Bradford W. Wright, *Comic Book Nation: The Transformation of Youth Culture in America* (Baltimore: Johns Hopkins University Press, 2001), 59.

4. Lizabeth Cohen, *A Consumer's Republics: The Politics of Mass Consumption in Postwar America* (New York: Vintage, 2003), 7–10. Stephanie Coontz, *The Way We Never Were: American Families and the Nostalgia Trap* (New York: Basic Books, 2000), 23–30. Steven Mintz, *Domestic Revolutions: A Social History of American Family Life* (New York: Free Press, 1989), 178–190.

5. Eugenia Kaledin, *Daily Life in the United States, 1940–1959: Shifting Worlds* (New York: Greenwood Press, 2000), 75–90. Douglas T. Miller, *The Fifties: The Way We Really Were* (New York: Doubleday, 1977), 147–170. Karal Ann Marling, *As Seen on TV: The Visual Culture of Everyday Life in the 1950s* (Cambridge, MA: Harvard University Press, 1996), 50–62.

6. Elaine Tyler May, *Homeward Bound: American Families in the Cold War Era* (New York: Basic Books,

2008), 19–27. Lynn Spigel, *Make Room for TV: Television and the Family Ideal in Postwar America* (Chicago: University of Chicago Press, 1992), 36–47.

7. "Oldest Baby Boomers Turn 60!" *U.S. Census Bureau*, January 3, 2006. http://www.census.gov/newsroom/releases/pdf/cb06-ffse01-2.pdf. Accessed on 19 August 2011.

8. Baby Boomer Headquarters, "The Boomer Stats," http://www.bbhq.com/bomrstat.htm. Accessed on 16 December 2009.

9. Victor D. Brooks, *Boomers: The Cold War Generation Grows Up* (Chicago: Ivan R. Dee, 2009), 25–34. Richard Cronker, *The Boomer Century, 1946–2046: How America's Most Influential Generation Changed Everything* (New York: Springboard Press, 2007), 86–92.

10. Wright 33–34.

11. Al Schwartz, "The People vs. Superman," *Superman* #62 (New York: DC Comics, January/February 1950).

12. Bill Finger, "The Case of the Mother Goose Mystery," *World's Finest* #83 (New York: DC Comics, July/August 1956).

13. Al Plastino, *Superman* #60, cover image (New York: DC Comics, September/October 1949).

14. Jeffrey K. Johnson, "The Countryside Triumphant: Jefferson's Ideal of Rural Superiority in Modern Superhero Mythology," *The Journal of Popular Culture* Vol. 43.4, 2010, 721–726.

15. Jeanne Pauline Williams, "The Evolution of Social Norms and the Life of Lois Lane: A Rhetorical Analysis of Popular Culture," Doctorial Dissertation, Ohio State University, 1986.

16. John Byrne, "Introduction by John Byrne from DC Comics Lois and Clark TPB Comic Compilation," *Lois Lane's Daily Journal*. http://www.loislanesdailyjournal.com/loislanehistory.htm#62123127. Accessed on 18 December 2009.

17. Al Plastino, *Superman* #67, cover image (New York: DC Comics, November/December 1950).

18. Al Plastino, *Action Comics* #149, cover image (New York: DC Comics, October 1950).

19. Win Mortimer, *Action Comics* #163, cover image (New York: DC Comics, December 1951).

20. Win Mortimer, *Superman* #94, cover image (New York: DC Comics, January 1955).

21. Haynes Johnson, *The Age of Anxiety: McCarthyism to Terrorism* (San Diego: Harcourt, 2005), 56–74. Griffin Fariello, *Red Scare: Memories of the American Inquisition* (New York: W.W. Norton, 1995), 23–31.

22. "Juvenile Delinquency," *Novel Guide*, http://www.novelguide.com/a/discover/adec_0001_0006_0/adec_0001_0006_0_01937.html Accessed on 22 December 2009.

23. Max F. Baer, "The National Juvenile Delinquency Picture," *Personnel and Guidance Journal* 38 (December 1959), 278–279. "Why Law Fails to Stop Teenage Crime," *U.S. News and World Report* (14 January 1955), 64–75.

24. David Hajdu, *The Ten-Cent Plague: The Great Comic-Book Scare and How It Changed America* (New York: Picador, 2008), 76.

25. Brian Cronin, "Comic Book Legends Revealed #235," *Comic Book Resources*, http://goodcomics.comicbookresources.com/2009/11/26/comic-book-legends-revealed-235/. Accessed on 21 December 2009.

26. Hajdu, 106–110.

27. Cronin; Amy Kiste Nyberg, *Seal of Approval: The History of the Comics Code* (Jackson: University Press of Mississippi, 1998), 24–25.

28. Hajdu 230–235. Bart Beaty, *Fredric Wertham and the Critique of Mass Culture* (Jackson: University Press of Mississippi, 2005), 136–139, 201.

29. Juvenile Delinquency (Comic Books) Hearings Before the United States Senate Committee on the Judiciary, Subcommittee to Investigate Juvenile Delinquency in the U.S., Eighty-third Congress, Second Session, on April 21–22, June 4, 1954. Wright, 161–175. Hajdu, 272.

30. "The Comics Code," *Lambiek.net*, http://lambiek.net/comics/code_text.htm. Accessed 22 on December 2009.

31. Hajdu, 326.

32. Otto Binder and Curt Swan, "The Supergirl from Krypton," *Action Comics* #252 (New York: DC Comics, May 1959).

33. Grant Morrison, *Supergods: What Masked Vigilantes, Miraculous Mutants, and a Sun God from Smallville Can Teach Us About Being Human* (New York: Spiegel and Grau, 2001), 63.

Chapter 5

1. Leonard Steinhorn, *The Greater Generation: In Defense of the Baby Boom Legacy* (New York: Thomas Dunne Books, 2006), 1–4.

2. John F. Kennedy, *Inaugural Address*, 20 January 1961. Reprinted at http://www.americanrhetoric.com/speeches/jfkinaugural.htm. Accessed on 10 January 2010.

3. Theodore C. Sorensen, *"Let the Word Go Forth": The Speeches, Statements, and Writings of John F. Kennedy, 1947 to 1963* (New York: Delacorte Press, 1988), 1–6.

4. "1960 Comic Book Sales Figures," *The Comics Chronicles: A Resource for Comics Research*, http://www.comichron.com/yearlycomicssales/1960s/1960.html. Accessed on 18 January 2010.

5. Jerry Siegel and Curt Swan, "The Death of Superman," *Superman* #149 (New York: DC Comics, 1961).

6. Otto Binder and Kurt Schaffenberger, "Mr. and Mrs. Clark (Superman) Kent," *Superman's Girlfriend Lois Lane* #19 (New York: DC Comics, 1960).

7. Bill Finger and Bob Kane, "Batman's New Secret Identity," *Batman* #151 (New York: DC Comics, 1962).

8. Jim Shooter and Curt Swan, "Superman and Batman-Brothers," *World's Finest Comics* #172 (New York: DC Comics, 1967).

9. Leo Dorfman and Curt Swan, "The Amazing Story of Superman-Red and Superman-Blue," *Superman* #162 (New York: DC Comics, 1963).

10. "1960 Comic Book Sales Figures," *The Comics Chronicles: A Resource for Comics Research*, http://www.comichron.com/yearlycomicssales/1960s/1960.html. Accessed on 18 January 2010.

11. "1961 Comic Book Sales Figures," *The Comics Chronicles: A Resource for Comics Research*, http://www.comichron.com/yearlycomicssales/1960s/1961.html. Accessed on 18 January 2010.

12. Gerald Jones, *Men of Tomorrow: Geeks, Gangsters, and the Birth of the Comic Book* (New York: Basic Books, 2004), 295–296.

13. For further explanation of the Marvel method see Stan Lee's autobiography, *Excelsior! The Amazing Life of Stan Lee*.

14. Stan Lee and George Mair, *Excelsior! The Amazing Life of Stan Lee* (New York: Fireside, 2002), 114.

15. Mark Evanier, *Kirby: King of Comics* (New York: Harry N. Abrams, 2008), 122.

16. Pierre Comtois, *Marvel Comics in the 1960s: An Issue by Issue Field Guide to a Pop Culture Phenomenon* (Raleigh, NC: TwoMorrows, 2009), 13.

17. Robert Genter, "'With Great Power Comes Great Responsibility': Cold War Culture and the Birth of Marvel Comics," *The Journal of Popular Culture* 40: 6, 2007, 4–7.

18. Capitano, 252–257.

19. Stan Lee and George Mair, 127.

20. Marvel did not release sales figures for 1962–1965 but in 1966 *Amazing Spider-Man* was Marvel's number one selling title; http://www.comichron.com/yearlycomicssales/1960s/1966.html. Accessed on 27 January 2010.

21. David Obst, *Too Good to Be Forgotten: Changing America in the '60s and '70s* (New York: John Wiley, 1998), 55–56.

22. Fredric Jameson, "Periodizing the 60s," *The 60s Without Apology*, editor Sohnya Sayres (Minneapolis: University of Minnesota Press, 1984), 182–183.

23. David R. Colburn and George E. Pozzetta, "Race, Ethnicity, and the Evolution of Political Legitimacy," *The Sixties: From Memory to History*, editor David Farber (Chapel Hill: University of North Carolina Press, 1994), 138–141.

24. Stanley Karnow, *Vietnam: A History* (New York: Penguin Books, 1997), 694–697.

25. Ibid., 695–697.

26. George Lipsitz, "Who'll Stop the Rain?" *The Sixties: From Memory to History*, editor David Farber (Chapel Hill: University of North Carolina Press, 1994), 206–221.

27. "Timothy Leary: Turn On, Tune In, Drop Out," http://turnontuneindropout.com/Timothy_Leary_files/leary2.html. Accessed 23 June 2011.

28. Steinhorn, 84–86.

29. Bradford W. Wright, *Comic Book Nation: The Transformation of Youth Culture in America* (Baltimore: Johns Hopkins University Press), 2001, 224.

30. In 1966, when Marvel titles were already well known among comic book readers, the top selling Marvel comic book, *The Amazing Spider-Man*, sold an average of 340,155 copies a month. Although this sales number was well above that of the average comic book and enough to make *The Amazing Spider-Man* a smashing success, it was not among the top ten superhero titles. Each of the top ten selling superhero titles were DC comic books. *Batman*, propelled by the television show's popularity, sold an average of 898,470 copies a month. The number two selling book, *Superman*, averaged 719,976 issues a month. Each of these titles sold more than double Marvel's top title. By the end of the decade in 1969, DC's sales had dropped dramatically, but the top four superhero titles were still DC comic books. *The Amazing Spider-Man* was artistically, creatively, socially, and culturally important but *Superman*, *Superboy*, and *Superman's Girlfriend Lois Lane* still outsold the top Marvel title. http://www.comichron.com/yearlycomicssales.html. Accessed 5 February 2010.

31. Scott MacFarlane, "The Counterculture," *Baby Boom: People and Perspectives* (Santa Barbara, CA: ABC-CLIO, 2010), 117–123.

32. Wright, 219.

33. Lawrence S. Wittner, *Cold War America: From Hiroshima to Watergate* (New York: Praeger, 1974), 268–269.

34. Ibid., 287–288.

35. Rexford G. Tugwell, *Off Course: From Truman to Nixon* (New York: Praeger, 1971), 270.

36. Wittner, 291–292.

37. Karnow, 697.

38. David Farber, "The Silent Majority and Talk About Revolution," *The Sixties: From Memory to History*, editor David Farber (Chapel Hill: University of North Carolina Press, 1994), 302–305.

39. "Political Notes: Chairman Daley's Maxims," *Time*, Online Edition, July 18, 1969, http://www.time.com/time/magazine/article/0,9171,901037,00.html. Accessed on 23 June 2011.

40. Wright, 235.

Chapter 6

1. Philip Jenkins, *Decade of Nightmares: The End of the Sixties and the Making of Eighties America* (New York: Oxford University Press, 2006), 4.

2. For the purposes of this study the 1970s include the years 1970–1979. Historians disagree about what years constitute the cultural 1970s and I define the decade using the traditional parameters. Although things associated with the 1960s, like the Kent State massacre, take place in the 1970s, I believe this reflects a nation in flux and reaffirms that notion that cultural change is often a slow, painstaking process.

3. Rick Hampson, "1970 Kent State shootings are an enduring history lesson," *USA Today*, Online Edition, May 4, 2010, http://www.usatoday.com/news/nation/2010–05–03-kent-state_N.htm. Accessed on 29 June 2011.

4. Les Daniels, *Superman: The Complete History* (San Francisco: Chronicle Books, 1998), 115–16.

5. Denny O'Neil, *Voices from Krypton*, http://www.earthsmightiest.com/fansites/justiceleague/news/?a=6620. Accessed on 27 September 2010.

6. Christopher Irving, "Carmine Infantino's Final Interview? No Way," *NYC Graphic*, 2 July 2009, http://graphicnyc.blogspot.com/2009/07/carmine-infantinos-final-interview.html. Accessed on 3 October 2010.

7. "The Blurbs of Jack Kirby," *Dial B for Blog*, http://www.dialbforblog.com/archives/401/. Accessed on 21 June 2011.

8. Mark Evanier, "Afterword," *Jack Kirby's Fourth World Omnibus*, Vol. 1 (New York: DC Comics, 2007).

9. "The Great One Is Coming," print advertisement in *Superman's Pal Jimmy Olsen* #130 (New York: DC Comics, July 1970), 19.

10. "The King Is Here," cover to *Superman's Pal Jimmy Olsen* #133 (New York: DC Comics, October 1970).

11. Jack Kirby, "Forever People in Search of a Dream," *Forever People* #1 in *The Greatest Superman Stories Ever Told* (New York: DC Comics, 1987), 231–254.

12. Mark Evanier, "Introduction," *Jack Kirby's OMAC: One Man Army Corps* Vol. 1 (New York: DC Comics, 2008), 4.

13. Denny O'Neil, "Introduction," *Green Lantern/Green Arrow* Vol. 1 (New York: DC Comics, 2004), 6.

14. Denny O'Neil, "No Evil Shall Escape My Sight," *Green Lantern/Green Arrow*. Vol. 1 (New York: DC Comics, 2004), 15.

15. John Wells, "Green Lantern/Green Arrow: And Through Them Change an Industry," *Back Issue*, December 2010, 52.

16. Denny O'Neil, "Introduction," *Green Lantern/Green Arrow*, Vol. 1 (New York: DC Comics, 2004), 7.

17. Wright, 233–234.

18. Brian Cronin, "Comic Book Urban Legends Revealed #119," *Comic Book Resources*, http://goodcomics.comicbookresources.com/2007/09/06/comic-book-urban-legends-revealed-119/. Accessed on 19 August 2011.

19. "Stan Lee on the Spider-Man Drug Story Too Hot for the Comics Code Authority [Video]," *Comics Alliance*, http://www.comicsalliance.com/2010/07/26/stan-lee-amazing-spider-man-drugs-comics-code-authority/. Accessed on 19 August 2011.

20. Amy Kiste Nyberg, *Seal of Approval: The History of the Comics Code* (Jackson: University Press of Mississippi, 1998), 142.

21. Stephen E. Ambrose, *Nixon: The Triumph of a Politician, 1962–1972* (New York: Simon & Schuster, 1987), 217–222.

22. Alan F. Westin, "Information, Dissent, and Political Power: Watergate Revisited," *Watergate and Afterward: The Legacy of Richard Nixon*, editors Leon Friedman and William F. Levantrosser (Westport, CT: Greenwood, 1992), 54–59.

23. Thomas Hine, *The Great Funk: Falling Apart and Coming Together (on a Shag Rug) in the Seventies* (New York: Sarah Crichton Books, 2007), 34–35, 198–199.

24. Steve Englehart, *Captain America and the Falcon* #156 (New York: Marvel Comics, December 1972).

25. Steve Englehart, *Captain America and the Falcon* #163–176 (New York: Marvel Comics, July 1973–August 1974).

26. Steve Engelhart, "Captain America II," http://www.steveenglehart.com/Comics/Captain%20America%20169–176.html. Accessed on 19 August 2011.

27. Steve Englehart, "Captain America Must Die," *Captain America and the Falcon* #176 (New York: Marvel Comics, August 1974).

28. Gerry Conway, "The Night Gwen Stacy Died" and "The Green Goblin's Last Stand," *The Amazing Spider-Man* #121–122 (New York: Marvel Comics, June–July 1973).

29. Gerry Conway, *Comic Geek Speak*, Episode 701, October 6, 2009, interview, http://comicgeekspeak.com/episodes/comic_geek_speak-891.php. Accessed on 19 August 2011.

30. Michael McAvennie, "1970s," *DC Comics: Year by Year, A Visual Chronicle* (New York: DK Publishing, 2010), 153.

31. Joe Simon, "The Making of the Prez," *Prez* #1 (New York: DC Comics, March 1974).

32. Jimmy Carter, "Primary Sources: The 'Crisis of Confidence' Speech," July 15, 1979, http://www.pbs.org/wgbh/amex/carter/filmmore/ps_crisis.html. Accessed on 19 August 2011.

33. James Cannon, *Time and Chance: Gerald Ford's Appointment with History* (New York: HarperCollins), 1994, 305–308; Douglas Brinkley, *Gerald R. Ford* (New York: Times Books, 2007), 64–70.

34. John Robert Greene, *The Presidency of Gerald R. Ford* (Lawrence: University of Kansas, 1995), 132–136.

35. Brinkley, 134–140.

36. Bill Mantlo, "Long Time Gone," *Iron Man* #78 (New York: Marvel Comics, September 1975).

37. Michael McAvennie, "1970s," *DC Comics: Year by Year, A Visual Chronicle* (New York: DK Publishing, 2010), 162.

38. Elliot S! Maggin, "The Invader from Hell!" *Batman Family* #1 (New York: DC Comics, October 1975).

39. Andrew Glass, "Carter Pardons Draft Dodgers Jan. 21, 1977," *Politico*, http://www.politico.com/news/stories/0108/7974.html. Accessed on 28 June 2011.

40. "The Blackout: Night of Terror," *Time*, Online Edition, July 25, 1977, http://www.time.com/time/magazine/article/0,9171,919089,00.html. Accessed on 12 May 2011.

41. Hine, 214–215.

42. Erwin C. Hargrove, *Jimmy Carter as President: Leadership and the Politics of the Public Good* (Baton Rouge: Louisiana State University Press, 1988), 137–141.

43. Ibid., 52–54. Jimmy Carter, *White House Diary* (New York: Farrar, Straus and Giroux, 2010), 278–285.

44. Carter, 367–69.

45. Henry S. Bradsher, *Afghanistan and the Soviet Union* (Durham, NC: Duke Press Policy Studies, 1983), 175–180.

46. Michael McAvennie, "1970s," *DC Comics: Year by Year, a Visual Chronicle* (New York: DK Publishing, 2010), 172–179

47. The New Gods' Black Racer and Vykin the Black, the Green Lantern's John Stewart, the Legion of Superheroes' Tyroc, and the Teen Titans' Mal Duncan appeared in DC Comics stories before Black Lightning. Each of these heroes only appeared briefly and arguably were of little consequence during the 1970s.

48. Jeffrey A. Brown. *Black Superheroes, Milestone Comics, and Their Fans* (Jackson: University Press of Mississippi, 2001), 19–24.

49. Tony Isabella, "Black Lightning and Me," *The Hembeck Files*, http://www.proudrobot.com/hembeck/blacklightning.html. Accessed on 19 August 2011.

50. Denny O'Neil and Neal Adams, *Superman vs. Muhammad Ali Deluxe Edition* (New York: DC Comics, 2010).

51. David R. Black, "The DC Implosion!" *Fanzing: The DC Comics Fan Site*, http://www.fanzing.com/mag/fanzing27/feature1.shtml. Accessed on 19 August 2011.

52. Jenette Kahn, "DC Publishorial: Onward and Upward," print advertisement in all DC Comics, New York: DC Comics, September 1978.

53. "Explosion and Implosion!" *Dial B for Blog*, http://www.dialbforblog.com/archives/252/. Accessed on 19 August 2011.

54. David Michelinie, *Invincible Iron Man* #120–128 (New York: Marvel Comics, March–November 1979).

Chapter 7

1. United States Department of Labor Bureau of Labor Statistics, "Unemployment Rate," http://data.bls.gov/pdq/SurveyOutputServlet. Accessed 20 August 2011, "Historical Inflation," *Inflationdata.com*, http://inflationdata.com/inflation/Inflation_Rate/HistoricalInflation.aspx?dsInflation_currentPage=2. Accessed on 20 August 2011.

2. Ronald Reagan, "Acceptance Speech at the 1980 Republican Convention," July 17, 1980, *The National Center for Public Policy Research*. http://www.nationalcenter.org/ReaganConvention1980.html. Accessed on 24 June 2011.

3. Sean Wilentz, *The Age of Reagan: A History, 1974–2008* (New York: HarperCollins, 2008), 135–139.

4. Dinesh D'Souza, *Ronald Reagan: How an Ordinary Man Became an Extraordinary Leader* (New York: Simon & Schuster, 1999), 11–15.

5. Frank Newport, Jeffrey M. Jones, and Lydia Saad, "Ronald Reagan From the People's Perspective: A Gallup Poll Review," Gallup, 7 June 2004, http://www.gallup.com/poll/11887/Ronald-Reagan-From-Peoples-Perspective-Gallup-Poll-Review.aspx. Accessed 20 August 2011.

6. United States Department of Labor Bureau of Labor Statistics, "Unemployment Rate," http://data.bls.gov/pdq/SurveyOutputServlet. Accessed on 20 August 2011.

7. Newport, Jones, and Saad.

8. David Gergen in D'Souza, 45

9. Hodding Carter, *The Reagan Years* (New York: George Braziller, 1988), 7–8.

10. Edwin Meese, *With Reagan: The Inside Story* (Washington, D.C.: Regnery Gateway, 1992), 163–170.

11. Wilentz, 278–279.

12. Ronald Reagan, "Lebanon and Grenada," speech, 27 October 1983, http://www.presidentreagan.info/speeches/lebanon_and_grenada.cfm, 20 August 2011.

13. Bradford W. Wright, *Comic Book Nation: The Transformation of Youth Culture in America* (Baltimore: Johns Hopkins University Press, 2003), 260–262.

14. Wright, 266.

15. Don Thompson and Maggie Thompson, "Epic Beginnings" *Camelot 3000* (New York: DC Comics, 1988), 1–2.

16. Greg Burgas, "Comics You Should Own Flashback: *Camelot 3000*," *Comic Book Resources*, May 4, 2010, http://goodcomics.comicbookresources.com/2010/05/04/comics-you-should-own-flashback-camelot-3000/ Accessed on 27 June 2011.

17. "Ronald Reagan TV ad: 'Its [*sic*] morning in America again.'" *You Tube*, http://www.youtube.com/watch?v=EU-IBF8nwSY. Accessed on 27 June 2011.

18. Ronald Reagan, "20 Years Later: Reagan's Westminster Speech," June 8, 1982, *The Heritage Foundation*, http://www.heritage.org/research/reports/2002/06/reagans-westminster-speech. Accessed on 27 June 2011.

19. Ronald Reagan, "President Ronald Reagan, 'Evil Empire' Speech," *You Tube*, http://www.youtube.com/watch?v=do0x-Egc6oA. Accessed on 27 June 2011.

20. Ronald Reagan, "Bloopers, Blunders, and Bombast: Uncensored Comments of American Politicians," http://www.historyplace.com/specials/different/bloopers.htm. Accessed 27 June 2011.

21. "Bernhard Goetz Biography," *Biography.com*, http://www.biography.com/articles/Bernhard-Goetz-578520. Accessed 27 June 2011.

22. Mike Baron. "Afterword," *The Punisher* (New York: Marvel Comics), 1988.

23. Cord Scott, "The Alpha and the Omega: Captain America and the Punisher," in *Captain America and the Struggle of the Superhero: Critical Essays*, editor Robert G. Weiner (Jefferson, NC: McFarland, 2009), 125–126.

24. Mike W. Barr. "Fear Grows in Brooklyn," *Captain America #241* (New York: Marvel Comics, January 1980).

25. It is difficult to even estimate *Crisis on Infinite Earths'* body count. If the series truly featured an infinite number of Earths then the number of characters or beings that died would also appear to be infinite.

26. Peter Rios, *Comic Geek Speak Presents The Crisis Tapes: Footnotes Vol. 5*. Podcast, August 2010, http://www.comicgeekspeak.com/episodes/crisis-1141.php. Accessed on 20 August 2011.

27. Adam C. Murdough, *Worlds Will Live, Worlds Will Die: Myth, Metatext, Continuity, and Cataclysm in DC Comics' Crisis on Infinite Earths*. Bowling Green University, August 2006.

28. John Byrne, "Rebirth: John Byrne's Superman," quoted in James Van Hise, *The Superman Files*. Canoga Park, CA: Heroes Publishing, 1986.

29. Frank Miller, quoted in Joe Strike, "Frank Miller's 'Dark Knight' Brought Batman Back to Life," *New York Daily News*, Online Edition, 16 July 2008. http://articles.nydailynews.com/2008-07-16/entertainment/17902060_1_dark-knight-returns-batman-superman. Accessed on 20 August 2011.

30. Frank Miller, *Batman: The Dark Knight Returns* (New York: DC Comics, 2002), 186.

31. Ibid., 192.

32. Ibid., 135.

33. Cary Bates, *The Flash* #324 (New York: Marvel Comics, August 1983).

34. J.M. DeMatteis, *Kraven's Last Hunt* (New York: Marvel Comics, 2006).

35. Shannon Cochran, "The Cold Shoulder: Saving Superheroines from Comic-book Violence," *Bitch Media*. Accessed 13 May 2011.

36. Wilentz, 202–205. M. Stephen Weatherford and Lorraine M. McDonnell, "Ideology and Economic Policy," *Looking Back at the Reagan Presidency*, Larry Bergman, editor (Baltimore: Johns Hopkins University Press, 1990), 127–132.

37. Wilentz, 208.

38. Benjamin Ginsberg and Martin Shefter, "After the Reagan Revolution: A Postelection Politics?" in *Look-*

ing Back at the Reagan Presidency, Larry Bergman, editor (Baltimore: Johns Hopkins University Press, 1990), 249–252. Wilentz, 236–240.

   39. For an in depth analysis of *Green Arrow: The Longbow Hunters*, listen to the *Raging Bullets: A DC Comics Fan Podcast* Episode #260. http://ragingbullets.libsyn.com/raging-bullets-episode-260-a-dc-comics-fan-podcast.

   40. Wright, 273.

Chapter 8

   1. "50s Adventures of Superman — Intro," *You Tube*, http://www.youtube.com/watch?v=Q2l4bz1FT8U. Accessed on 27 June 2011.

   2. Martin Walker, *The Cold War: A History* (New York: Henry Holt, 1993), 315–321.

   3. "Timeline: South Africa," *BBC News*, June 21, 2011. http://news.bbc.co.uk/2/hi/africa/1069402.stm. Accessed on 29 June 2011.

   4. Josef Joffe, "The Wall and the End of History," *Newsweek*, Online Edition, November 6, 2009, http://www.newsweek.com/2009/11/05/the-wall-and-the-end-of-history.html. Accessed 29 June 2011.

   5. Herbert S. Parmet, *George Bush: The Life of a Lone Star Yankee* (New York: Scribner, 1997), 416–420.

   6. Ibid., 302–308. Stephen R. Graubard, *Mr. Bush's War: Adventures in the Politics of Illusion* (New York: Hill and Wang, 1992), 125–130.

   7. Grant Morrison *Arkham Asylum* 15th anniversary edition (New York: DC Comics), 1989.

   8. Morrison, *Arkham Asylum*, 38.

   9. Stan Lee, *Fantastic Four Annual #3* (New York: Marvel Comics, October 1965). Elliot S! Maggin, "The Last Earth-Prime Story," *Superman* #411 (New York: DC Comics, September 1985).

   10. There are other examples of superheroes understanding their fictional existences, including John Byrne's stories in *Sensational She-Hulk*, which also began in 1989. Morrison's *Animal Man* is arguably the first superhero comic book storyline to use the quest to gain complete self-awareness as a major plot device.

   11. Grant Morrison, *Animal Man: Deus Ex Machina* (New York: DC Comics, 2003), 208.

   12. "Ultron Unlimited (Part 1 of 4)," *Snikt! The Comics of the Nineties*, June 14, 2009, http://marincomics.tumblr.com/. Accessed on 27 June 2011.

   13. Derek Chollet and James Goldgeier, *America Between the Wars: From 11/9 to 9/11, the Misunderstood Years Between the Fall of the Berlin Wall and the Start of the War on Terror* (New York: PublicAffairs, 2008), 54–55, 72–84.

   14. Haynes Johnson, *The Best of Times: America in the Clinton Years* (New York: Harcourt, 2001),168.

   15. "Image Comics," *The Unknown*, http://www.unknowncomicsandgames.com/image-comics. Accessed 5 June 2011.

   16. "February 1996 Comic Book Sales Rankings," *The Comics Chronicles*, http://www.comichron.com/monthlycomicssales/1996/1996–02Diamond.html, Accessed on 6 August 2011.

   17. "1992 Comic Book Sales Figures," *The Comics Chronicles*, http://www.comichron.com/monthlycomics sales/1992.html. Accessed 5 May 2011.

   18. "Reign of the Supermen," *Comic Vine*, http://www.comicvine.com/reign-of-the-supermen/39–56339/. Accessed on 12 June 2011.

   19. Graham Nolan, "Comics: Meet the Artist," *The Washington Post*, May 16, 2003, Online Edition, http://www.washingtonpost.com/wp-srv/liveonline/03/regular/style/comics/r_style_comics051603.htm. Accessed on 15 May 2011.

   20. "Knightfall" *Comic Vine*, http://www.comicvine.com/knightfall/39–40761/. Accessed on 12 June 2011.

   21. Glenn Greenberg, *The Life of Reilly*, Part 19, March 5, 2008, http://lifeofreillyarchives.blogspot.com/2008/03/part-19.html. Accessed on 13 June 2011.

   22. "1993 Comic Book Sales Figures," *The Comics Chronicles*, http://www.comichron.com/monthlycomics sales/1992.html, Accessed on 5 May 2011, http://www.comichron.com/monthlycomicssales/1993.html.

   23. Mark Voger, *The Dark Age: Grim, Great and Gimmicky Post-Modern Comics* (Raleigh, NC: TwoMorrows, 2006), 124–144.

   24. Wayne Bert, *The Reluctant Superpower: United States Policy in Bosnia, 1991–95* (New York: St. Martin's, 1997), 202–209.

   25. Johnson, 108–120.

   26. Peter B. Levy, *Encyclopedia of the Clinton Presidency* (Westport, CT: Greenwood, 2002), 265–266.

   27. Chollet and Goldgeier, 86–89. Levy, 159–160.

   28. Dan Raviv, *Comic Wars: How Two Tycoons Battled Over the Marvel Comics Empire — And Both Lost* (New York: Broadway, 2001).

   29. Adrian Watts, "Avengers: Heroes Reborn," *White Rocket Books*, Accessed on 9 June 2011.

   30. Mark Waid and Alex Ross, *Kingdom Come* (New York: DC Comics, 1997).

   31. Elliot S! Maggin, "The New Bards" in *Kingdom Come* (New York: DC Comics, 1997), 7.

32. Levy, 258, 260.

33. Johnson, 417–419.

34. Matthew K. Manning, "1979s," *DC Comics: Year by Year, a Visual Chronicle* (New York: DK Publishing, 2010), 272, 279.

35. Ibid., 275, 279.

Chapter 9

1. For this study's purposes, I consider the year 2000 to be the start of the third millennium. I understand that officially the new millennium did not begin until January 1, 2001, but most popular and mass culture venues refer to the year 2000 as the millennium's starting year and I chose to follow this popular interpretation.

2. Richard Lacayo, John Cloud, Emily Mitchell, Wendy Cole, Declan McCullagh, Timothy Roche, and Richard Woodbury, "The End of the World as We Know It?" *Time*, 18 January 1999, Online edition, http://www.time.com/time/magazine/article/0,9171,990020,00.html. Accessed 17 April 2010.

3. "Watching for the Y2K Bug," *New York Times*, editorial, 30 December 1999, Online edition, http://www.nytimes.com/1999/12/30/opinion/watching-for-the-y2k-bug.html?scp=3&sq=y2k&st=nyt. Accessed 17 April 2010.

4. Ibid.

5. Robert Draper, *Dead Certain: The Presidency of George W. Bush* (New York: Free Press, 2007), 82–83.

6. "Timeline: How the Anthrax Terror Unfolded," *NPR.org*, 1 August 2008, http://www.npr.org/templates/story/story.php?storyId=93170200. Accessed 1 August 2010.

7. William Robert Johnston, "Review of Fall 2001 Anthrax Bioattacks," 28 September 2007, http://www.johnstonsarchive.net/terrorism/anthrax.html. Accessed 1 August 2010.

8. Murat Kurnaz, *Five Years of My Life: An Innocent Man in Guantanamo* (New York: Palgrave Macmillan, 2007), 15–18. Weisberg, Jacob, *The Bush Tragedy* (New York: Random House, 2008), 177–178.

9. J. Michael Straczynski and John Romita, Jr., *The Amazing Spider-Man* #36 (New York: Marvel Comics, 2002), 9.

10. Bill Jourdain, "Big All-American Comic Book," *Golden Age of Comic Books*, 20 December 2008, http://goldenagecomics.org/wordpress/2008/12/20/big-all-american-comic-book/. Accessed 3 August 2010.

11. "Aggregated 2003 Comic Book Sales Figures," *The Comics Chronicles*, http://www.comichron.com/monthlycomicssales/2003.html. Accessed 2 May 2010.

12. "George W. Bush 2004 TV Ads 'Wolves.'" *4President.tv*, http://tv.4president.us/2004/bush2004wolves.htm. Accessed on 4 August 2010.

13. Stan Lee and Jack Kirby, *Marvel Masterworks: Avengers, Vol. 1* (New York: Marvel, 2002).

14. "Avengers Disassembled," *BD Comics*, 13 February 2007, http://bdcomics.bdgamers.net/2007/02/13/avengers-disassembled/. Accessed 3 August 2010.

15. Brian Michael Bendis, *Avengers Disassembled* (New York: Marvel Comics, 2006).

16. Brad Meltzer, *Identity Crisis* (New York: DC Comics, 2006).

17. Valerie D'Orazio, "Goodbye to Comics #7: 'We Need A Rape.'" *The Occasional Superheroine*, http://occasionalsuperheroine.blogspot.com/search/label/Goodbye%20To%20Comics?updated-max=2006-11-17T07%3A31%3A00-05%3A00&max-results=20. Accessed on 4 May 2010.

18. Ibid.

19. Ibid.

20. "Poll Shows Dissatisfaction with Iraq War," *CNN.com*, http://www.cnn.com/2005/POLITICS/06/20/poll/. Accessed on 2 May 2010.

21. "Chronology of Abu Ghraib," *The Washington Post*, Online Edition, http://www.washingtonpost.com/wp-srv/world/daily/graphics/abughraib_050904.htm. Accessed on 2 May 2010.

22. Simon Jeffrey, "George Bush's Approval Ratings: 2001–2009," *The Guardian*, Online Edition, 16 January 2009, http://www.guardian.co.uk/world/interactive/2009/jan/16/george-bush-approval-ratings-america. Accessed on 2 May 2010.

23. Brian Michael Bendis, *House of M* (New York: Marvel Comics, 2008).

24. Geoff Johns, *Infinite Crisis* (New York: DC Comics, 2008).

25. George Gene Gustines, "Recalibrating DC Heroes for a Grittier Century," *The New York Times*, Online Edition, 12 October 2005, http://query.nytimes.com/gst/fullpage.html?res=9B02E6D8163FF931A25753C1A9639C8B63&sec=&spon=&pagewanted=1. Accessed 11 August 2010.

26. Geoff Johns, Grant Morrison, Greg Rucka, and Mark Waid, *52* (New York: DC Comics, 2007).

27. Sharon Squassoni, "North Korea's Nuclear Weapons: Latest Developments," *CRS Report for Congress*, 18 October 2006, http://www.fas.org/sgp/crs/nuke/RS21391.pdf . Accessed on 4 August 2010.

28. "North Korea's Nuclear Ambitions," *NPR.org*, 10 October 2006, http://www.npr.org/worldopinion/20061010_worldopinion_northkorea.html. Accessed on 6 August 2010.

29. Julie Creswell and Vikas Bajaj, "$3.2 Billion Move by Bear Stearns to Rescue Fund," *The New York Times*, 23 June 2007, Electronic Edition, http://www.nytimes.com/2007/06/23/business/23bond.html?_r=1. Accessed on 9 May 2010.

30. Matthew Benjamin, "Most Americans See Recession in the Next 12 Months," *Bloomberg.com*, 11 April 2007, http://www.bloomberg.com/apps/news?pid=20601068&sid=avYkRibHRfDk&refer=economy. Accessed on 9 May 2010.

31. "China Raises 2007 Growth Figure," *BBC News*, Electronic Edition, 10 April 2008, http://news.bbc.co.uk/2/hi/business/7340018.stm. Accessed on 9 May 2010.

32. "U.S. Trade Deficit Declined in 2007," *MSNBC.com*, 14 February 2008, http://www.msnbc.msn.com/id/23163519/. Accessed on 9 May 2010.

33. T. Rees Shapiro, "Virginia Tech Student Remember Those Who Died in Shooting," *The Washington Post*, 16 April 2010, http://www.washingtonpost.com/wp-dyn/content/article/2010/04/15/AR2010041505727.html. Accessed on 9 May 2009.

34. Mark Millar, *Civil War* (New York: Marvel, 2008).

35. Erik Henriksen, "This Is What It Sounds Like When Nerds Cry," *The Portland Mercury*, 7 March 2007, http://blogtown.portlandmercury.com/2007/03/this_is_what_it_sounds_like_wh.php. Accessed on 9 May 2010.

36. Ed Brubaker, *The Death of Captain America Omnibus* (New York: Marvel Comics, 2009).

37. George Gene Gustines, "Captain America Is Dead; National Hero Since 1941," *The New York Times*, Online Edition, 7 March 2007, http://www.nytimes.com/2007/03/08/books/08capt.html. Accessed 3 May 2010.

38. Bryan Robinson, "What the Death of Captain America Really Means: Bullets Killed Him, but the War on Terror Really Did Cap In," *ABC News*, Online Edition, 8 March 2007, http://abcnews.go.com/US/story?id=2934283&page=1. Accessed 5 May 2010.

39. Ibid.

40. Daniel Taverne, "Does the Death of Captain America Predict the Death of the American Way?" *American Chronicle*, March 7, 2007, http://www.americanchronicle.com/articles/view/21785. Accessed 10 May 2010.

41. Leonard Pitts, Jr., "Come Back, Captain, We Need You," *The Seattle Times*, Electronic Edition, 14 March 2007, http://seattletimes.nwsource.com/html/opinion/2003616520_pitts14.html. Accessed on 11 May 2010.

42. Colleen Long, "Marvel Comics Buries Captain America," *The Washington Post*, Electronic Edition, 1 July 2007, http://www.washingtonpost.com/wp-dyn/content/article/2007/06/30/AR2007063000511.html. Accessed 10 May 2010.

43. Ibid.

44. Stephen Colbert, *The Colbert Report*, Electronic Edition, 12 March 2007, http://www.colbertnation.com/the-colbert-report-videos/83567/march-12-2007/sign-off---captain-america-shield. 10 May 2010.

45. Brian Michael Bendis, *Secret Invasion* (New York: Marvel, 2010).

46. David Paul Kuhn and Jonathan Martin, "Republican Candidates Begin Snubbing Bush," Politico, 18 June 2007, http://www.politico.com/news/stories/0607/4538.html. Accessed on 3 August 2010.

47. Michael Abramowitz and Michael D. Shear, "McCain Emphasizes Distance from Bush: Criticism of Administration Stepped Up," *The Washington Post*, 21 October 2008, http://www.washingtonpost.com/wp-dyn/content/article/2008/10/20/AR2008102003638.html. 6 August 2010.

48. Geoff Johns, *Superman and the Legion of Super-heroes* (New York: DC Comics, 2009).

49. Richard George, "NYCC 08: Grant Morrison and J.G. Jones on Final Crisis, DC's last NYCC panel focuses on its biggest 2008 storyline," *IGN.com*, http://comics.ign.com/articles/868/868035p1.html.

50. Jeffrey Renaud, "All Star Grant Morrison I: Final Crisis," *Comic Book Resources*, 15 April 2008, http://www.comicbookresources.com/?page=article&id=16005. Accessed 2 August 2010.

51. Grant Morrison, *Final Crisis* #1 (New York: DC Comics, 2009), 18.

52. Morrison, *Final Crisis* #5 (New York: DC Comics, 2009), 23.

53. Veneta Rogers, "Brian Bendis — Wrapping It All Up and Starting Dark Reign," *Newsarama*, http://www.newsarama.com/comics/120805-Bendis-Dark-Reign.html. Accessed on 5 December 2008.

Conclusion

1. Neil Gaiman quoted in Hank Wagner, Christopher Golden, and Stephen R. Bissette, *Prince of Stories: The Many Worlds of Neil Gaiman* (New York: St. Martin's Press, 2008), 27.

BIBLIOGRAPHY

Abramowitz, Michael, and Michael D. Shear. "McCain Emphasizes Distance from Bush: Criticism of Administration Stepped Up." *The Washington Post*. 21 October 2008. http://www.washingtonpost.com/wp-dyn/content/article/2008/10/20/AR2008102003638.html. Accessed 6 August 2010.

Action Comics #58. New York: DC Comics, 1943.

Action Comics #59. New York: DC Comics, 1943.

"Aggregated 2003 Comic Book Sales Figures." *The Comics Chronicles*. http://www.comichron.com/monthlycomicssales/2003.html. Accessed 2 May 2010.

Ambrose, Stephen E. *Nixon: The Triumph of a Politician, 1962–1972*. New York: Simon & Schuster, 1987.

"Atomic Style." *Atom-A*. http://www.atom-a.com/atomic.html. Accessed 19 September 2009.

"Atomic Toys — Comics." *Oak Ridge Associated Universities*. http://www.orau.org/ptp/collection/atomictoys/atomictoys.htm. Accessed 11 October 2009.

"Avengers Disassembled." *BD Comics*. 13 February 2007. http://bdcomics.bdgamers.net/2007/02/13/avengers-disassembled/. Accessed 3 August 2010.

Baby Boomer Headquarters. "The Boomer Stats." http://www.bbhq.com/bomrstat.htm. Accessed 16 December 2009.

Baer, Max F. "The National Juvenile Delinquency Picture," *Personnel and Guidance Journal* 38 (December 1959).

Barclay, McClelland. "Man the Guns — Join the Navy." Print advertisement, 1942. *Powers of Persuasion: Poster Art from World War II: The National Archives*. http://www.archives.gov/exhibits/powers_of_persuasion/man_the_guns/man_the_guns.html. Accessed on 21 August 2009.

Baron, Mike. "Afterword." *The Punisher*. New York: Marvel Comics, 1988.

Barr, Mike W. *Captain America* #241. "Fear Grows in Brooklyn." New York: Marvel Comics, January 1980.

Bates, Cary, and Dave Cockrum. *Superboy and the Legion of Super-Heroes* #195. New York: DC Comics, 1973.

_____. *The Flash* #324. New York: Marvel Comics, August 1983.

Batman #12. New York: DC Comics, 1942.

Batman #15. New York: DC Comics, 1943.

Batman #17. New York: DC Comics, 1943.

Beall, C.C. "Don't Let Him Down." Print advertisement, 1941. Northwestern University Library Collection. http://digital.library.northwestern.edu/otcgi/digilib/llscgi60.exe?DB=0&ACTION=View&QUERY=home%20efforts&RGN=M653&OP=and&SUBSET=SUBSET&FROM=1&SIZE=10&ITEM=5. Accessed on 19 August 2011.

Beaty, Bart. *Fredric Wertham and the Critique of Mass Culture*. Jackson: University Press of Mississippi, 2005.

Beck, C.C. "Captain Marvel and the Atomic War." *DC's Greatest Imaginary Stories*. New York: DC Comics, 2005.

Beerbohm, Robert Lee. "The Mainline Comics Story: An Initial Examination." *The Jack Kirby Collector* #25. http://www.twomorrows.com/kirby/articles/25mainline.html. 11 December 2009.

Bendis, Brian Michael. *Avengers Disassembled*. New York: Marvel Comics, 2006.

_____. *House of M*. New York: Marvel Comics, 2008.

_____. *Secret Invasion*. New York: Marvel, 2010.

Benjamin, Matthew. "Most Americans See Recession in the Next 12 Months." *Bloomberg.com*. 11 April 2007. http://www.bloomberg.com/apps/news?pid=20601068&sid=avYkRibHRfDk&refer=economy. Accessed on 9 May 2010.

Benton, Mike. *Superhero Comics of the Golden Age: The Illustrated History.* Dallas: Taylor, 1992.

"Bernhard Goetz Biography." *Biography.com.* http://www.biography.com/articles/Bernhard-Goetz-578520. Accessed 27 June 2011.

Bert, Wayne. *The Reluctant Superpower: United States Policy in Bosnia, 1991–95.* New York: St. Martin's, 1997.

"Bikini 60 Years Old and Still Turning Heads." 17 August 2006. *The Paramus Post.* http://www.paramus post.com/article.php/20060816162140460. Accessed on 19 August 2011.

Binder, Otto, and Curt Swan. "The Supergirl from Krypton." *Action Comics* #252. New York: DC Comics, May 1959.

_____, and Kurt Schaffenberger. "Mr. and Mrs. Clark (Superman) Kent." *Superman's Girlfriend Lois Lane* #19. New York: DC Comics, 1960.

Black, David R. "The DC Implosion!" *Fanzing: The DC Comics Fan Site,* http://www.fanzing.com/mag/ fanzing27/feature1.shtml. Accessed 19 August 2011.

"The Blackout: Night of Terror." *Time.* Online Edition. July 25, 1977. http://www.time.com/time/mag azine/article/0,9171,919089,00.html. Accessed 12 May 2011.

Blanchard, B. Wayne. "American Civil Defense, 1945–1985: The Evolution of Programs and Policies." Emmitsburg, MD, 1985.

"The Blurbs of Jack Kirby." *Dial B for Blog.* http://www.dialbforblog.com/archives/401/. Accessed 21 June 2011.

"Bomb Shelters." http://www.lilesnet.com/memories/past/bomb_shelters.htm. Accessed 14 December 2009.

Boyer, Paul. *By the Bomb's Early Light: American Thought and Culture at the Dawn of the Atomic Age.* Chapel Hill: University of North Carolina Press, 1994.

Bradsher, Henry S. *Afghanistan and the Soviet Union.* Durham, NC: Duke Press Policy Studies, 1983.

Brevoort, Tom. "No Prize!" *Marvel.com.* 22 March 2007. http://marvel.com/blogs/Tom%20Brevoort/ entry/361. Accessed 14 December 2009.

Brinkley, Douglas. *Gerald R. Ford.* New York: Times Books, 2007, 64–70.

Brooks, Victor D. *Boomers: The Cold War Generation Grows Up.* Chicago: Ivan R. Dee, 2009.

Brown, Jeffrey A. *Black Superheroes, Milestone Comics, and Their Fans.* Jackson: University Press of Mississippi, 2001.

Brubaker, Ed. *The Death of Captain America Omnibus.* New York: Marvel Comics, 2009.

Bulletman #1. New York: Fawcett Comics, 1940.

Burgas, Greg. "Comics You Should Own Flashback: *Camelot 3000.*" *Comic Book Resources.* May 4, 2010. http://goodcomics.comicbookresources.com/2010/05/04/comics-you-should-own-flashback-camelot-3000/. Accessed 27 June 2011.

Byrne, John. "Introduction by John Byrne from DC Comics Lois and Clark TPB Comic Compilation." *Lois Lane's Daily Journal.* http://www.loislanesdailyjournal.com/loislanehistory.htm#62123127. Accessed 18 December 2009.

_____. "Rebirth: John Byrne's Superman." Quoted in Van Hise, James. *The Superman Files.* Canoga Park, CA: Heroes Publishing, 1986.

Cannon, James. *Time and Chance: Gerald Ford's Appointment with History.* New York: HarperCollins, 1994.

Capitanio, Adam. "'The Jekyll and Hyde of the Atomic Age': The Incredible Hulk at the Ambiguous Embodiment of Nuclear Power." *The Journal of Popular Culture,* Vol. 43.2, 2010.

Captain America #77 and #78. New York: Marvel Comics, 1954.

Captain Marvel Adventures #14. New York: Fawcett, 1942.

Carbonell, Nestor T. *And the Russians Stayed: The Sovietization of Cuba.* New York: William Morrow, 1989.

Carter, Hodding. *The Reagan Years.* New York: George Braziller, 1988.

Carter, Jimmy. "Primary Sources: The 'Crisis of Confidence' Speech." July 15, 1979. http://www.pbs.org/ wgbh/amex/carter/filmmore/ps_crisis.html.

_____. *White House Diary.* New York: Farrar, Straus and Giroux, 2010.

Chabon, Michael. "Secret Skin: An Essay in Unitard Theory." *The New Yorker.* March 10, 2008. http://www. newyorker.com/reporting/2008/03/10/080310fa_fact_chabon/?currentPage=all. Accessed 8 December 2009.

"China Raises 2007 Growth Figure." *BBC News.* Electronic Edition. 10 April 2008. http://news.bbc.co. uk/2/hi/business/7340018.stm. Accessed on 9 May 2010.

Chollet, Derek, and James Goldgeier. *America Between the Wars: From 11/9 to 9/11, the Misunderstood Years Between the Fall of the Berlin Wall and the Start of the War on Terror.* New York: Public Affairs, 2008.

"Chronology of Abu Ghraib." *The Washington Post.* Online Edition. http://www.washingtonpost.com/wp-srv/world/daily/graphics/abughraib_050904.htm. Accessed on 2 May 2010.

Cochran, Shannon. "The Cold Shoulder-saving Superheroines from Comic-book Violence." *Bitch Media.* Accessed 13 May 2011.

Colbert, Stephen. *The Colbert Report*. Electronic Edition. 12 March 2007. http://www.colbertnation.com/the-colbert-report-videos/83567/march-12-2007/sign-off-captain-america-shield. Accessed 10 May 2010.

Colburn, David R., and George E. Pozzetta. "Race, Ethnicity, and the Evolution of Political Legitimacy." *The Sixties: From Memory to History*, editor David Farber. Chapel Hill: University of North Carolina Press, 1994.

Cohen, Lizabeth. *The Politics of Mass Consumption in Postwar America*. New York: Vintage, 2003.

"The Comics Code." *Lambiek.net*. http://lambiek.net/comics/code_text.htm. Accessed 22 December 2009.

Commager, Henry Steele. *The Story of the Second World War*. Washington, D.C.: Brassey's, 1991, 2–8.

Comtois, Pierre. *Marvel Comics in the 1960s: An Issue by Issue Field Guide to a Pop Culture Phenomenon*. Raleigh, NC: TwoMorrows, 2009.

Conway, Gerry. "A Conversation with Gerry Conway." Audio Interview. *Comic Geek Speak*, Episode 701. October 6, 2009, 34:10. http://comicgeekspeak.com/episodes/comic_geek_speak-891.php Accessed 19 August 2011.

_____."The Night Gwen Stacy Died" and "The Green Goblin's Last Stand." *The Amazing Spider-Man* #121–122, New York: Marvel Comics, June-July 1973.

_____, and Al Milgrom. *Firestorm, the Nuclear Man* #1. New York: DC Comics, 1978.

Coontz, Stephanie. *The Way We Never Were: American Families and the Nostalgia Trap*. New York: Basic Books, 2000.

Costello, Matthew J. *Secret Identity Crisis: Comic Books and the Unmasking of Cold War America*. New York: Continuum, 2009.

Creswell, Julie, and Vikas Bajaj. "$3.2 Billion Move by Bear Stearns to Rescue Fund." *The New York Times*, 23 June 2007. Electronic Edition. http://www.nytimes.com/2007/06/23/business/23bond.html?_r=1. Accessed on 9 May 2010.

Cronin, Brian. "Comic Book Urban Legends Revealed #7!" *Comic Book Resources*. July 14, 2005.

_____. "Comic Book Urban Legends Revealed #119." *Comic Book Resources*. http://goodcomics.comicbookresources.com/2007/09/06/comic-book-urban-legends-revealed-119. Accessed 19 August 2011.

_____. "Comic Book Legends Revealed #235." *Comic Book Resources*. http://goodcomics.comicbookresources.com/2009/11/26/comic-book-legends-revealed-235/. Accessed 21 December 2009.

Cronker, Richard. *The Boomer Century, 1946–2046: How America's Most Influential Generation Changed Everything*. New York: Springboard Press, 2007.

Daniels, Les. *A Celebration of the World's Favorite Comic Book Heroes*. New York: Billboard Books, 2003.

_____. *Superman: The Complete History*. San Francisco: Chronicle Books, 1998.

David, Larry, and Jerry Seinfeld. "The Stock Tip." Seinfeld Lists. http://www.seinfeldscripts.com/TheStockTip.htm. Accessed on 9 July 2009.

"Defense needs rubber: Save your tires." Print advertisement, 1941. Northwestern University Library Collection. http://www.library.northwestern.edu/otcgi/digilib/llscgi60.exe?DB=2&SORTBY=%4D%32%36%30%43&ACTION=View&QUERY=%6A%70%65%67&RGN=%4D%38%35%36%31%5A&OP=and&QUERY=%74%69%72%65%73&OP=and&SUBSET=SUBSET&FROM=1&SIZE=5&ITEM=1 Accessed on 6 December 2009.

DeMatteis, J.M. "Kraven's Last Hunt." New York: Marvel Comics, 2006.

Dinerstein, Herbert S. *The Making of a Missile Crisis: October 1962*. Baltimore: Johns Hopkins University Press, 1976.

D'Orazio, Valerie. "Goodbye to Comics #7: 'We Need A Rape.'" *The Occasional Superheroine*. http://occasionalsuperheroine.blogspot.com/search/label/Goodbye%20To%20Comics?updated-max=2006-11-17T07%3A31%3A00–05%3A00&max-results=20. Accessed on 4 May 2010.

Dorfman, Leo, and Curt Swan. "The Amazing Story of Superman-Red and Superman-Blue." *Superman* #162. New York: DC Comics, 1963.

Dorne, Albert. "Less dangerous than careless talk: don't discuss troop movements, ship sailings, war equipment." Print advertisement, 1944. Northwestern University Library Collection. http://digital.library.northwestern.edu/otcgi/digilib/llscgi60.exe?DB=0&ACTION=View&QUERY=%74%61%6C%6B&OP=and&SUBSET=SUBSET&FROM=1&SIZE=20&ITEM=7. Accessed on 19 August 2011.

Draper, Robert. *Dead Certain: The Presidency of George W. Bush*. New York: Free Press, 2007.

D'Souza, Dinesh. *Ronald Reagan: How an Ordinary Man Became an Extraordinary Leader*. New York: Simon & Schuster, 1999, 11–15.

"Duck and Cover: The Citizen Kane of Civil Defense." *Conelrad.com*. http://www.conelrad.com/duckandcover/cover.php?turtle=01. Accessed 14 December 2009.

Dungan, Tracie. "Bentonville: Crystal Bridges Museum Obtains Rosie the Riveter." *Arkansas Democrat Gazette*, June 9, 2009. http://www.rosietheriveter.org/painting.htm. Accessed 2 August 2009.

"The End: Nuclear Nostalgia." *FLYP*. Issue 28, April 27–May 9, 2009. http://www.flypmedia.com/con tent/end-nuclear-nostalgia. Accessed 14 December 2009.

Engelhardt, Tom. *The End of Victory Culture: Cold War America and the Disillusioning of a Generation*. Basic Books, 1995.

Englehart, Steve. *Captain America and the Falcon* #163–#176, New York: Marvel Comics, July 1973–August 1974.

_____. "Captain America II." http://www.steveenglehart.com/Comics/Captain%20America%20169–176. html. Accessed 19 August 2011.

_____. "Two into One Won't Go." *Captain America and the Falcon* #156. New York: Marvel Comics, December 1972.

Ericson, Eric. "The sound that kills: Don't murder men with idle words." Print advertisement, 1942. Northwestern University Library Collection. http://digital.library.northwestern.edu/wwii-posters/ img/ww1646–71.jpg. Accessed on 19 August 2011.

Evanier, Mark. "Afterword." *Jack Kirby's Fourth World Omnibus*. Vol. 1, New York: DC Comics, 2007.

_____. "Introduction." *Jack Kirby's OMAC: One Man Army Corps*. Vol. 1. New York: DC Comics, 2008.

_____. *Kirby: King of Comics*. New York: Harry N. Abrams, 2008. "1961 Comic Book Sales Figures." *The Comics Chronicles: A Resource for Comics Research*. http://www.comichron.com/yearlycomicssales/1960s/ 1961.html. Accessed 18 January 2010.

Ewalt, David M. "Becoming Batman." *Forbes.com*. June 20, 2005. http://www.forbes.com/2005/06/20/bat man-movies-superheroes-cx_de_0620batman.html. Accessed on 15 July 2009.

"Explosion and Implosion!" *Dial B for Blog*. http://www.dialbforblog.com/archives/252/. Accessed on 19 August 2011.

Farber, David. "The Silent Majority and Talk About Revolution." *The Sixties: From Memory to History*, editor David Farber. Chapel Hill: University of North Carolina Press, 1994.

Fariello, Griffin. *Red Scare: Memories of the American Inquisition*. New York: W.W. Norton, 1995.

"Farm Scrap Builds Destroyers: 900 Tons of Scrap Metal Goes into a Destroyer." Print advertisement, 1942. Northwestern University Library Collection. http://digital.library.northwestern.edu/otcgi/digi lib/llscgi60.exe?DB=0&ACTION=View&QUERY=%43%6F%6E%73%65%72%76%65%20%6D %61%74%65%72%69%61%6C%73&RGN=%4D%36%35%33&OP=and&SUBSET=SUBSET& FROM=1&SIZE=10&ITEM=6. Accessed on 19 August 2011.

Feiffer, Jules. *The Great Comic Book Heroes*. Seattle: Fantagraphic, 2003.

"50s Adventures of Superman: Intro." You Tube. http://www.youtube.com/watch?v=Q2l4bz1FT8U. Accessed 27 June 2011.

Finger, Bill. "The Case of the Mother Goose Mystery." *World's Finest* #83. New York: DC Comics, July/August 1956.

_____, and Bob Kane. "Batman's New Secret Identity." *Batman* #151. New York: DC Comics, 1962.

Fischer, Anton. "A careless word — A needless loss." Print advertisement, 1943. Northwestern University Library Collection. http://digital.library.northwestern.edu/otcgi/digilib/llscgi60.exe?DB=0&SORT BY=%4D%32%34%35&ACTION=View&QUERY=%6A%70%65%67&RGN=%4D%38% 35%36%31%5A&OP=and&SUBSET=SUBSET&FROM=1&SIZE=10&ITEM=5. Accessed on 19 August 2011.

Gallup, George. *The Gallup Poll: Public Opinion 1935–1971*. Vol. 1. Random House: New York, 1972.

Genter, Robert. "'With Great Power Comes Great Responsibility': Cold War Culture and the Birth of Marvel Comics," *The Journal of Popular Culture* 40: 6, 2007.

George, Richard. "NYCC 08: Grant Morrison and J.G. Jones on Final Crisis: DC's last NYCC panel focuses on its biggest 2008 storyline." *IGN.com*. http://comics.ign.com/articles/868/868035p1.html.

"George W. Bush 2004 TV Ads 'Wolves.'" *4President.tv*. http://tv.4president.us/2004/bush2004wolves.htm. Accessed on 4 August 2010.

Ginsberg, Benjamin, and Martin Shefter. "After the Reagan Revolution: A Postelection Politics?" *Looking Back at the Reagan Presidency*. Larry Bergman, ed. Baltimore: Johns Hopkins University Press, 1990.

Glass, Andrew. "Carter Pardons Draft Dodgers Jan. 21, 1977." *Politico*. http://www.politico.com/news/sto ries/0108/7974.html. Accessed 28 June 2011.

Goulart, Ron. *Comic Book Culture: An Illustrated History*. Portland: Collectors Press, 2007.

Graubard, Stephen R. *Mr. Bush's War: Adventures in the Politics of Illusion*. New York: Hill and Wang, 1992.

"The Great One Is Coming." Print advertisement in *Superman's Pal Jimmy Olsen* #130. New York: DC Comics, July 1970.

Greenberg, Glenn. *The Life of Reilly*. Part 19. March 5, 2008. http://lifeofreillyarchives.blogspot.com/2008/ 03/part-19.html. Accessed 13 June 2011.

Greene, John Robert. *The Presidency of Gerald R. Ford*. Lawrence, KS: University of Kansas, 1995.

Gresh, Lois, and Robert Weinberg. *The Science of Superheroes.* Hoboken, New Jersey: John Wiley and Sons, 2002.

Gustines, George Gene. "Captain America Is Dead; National Hero Since 1941." *The New York Times.* Online Edition. 7 March 2007. http://www.nytimes.com/2007/03/08/books/08capt.html. Accessed 3 May 2010.

_____. "Recalibrating DC Heroes for a Grittier Century," *The New York Times.* Online Edition. 12 October 2005. http://query.nytimes.com/gst/fullpage.html?res=9B02E6D8163FF931A25753C1A9639C8B 63&sec=&spon=&pagewanted=1. Accessed 11 August 2010.

Hajdu, David. *The Ten-Cent Plague: The Great Comic-Book Scare and How It Changed America.* New York: Picador, 2009.

Hampson, Rick. "1970 Kent State Shootings are an Enduring History Lesson." *USA Today.* Online Edition. May 4, 2010. http://www.usatoday.com/news/nation/2010-05-03-kent-state_N.htm. Accessed 29 June 2011.

Hargrove, Erwin C. *Jimmy Carter as President: Leadership and the Politics of the Public Good.* Baton Rouge, LA: Louisiana State University Press, 1988.

Hart, B.H. Liddell. *History of the Second World War.* New York: Putnam's, 1970.

Henriksen, Erik. "This Is What It Sounds Like When Nerds Cry." *The Portland Mercury.* 7 March 2007. http://blogtown.portlandmercury.com/2007/03/this_is_what_it_sounds_like_wh.php. Accessed on 9 May 2010.

Henriksen, Margot A. *Dr. Strangelove's America: Society and Culture in the Atomic Age.* Berkeley: University of California Press, 1997.

Hine, Thomas. *The Great Funk: Falling Apart and Coming Together (on a Shag Rug) in the Seventies.* New York: Sarah Crichton Books, 2007.

"Historical Inflation." *Inflationdata.com.* http://inflationdata.com/inflation/Inflation_Rate/HistoricalInfla tion.aspx?dsInflation_currentPage=2. Accessed on 20 August 2011.

"I gave a man! Will you give at least 10% of your pay in war bonds?" Print advertisement, 1942. Butter funk.com. http://www.butterfunk.com/image-109/northwestern+university.html. Accessed on 19 August 2011.

"I'll carry mine too! Trucks and tires must last till victory." Print advertisement, 1943. Northwestern University Library Collection. http://www.library.northwestern.edu/otcgi/digilib/llscgi60.exe?DB=2& SORTBY=%4D%32%36%30%43&ACTION=View&QUERY=%6A%70%65%67&RGN=%4D% 38%35%36%31%5A&OP=and&QUERY=%74%69%72%65%73&OP=and&SUBSET=SUB SET&FROM=1&SIZE=5&ITEM=4. Accessed on 7 December 2009.

"I'll carry mine too! Trucks and tires must last till victory." Print advertisement, 1943. Militarywives.com http://www.militarywives.com/index.php?option=com_content&view=article&id=311:ill-carry-mine-too&catid=38:conserve-materials&Itemid=254. Accessed on 18 August 2011.

"Image Comics." *The Unknown.* http://www.unknowncomicsandgames.com/image-comics. Accessed 5 June 2011.

Irving, Christopher. "Carmine Infantino's Final Interview? No Way." *NYC Graphic.* 2 July 2009. http:// graphicnyc.blogspot.com/2009/07/carmine-infantinos-final-interview.html. Accessed on 3 October 2010.

Isabella, Tony. "Black Lightning and Me." *The Hembeck Files.* http://www.proudrobot.com/hembeck/black lightning.html. Accessed 19 August 2011.

Jameson, Fredric. "Periodizing the 60s." *The 60s Without Apology*, editor Sohnya Sayres. Minneapolis: University of Minnesota Press, 1984.

Jeffrey, Simon. "George Bush's Approval Ratings: 2001–2009." *The Guardian.* Online Edition. 16 January 2009. http://www.guardian.co.uk/world/interactive/2009/jan/16/george-bush-approval-ratings-amer ica. Accessed on 2 May 2010.

Jenkins, Philip. *Decade of Nightmares: The End of the Sixties and the Making of Eighties America.* New York: Oxford University Press, 2006.

Joffe, Josef. "The Wall and the End of History." Newsweek. Online Edition. November 6, 2009. http:// www.newsweek.com/2009/11/05/the-wall-and-the-end-of-history.html. Accessed 29 June 2011.

Johns, Geoff, Grant Morrison, Greg Rucka, and Mark Waid. *52.* New York: DC Comics, 2007.

_____. *Infinite Crisis.* New York: DC Comics, 2008.

_____. *Superman and the Legion of Super-Heroes.* New York: DC Comics, 2009.

Johnson, Haynes. *The Age of Anxiety: McCarthyism to Terrorism.* San Diego: Harcourt, 2005.

_____. *The Best of Times: America in the Clinton Years.* New York: Harcourt, 2001.

Johnson, Jeffrey K. "The Countryside Triumphant: Jefferson's Ideal of Rural Superiority in Modern Super-hero Mythology." *The Journal of Popular Culture.* Vol. 43.4, 2010.

Johnston, William Robert. "Review of Fall 2001 Anthrax Bioattacks." 28 September 2007. http://www.johnstonsarchive.net/terrorism/anthrax.html. Accessed 1 August 2010.

Jones, Gerald. *Men of Tomorrow: Geeks, Gangsters, and the Birth of the Comic Book*. New York: Basic Books, 2004.

Jourdain, Bill. "Big All-American Comic Book." *Golden Age of Comic Books*. 20 December 2008. http://goldenagecomics.org/wordpress/2008/12/20/big-all-american-comic-book/. Accessed 3 August 2010.

Juvenile Delinquency (Comic Books) Hearings Before the United States Senate Committee on the Judiciary, Subcommittee to Investigate Juvenile Delinquency in the U.S., Eighty-Third Congress, Second Session, on April 21–22 and June 4, 1954.

"Juvenile Delinquency." *Novel Guide*. http://www.novelguide.com/a/discover/adec_0001_0006_0/adec_0001_0006_0_01937.html. Accessed on 22 December 2009.

Kahn, Jenette. "DC Publishorial: Onward and Upward." Print advertisement in all DC Comics. New York: DC Comics, September 1978.

Kaledin, Eugenia. *Daily Life in the United States, 1940–1959: Shifting Worlds*. New York: Greenwood Press, 2000.

Kane, Bob. *Batman Archives Vol. 1*. New York: DC Comics, 1990.

Karnow, Stanley. *Vietnam: A History*. New York: Penguin Books, 1997.

Keegan, John. *The Second World War*. New York: Viking, 1990.

Kennedy, John F. *Inaugural Address*. 20 January 1961. Reprinted at http://www.americanrhetoric.com/speeches/jfkinaugural.htm 10 January 2010.

"The King Is Here." Cover to *Superman's Pal Jimmy Olsen* #133. New York: DC Comics, October 1970.

Kirby, Jack. "Forever People in Search of a Dream." From *Forever People* #1 in *The Greatest Superman Stories Ever Told*. New York: DC Comics, 1987.

"Knightfall." *Comic Vine*. http://www.comicvine.com/knightfall/39–40761/. Accessed on 12 June 2011.

Koerner, Henry. "Save waste fats for explosives. Take them to your meat dealer." Print advertisement, 1943. *Powers of Persuasion: Poster Art from World War II: The National Archives*. http://www.archives.gov/exhibits/powers_of_persuasion/use_it_up/images_html/save_waste_fats.html. Accessed on 6 August 2009.

Kuhn, David Paul, and Jonathan Martin. "Republican Candidates Begin Snubbing Bush." *Politico*. 18 June 2007. http://www.politico.com/news/stories/0607/4538.html. Accessed on 3 August 2010.

Kurnaz, Murat. *Five Years of My Life: An Innocent Man in Guantanamo*. New York: Palgrave Macmillan, 2007, 15–18.

Lacayo, Richard, John Cloud, Emily Mitchell, Wendy Cole, Declan McCullagh, Timothy Roche, and Richard Woodbury. "The End of the World as We Know It?" *Time*. 18 January 1999. Online Edition. http://www.time.com/time/magazine/article/0,9171,990020,00.html. Accessed 17 April 2010.

Lee, Stan, and Bill Everett. *Daredevil* #1. New York: Marvel Comics, 1964.

_____, and George Mair. *Excelsior! The Amazing Life of Stan Lee*. New York: Fireside, 2002.

_____, and Jack Kirby. *Fantastic Four* #1. New York: Marvel Comics, 1961.

_____. *Fantastic Four Annual* #3. New York: Marvel Comics, October 1965.

_____. *Marvel Masterworks: Avengers*, Vol. 1. New York: Marvel, 2002.

_____, and Steve Ditko. *Amazing Fantasy* #15. New York: Marvel Comics, 1962.

Leuchtenburg, William E. *Franklin D. Roosevelt and the New Deal, 1932–1940*. New York: Harper & Row, 1963.

Levy, Peter B. *Encyclopedia of the Clinton Presidency*. Westport, CT: Greenwood Press, 2002.

The Library of Congress World War II Companion. David M. Kennedy, ed. New York: Simon & Schuster, 2007.

Lipsitz, George. "Who'll Stop the Rain?" *The Sixties: From Memory to History*. David Farber, ed. Chapel Hill: University of North Carolina Press, 1994.

Long, Colleen. "Marvel Comics Buries Captain America." *The Washington Post*. Electronic Edition. 1 July 2007. http://www.washingtonpost.com/wp-dyn/content/article/2007/06/30/AR2007063000511.html. Accessed 10 May 2010.

"Loose Lips Sink Ships." Ad Council advertising campaign, 1942–1945. http://www.adcouncil.org/default.aspx?id=127. Accessed on 10 December 2009.

MacFarlane, Scott. "The Counterculture." *Baby Boom: People and Perspectives*. Santa Barbara, CA: ABC-CLIO, 2010.

Maddox, Robert James. *The United States and World War II*. Boulder, CO: Westview Press, 1992.

Madrid, Mike. *The Supergirls: Fashion, Feminism, Fantasy, and the History of Comic Book Heroines*. New York: Exterminating Angel Press, 2009.

Maggin, Elliot S!. "The Invader from Hell!" *Batman Family* #1. New York: DC Comics, October 1975.

_____. "The Last Earth-Prime Story." *Superman* #411. New York: DC Comics, September 1985.

"Man of Steal." *Time Bullet*. http://timebulleteer.wordpress.com/2011/01/10/the-man-of-steal/. Accessed on 22 July 2011.

_____. "The New Bards" in *Kingdom Come*. New York: DC Comics, 1997.

Manning, Matthew K. "1979s." *DC Comics: Year by Year, a Visual Chronicle*. New York: DK Publishing, 2010.

Mantlo, Bill, and George Tuska. "Long Time Gone." *Invincible Iron Man* #78, New York: Marvel Comics, September 1975.

Markstein, Donald D. "Don Markstein's Toonopedia." http://www.toonopedia.com/index.htm. Accessed 13 December 2009.

Marling, Karal Ann. *As Seen on TV: The Visual Culture of Everyday Life in the 1950s*. Cambridge, MA: Harvard University Press, 1996.

Marschall, Rick. "Foreword" in *Batman Archives* Vol. 1. New York: DC Comics, 1990.

Marvel Mystery Comics #32. New York: Marvel Comics, 1942.

Master Comics #29. New York: Fawcett, 1942.

May, Elaine Tyler. *Homeward Bound: American Families in the Cold War Era*. New York: Basic Books, 2008.

McAvennie, Michael. "1970s." *DC Comics: Year by Year, a Visual Chronicle*. New York: DK Publishing, 2010.

Meese, Edwin. *With Reagan: The Inside Story*. Washington, D.C.: Regnery Gateway, 1992.

Meltzer, Brad. *The Book of Lies*. New York: Grand Central, 2008.

_____. *Identity Crisis*. New York: DC Comics, 2006.

Michelinie, David. *Invincible Iron Man* #120–128. New York: Marvel Comics, March–November 1979.

Millar, Mark. *Civil War*. New York: Marvel, 2008.

Miller, Douglas T. *The Fifties: The Way We Really Were*. New York: Doubleday, 1977.

Miller, Frank. *Batman: The Dark Knight Returns*. New York: DC Comics, 2002.

_____. Quoted in Joe Strike, "Frank Miller's 'Dark Knight' Brought Batman Back to Life." *New York Daily News*. Online Edition. 16 July 2008. http://articles.nydailynews.com/2008–07–16/entertainment/17902060_1_dark-knight-returns-batman-superman. Accessed on 20 August 2011.

Mintz, Steven. *Domestic Revolutions: A Social History of American Family Life*. New York: Free Press, 1989.

Moore, Alan, and Dave Gibbons. *Watchmen* #1. New York: DC Comics, 1986.

Morrison, Grant. *Animal Man: Deus Ex Machina*. New York: DC Comics, 2003.

_____. *Arkham Asylum*, 15th anniversary edition. New York: DC Comics, 1989.

_____. *Final Crisis* #1. New York: DC Comics, 2009.

_____. *Final Crisis* #5. New York: DC Comics, 2009.

_____. *Superergods: What Masked Vigilantes, Miraculous Mutants, and a Sun God from Smallville Can Teach Us About Being Human*. New York: Spiegel and Grau, 2011.

Mortimer, Win. *Action Comics* #163. Cover image. New York: DC Comics, December 1951.

_____. *Superman* #94. Cover image. New York: DC Comics, January 1955.

"The Most Famous Poster," Library of Congress. http://www.loc.gov/exhibits/treasures/trm015.html Accessed on 10 December 2009.

Murdough, Adam C. *Worlds Will Live, Worlds Will Die: Myth, Metatext, Continuity, and Cataclysm in DC Comics' Crisis on Infinite Earths*. Bowling Green University, August 2006.

National Archives. "World War II Causalities." http://www.archives.gov/research/arc/ww2/. Accessed on December 13, 2009.

Newport, Frank, Jeffrey M. Jones, and Lydia Saad. "Ronald Reagan from the People's Perspective: A Gallup Poll Review." Gallup. 7 June 2004. http://www.gallup.com/poll/11887/Ronald-Reagan-From-Peoples-Perspective-Gallup-Poll-Review.aspx. Accessed 20 August 2011.

"1960 Comic Book Sales Figures." *The Comics Chronicles: A Resource for Comics Research*. http://www.comichron.com/yearlycomicssales/1960s/1960.html. Accessed 18 January 2010.

"1992 Comic Book Sales Figures." *The Comics Chronicles*. http://www.comichron.com/monthlycomicssales/1992.html. Accessed 5 May 2011.

"1993 Comic Book Sales Figures." *The Comics Chronicles*. http://www.comichron.com/monthlycomicssales/1992.html. Accessed 5 May 2011.

Nolan, Graham. "Comics: Meet the Artist." *The Washington Post*. May 16, 2003. Online Edition. http://www.washingtonpost.com/wp-srv/liveonline/03/regular/style/comics/r_style_comics051603.htm. Accessed 15 May 2011.

"North Korea's Nuclear Ambitions." *NPR.org*. 10 October 2006. http://www.npr.org/worldopinion/20061010_worldopinion_northkorea.html. Accessed on 6 August 2010.

Nyberg, Amy Kiste. *Seal of Approval: The History of the Comics Code*. Jackson: University Press of Mississippi, 1998.

Obst, David. *Too Good to Be Forgotten: Changing America in the '60s and '70s*. New York: John Wiley, 1998.

"Oldest Baby Boomers Turn 60!" *U.S. Census Bureau*. January 3, 2006. http://www.census.gov/newsroom/releases/pdf/cb06-ffse01-2.pdf. Accessed 19 August 2011.

O'Neil, Denny. "Introduction." *Green Lantern/ Green Arrow*. Vol. 1. New York: DC Comics, 2004.

_____. "No Evil Shall Escape My Sight." *Green Lantern/Green Arrow*. Vol. 1. New York: DC Comics, 2004.

_____. *Voices from Krypton*. http://www.earthsmightiest.com/fansites/justiceleague/news/?a=6620. Accessed on 27 September 2010.

_____, and Neal Adams. *Superman vs. Muhammad Ali Deluxe Edition*. New York: DC Comics, 2010.

"Operation Crossroads." *Radiochemistry Society U.S. Nuclear Tests: Info Gallery, 1945–1962*. http://www.radiochemistry.org/history/nuke_tests/crossroads/index.html. Accessed on 6 September 2009.

Parker, Bill, and Jon Smalle. *Nickel Comics* #1. New York: Fawcett Comics, 1940.

Parmet, Herbert S. *George Bush: The Life of a Lone Star Yankee*. New York: Scribner, 1997.

Pipes, Richard. "Ash Heap of History: President Reagan's Westminster Address 20 Years Later." *Ronald Reagan: The Heritage Foundation Remembers*. 3 June 2002. http://www.reagansheritage.org/reagan/html/reagan_panel_pipes.shtml. Accessed on 29 December 2009.

Pitts, Leonard, Jr. "Come Back, Captain, We Need You." *The Seattle Times*. Electronic Edition. 14 March 2007. http://seattletimes.nwsource.com/html/opinion/2003616520_pitts14.html. Accessed on 11 May 2010.

Plastino, Al. *Superman* #60. Cover image. New York: DC Comics, September/October 1949.

_____. *Superman* #67. Cover image. New York: DC Comics, November/December 1950.

_____. *Action Comics* #149. Cover image. New York: DC Comics, October 1950.

"Political Notes: Chairman Daley's Maxims." *Time Magazine*. Online Edition. July 18, 1969. http://www.time.com/time/magazine/article/0,9171,901037,00.html. Accessed on 23 June 2011.

"Poll Shows Dissatisfaction with Iraq War." *CNN.com*. http://www.cnn.com/2005/POLITICS/06/20/poll/. Accessed on 2 May 2010.

"The Presidency." *Time*. July 11, 1932, Vol. 20.2. http://www.time.com/time/magazine/article/0,9171,743953,00.html. Accessed on 2 July 2009.

"Private Joe Lewis Says." Print advertisement, date unknown. *Powers of Persuasion: Poster Art from World War II: The National Archives*. Print advertisement, http://www.archives.gov/exhibits/powers_of_persuasion/united_we_win/images_html/private_joe_louis_says.html. Accessed on 21 August 2009.

Pursell, Weimer. "When you ride ALONE you ride with Hitler! Join a Car-Sharing Club Today!" Print advertisement, 1943. *Powers of Persuasion: Poster Art from World War II: The National Archives*. http://www.archives.gov/exhibits/powers_of_persuasion/use_it_up/images_html/ride_with_hitler.html. Accessed on 5 August 2009.

Raviv, Dan. *Comic Wars: How Two Tycoons Battled Over the Marvel Comics Empire—And Both Lost*. New York: Broadway Books, 2001.

Reagan, Ronald. "20 Years Later: Reagan's Westminster Speech." June 8, 1982. *The Heritage Foundation*. http://www.heritage.org/research/reports/2002/06/reagans-westminster-speech. Accessed on 27 June 2011.

_____. "Acceptance Speech at the 1980 Republican Convention." July 17, 1980. *The National Center for Public Policy Research*. http://www.nationalcenter.org/ReaganConvention1980.html. Accessed on 24 June 2011.

_____. "Bloopers, Blunders, and Bombast: Uncensored Comments of American Politicians." http://www.historyplace.com/specials/different/bloopers.htm. Accessed 27 June 2011.

_____. "Lebanon and Grenada," Speech. 27 October 1983, http://www.presidentreagan.info/speeches/lebanon_and_grenada.cfm. Accessed on 20 August 2011.

_____. "President Ronald Reagan: 'Evil Empire' Speech." *You Tube*. http://www.youtube.com/watch?v=do0x-Egc6oA. Accessed on 27 June 2011.

Rebel Without a Cause. Motion picture. Director Nicholas Ray, Warner Bros., 1955.

"Reign of the Supermen." *Comic Vine*. http://www.comicvine.com/reign-of-the-supermen/39–56339/. Accessed 12 June 2011.

Renaud, Jeffrey. "All Star Grant Morrison I: Final Crisis." *Comic Book Resources*. 15 April 2008. http://www.comicbookresources.com/?page=article&id=16005. Accessed 2 August 2010.

Richards, Walter DuBois. "They've Got More Important Places to Go Than You! ... Save Rubber. Check Your Tires Now." Print advertisement, 1942. Northwestern University Library Collection. http://www.library.northwestern.edu/otcgi/digilib/llscgi60.exe?DB=2&SORTBY=%4D%32%36%30%43&ACTI

ON=View&QUERY=%6A%70%65%67&RGN=%4D%38%35%36%31%5A&OP=and&QUERY=%74%69%72%65%73&OP=and&SUBSET=SUBSET&FROM=1&SIZE=5&ITEM=2. Accessed on 12 August 2009.

Rios, Peter. *Comic Geek Speak—The Crisis Tapes: Footnotes Vol. 5.* Podcast. August 2010. http://www.comic geekspeak.com/episodes/crisis-1141.php. Accessed on 20 August 2011.

Ro, Ronin. *Tales to Astonish: Jack Kirby, Stan Lee, and the American Comic Book Revolution.* New York: Bloomsbury, 2004.

Robinson, Bryan. "What the Death of Captain America Really Means: Bullets Killed Him, But the War on Terror Really Did Cap In." *ABC News.* Online Edition. 8 March 2007. http://abcnews.go.com/US/story?id=2934283&page=1. Accessed 5 May 2010.

Roese, Herbert. "Kinda give it your personal attention, will you? More Production." Print advertisement, 1942. University of North Texas Digital Library. http://digital.library.unt.edu/ark:/67531/metadc210/. Accessed on 19 August 2011.

Rogers, Veneta. "Brian Bendis — Wrapping It All Up and Starting Dark Reign." *Newsarama.* http://www.newsarama.com/comics/120805-Bendis-Dark-Reign.html. Accessed on 5 December 2008.

"Ronald Reagan TV ad: 'Its [*sic*] morning in America again.'" *You Tube.* http://www.youtube.com/watch?v=EU-IBF8nwSY. Accessed 27 June 2011.

Roosevelt, Franklin. December 9, 1941, Radio Address. http://www.mtholyoke.edu/acad/intrel/World War2/radio.htm. Accessed on 9 December 2009.

Rushin, Steve. "Bikini Waxing: From Bardot to Graf, from Ground Zero to Grass, Here's the Skinny on the Two Piece." 21 February 1997. *Sports Illustrated.* Online. http://sportsillustrated.cnn.com/vault/article/magazine/MAG1009487/index.htm. Accessed 22 September 2009.

Sarra, Valentino. "If you talk too much." Print advertisement, 1942. University of North Texas Digital Library. http://digital.library.unt.edu/ark:/67531/metadc517/m1/1/. Accessed 9 July 2011.

Schatt, Roy. "Scrap." Print advertisement, 1942. Northwestern University Library Collection. http://digital.library.northwestern.edu/otcgi/digilib/llscgi60.exe?DB=0&ACTION=View&QUERY=Conserve%20materials&RGN=M653&OP=and&SUBSET=SUBSET&FROM=1&SIZE=10&ITEM=2. Accessed on 19 August 2011.

Schwartz, Al. "The People vs. Superman." *Superman* #62. New York: DC Comics, January/February 1950.

Scott, Cord. "The Alpha and the Omega: Captain America and the Punisher," in *Captain America and the Struggle of the Superhero: Critical Essays*, editor Robert G. Weiner. Jefferson, NC: McFarland, 2009, 125–126.

Shapiro, T. Rees. "Virginia Tech Students Remember Those Who Died in Shooting." *The Washington Post*, 16 April 2010. http://www.washingtonpost.com/wp-dyn/content/article/2010/04/15/AR2010 041505727.html. Accessed on 9 May 2009.

"Share the Meat." Print advertisement, 1942. Northwestern University Library Collection. http://digital.library.northwestern.edu/wwii-posters/img/ww1645–33.jpg. Accessed on 19 August 2011.

Shooter, Jim, and Curt Swan. "Superman and Batman — Brothers." *World's Finest Comics* #172. New York: DC Comics, 1967.

Siegel, Jerome, and Curt Swan. "The Death of Superman." *Superman* #149. New York: DC Comics, 1961.

_____, and Joe Shuster. "Superman." *Action Comics* #1. New York: DC Comics, 1938.

_____, and _____. *Superman: The Dailies, Part I.* New York: Sterling, 2006.

_____. *Superman: Sunday Classics 1939–1943.* New York: Sterling, 2006.

Silva, Francisco. "284. Artists and Models (1955)" *1001 Flicks.* August 22, 2008. http://1001flicks.blogspot.com/2008_08_01_archive.html. Accessed 15 December 2009.

Simon, Joe. "The Making of the Prez," *Prez* #1, New York: DC Comics, March 1974.

_____, and Jack Kirby. *Captain America* #1. New York: Marvel Comics, 1941.

_____, and Jim Simon. *The Comic Book Makers.* Lebanon, NJ: Vanguard Production, 2003.

Snyder, Louis L. *The War: A Concise History, 1939–1945.* New York: Simon & Schuster, 1960.

"Someone Talked!" Print advertisement, 1942. Northwestern University Library Collection. http://www.library.northwestern.edu/govinfo/collections/wwii-posters/img/ww0207–04.jpg. Accessed 11 August 2009.

Sorensen, Theodore C. *"Let the Word Go Forth": The Speeches, Statements, and Writings of John F. Kennedy, 1947 to 1963.* New York: Delacorte Press, 1988.

Spigel, Lynn. *Make Room for TV: Television and the Family Ideal in Postwar America.* Chicago: University of Chicago Press, 1992.

Squassoni, Sharon. "North Korea's Nuclear Weapons: Latest Developments." *CRS Report for Congress.* 18 October 2006. http://www.fas.org/sgp/crs/nuke/RS21391.pdf . Accessed on 4 August 2010.

"Stan Lee on the Spider-Man Drug Story Too Hot for the Comics Code Authority [Video]." Comics

Alliance. http://www.comicsalliance.com/2010/07/26/stan-lee-amazing-spider-man-drugs-comics-code-authority/. Accessed 19 August 2011.

Stand by Me. Rob Reiner, director. Sony Pictures, 1986.

Steele, Diana. "America's Reaction to the Atomic Bombings of Hiroshima and Nagasaki." http://users.dickinson.edu/~history/product/steele/seniorthesis.htm. Accessed 14 December 2009.

Steinhorn, Leonard. *The Greater Generation: In Defense of the Baby Boom Legacy.* New York: Thomas Dunne Books, 2006.

Straczynski, J. Michael, and John Romita, Jr. *The Amazing Spider-Man #36.* New York: Marvel Comics, 2002.

Sunderland, Jake. "Cannon: It's About Objective Facts." *The Donald W. Reynolds School of Journalism.* 8 November 2006. http://www.unr.edu/journalism/content/061108/061108page2.htm. Accessed 29 December 2009.

Superman #17. New York: DC Comics, 1942.

Sussmann, Leila. "FDR and the White House Mail." *The Public Opinion Quarterly.* Vol. 20.1. Spring 1956.

Taverne, Daniel. "Does the Death of Captain America Predict the Death of the American Way?" *American Chronicle.* March 7, 2007. http://www.americanchronicle.com/articles/view/21785. Accessed 10 May 2010.

Terkel, Studs. *Hard Times: An Oral History of the Great Depression.* New York: Pantheon Books, 1970.

Thompson, Don. "OK, Axis, Here We Come." *All in Color for a Dime.* Krause, 1997, 122–123.

_____, and Maggie Thompson. "Epic Beginnings." *Camelot 3000.* New York: DC Comics, 1988.

"Timeline: How the Anthrax Terror Unfolded." *NPR.org.* 1 August 2008. http://www.npr.org/templates/story/story.php?storyId=93170200. Accessed 1 August 2010.

"Timeline: South Africa." *BBC News.* June 21, 2011. http://news.bbc.co.uk/2/hi/africa/1069402.stm. Accessed 29 June 2011.

"Tomorrow's Legacy." *The 1939–40 New York World's Fair.* http://xroads.virginia.edu/~1930s/DISPLAY/39wf/frame.htm. Accessed on 16 July 2009.

"Timothy Leary: Turn On, Tune In, Drop Out." http://turnontuneindropout.com/Timothy_Leary_files/leary2.html. Accessed 23 June 2011.

Tugwell, Rexford G. *Off Course: From Truman to Nixon.* New York: Praeger.

"Ultron Unlimited (Part 1 of 4)." *Snikt! The Comics of the Nineties.* June 14, 2009. http://marincomics.tumblr.com/. Accessed 27 June 2011.

"U.S. Trade Deficit Declined in 2007." *MSNBC.com.* 14 February 2008. http://www.msnbc.msn.com/id/23163519/. Accessed on 9 May 2010.

The United States Constitution. First Amendment, 1787.

United States Department of Labor, Bureau of Labor Statistics. "Unemployment Rate." http://data.bls.gov/pdq/SurveyOutputServlet. Accessed 20 August 2011.

"Uranium Rush Board Game." Oak Ridge Associated Universities. http://www.orau.org/ptp/collection/atomictoys/uraniumrush.htm. Accessed 19 September 2009.

Voger, Mark. *The Dark Age: Grim, Great and Gimmicky Post-modern Comics.* Raleigh, NC: TwoMorrows, 2006.

Wagner, Hank, Christopher Golden, and Stephen R. Bissette. *Prince of Stories: The Many Worlds of Neil Gaiman.* New York: St. Martin's, 2008.

Waid, Mark, and Alex Ross. *Kingdom Come.* New York: DC Comics, 1997.

Walker, Martin. *The Cold War: A History.* New York: Henry Holt, 1993.

"Wanted!" Print advertisement, 1944. Northwestern University Library Collection. http://digital.library.northwestern.edu/otcgi/digilib/llscgi60.exe?DB=0&ACTION=View&QUERY=%77%61%6E%74%65%64&OP=and&SUBSET=SUBSET&FROM=1&SIZE=20&ITEM=1. Accessed on 19 August 2011.

Warner, Philip. *World War II: The Untold Story.* London: Bodley Head, 1988.

Washington, George. "Farewell Address to the People of the United States." Archiving Early America. http://www.earlyamerica.com/earlyamerica/milestones/farewell/text.html. Accessed 19 July 2009.

"Watching for the Y2K Bug." *New York Times.* Editorial. 30 December 1999. Online edition. http://www.nytimes.com/1999/12/30/opinion/watching-for-the-y2k-bug.html?scp=3&sq=y2k&st=nyt. Accessed 17 April 2010.

Watts, Adrian. "Avengers: Heroes Reborn." *White Rocket Books.* Accessed on 9 June 2011.

Weatherford, M. Stephen, and Lorraine M. McDonnell. "Ideology and Economic Policy." *Looking Back at the Reagan Presidency.* Larry Bergman, editor. Baltimore: Johns Hopkins University Press, 1990.

Wecter, Dixon. *The Age of the Great Depression: 1929–1941.* New York: Macmillan, 1948.

Weinberg, Gerhard L. *A World at Arms: A Global History of World War II.* New York: Cambridge University Press, 2005.

Weisberg, Jacob. *The Bush Tragedy*. New York: Random House, 2008.

Wells, John. "Green Lantern/Green Arrow: And Through Them Change an Industry." *Back Issue*. December 2010.

Westin, Alan F. "Information, Dissent, and Political Power: Watergate Revisited." *Watergate and Afterward: The Legacy of Richard Nixon*. Leon Friedman and William F. Levantrosser, eds. Westport, CT: Greenwood, 1992.

"Why Law Fails to Stop Teenage Crime," *U.S. News and World Report*, 14 January 1955.

Wilentz, Sean. *The Age of Reagan: A History, 1974–2008*. New York: HarperCollins, 2008.

Williams, Jeanne Pauline. "The Evolution of Social Norms and the Life of Lois Lane: A Rhetorical Analysis of Popular Culture." Doctorial dissertation, Ohio State University, 1986.

Wittner, Lawrence S. *Cold War America: From Hiroshima to Watergate*. New York: Praeger, 1974.

"Women in War Jobs: Rosie the Riveter (1942–1945)." Ad Council advertising campaign, 1942–1945. http://www.adcouncil.org/default.aspx?id=128. Accessed 11 August 2009.

Zehr, E. Paul. *Becoming Batman: The Possibility of a Superhero*. Baltimore: Johns Hopkins University Press, 2008.

Zorbaugh, Harvey A. "The Comics: There They Stand!" *Journal of Educational Sociology*, December 1944, Vol. 18.

INDEX